The Dialectic in Journalism

The Dialectic
in Journalism

TOWARD A RESPONSIBLE USE
OF PRESS FREEDOM

John C. Merrill

LOUISIANA STATE UNIVERSITY PRESS
BATON ROUGE AND LONDON

Copyright © 1989 by Louisiana State University Press
All rights reserved
Manufactured in the United States of America
First printing
98 97 96 95 94 93 92 91 90 89   5 4 3 2 1
Typeface: Linotron Sabon
Typesetter: The Composing Room of Michigan, Inc.
Printer: Thomson-Shore, Inc.
Binder: John H. Dekker & Sons, Inc.

Library of Congress Cataloging-in-Publication Data
Merrill, John Calhoun, 1924–
    The dialectic in journalism : toward a responsible use of press
freedom / John C. Merrill.
       p.   cm.
    Bibliography: p.
    Includes index.
    ISBN 0-8071-1497-9 (alk. paper)
    1. Journalism—Philosophy.   2. Dialectic.   3. Freedom of the
press—United States—20th century.   4. Journalism—United States—
Objectivity.   I. Title.
PN4731.M429   1989
070'.01—dc19   88-7851
                                                                                  CIP

The paper in this book meets the guidelines for permanence and durability of the
Committee on Production Guidelines for Book Longevity of the Council on
Library Resources. ∞

In memory of
WALTER WOOD HITESMAN
of Louisiana, New York, and Massachusetts—magazine executive,
journalist, and gentleman—who appreciated my work when I needed
encouragement and urged me to continue tilling the fields of journalism
and philosophy

THE DIALECTIC

Everywhere, even in a person's mind, we find a process of unfolding. The great nineteenth-century German philosopher Georg W. F. Hegel called this process the *dialectic,* or the principle of contradiction. Everything tends to clash and merge with its opposite. Development is everywhere. And the development proceeds by the dialectical process.

First there is a *thesis,* then an *antithesis*—its opposite or contradiction. And these two are at last reconciled in a *synthesis,* which becomes another thesis, and the process begins again. This, believed Hegel, is the process of nature and the process of history. It also has a spiritual dimension: the development of consciousness, of discernment, of personality, of enlightenment.

This dialectic is found in journalism—this triadic movement that pushes thought forward and to higher levels through the recognition of flux and the merger of conflicting concepts. Journalism is filled with such concepts needing reconciliation, two of the chief among them being freedom and responsibility.

CONTENTS

Introduction   1

Part I/The Dialectical Approach

1 / The Search for Freedom   19

2 / In Search of Responsibility   37

3 / The Power of Antinomies   55

4 / A Nietzschean Dialectic   76

Part II/Freedom and Ethics

5 / Journalistic Freedom   97

6 / Freedom's Middle Way   131

7 / Merging Ethical Paths   156

8 / Definers of Journalistic Ethics   177

9 / Deontelic Ethics: A Synthesis   195

10 / Global Concerns   215

Conclusion: The Free and Ethical Journalist   234

Selected Bibliography   245

Index   251

The Dialectic in Journalism

INTRODUCTION

This book is an outgrowth of, or logical follow-up to, *The Imperative of Freedom* (1974), in which I emphasized the importance of freedom (both institutional and existential) in journalism. Whereas in that volume I gave major emphasis to freedom, in this book I have balanced the necessity for freedom in journalism with a concomitant need for responsibility. This is consistent with the underlying theme of the present work: that the pre-Socratic philosophy of flux and paradox, exemplified by Heraclitus, and the very similar dialectical philosophy of the eighteenth- and nineteenth-century German idealists, exemplified by Kant, Fichte, and Hegel, can, and should, be applied to the problems of journalism in the modern world.

Critics of *The Imperative of Freedom,* a book that caused considerable controversy because of its heavy libertarian emphasis, believed that it deprecated morality and the ethical use of freedom.[1] Although this "weakness" of the earlier volume was, I think, exaggerated, I have tried in the present work to right this real (or perceived) wrong by infusing these pages with an ethical strain that, I sincerely believe, must form a synthesis with freedom to support a vital and viable journalism.

Make no mistake: I have not lessened my concern for freedom. The Lockean, Millian, and Jeffersonian emphases are still present. But now the reader will also find a dialectical emphasis throughout the book—some-

---

1 Certainly *The Imperative of Freedom* did not ignore responsibility. The very purpose of the book, excluding its large concern with freedom, was to emphasize ethical and responsible journalism as it had seldom been emphasized before. From a philosophical perspective, it was an emphasis, to be sure, that stressed the virtues of freedom, rationalism, and humanism.

I

thing that was absent from the 1974 volume. Out of the clash or merger of freedom and ethics will come (and should come) the most desirable result: *responsible freedom*—or the ethical use of journalistic self-determination.

Back to Plato and Aristotle

It is said that all of us are either Platonists or Aristotelians in general philosophical orientation. If we are Platonists, we tend to be collectivist, altruistic, and romantic. If we are Aristotelians, we tend to be individualistic, egoistic, scientific, and realistic. Plato is often seen as the contrary of Aristotle. Plato is seen as the authoritarian, the elitist, the collectivist, the mystic; Aristotle, as the democrat, the individualist, the empiricist, the rationalist. Plato is portrayed as the idealist, Aristotle as the realist.

Plato is usually considered the intellectual father of such philosophers as St. Augustine, Kant, Hegel, and a whole succession of idealists, romantics, and relativists. Aristotle, on the other hand, is seen as progenitor of such philosophers as Thomas Aquinas, John Locke, and a whole succession of realists, empiricists, and absolutists.

Of course, this picture is superficial and overdrawn. It presents stereotypes of these classical Greek philosophers and their ideas, and it downplays the similarities or mergers (dialectical syntheses) of their thought. It ignores the multidimensionality of their belief systems and stresses extremes and generalizations.

A recent book by Leonard Peikoff gives such a picture of Plato and Aristotle and their impact on the history of ideas; it also traces the impact of Plato, Kant, and especially Hegel on the growth of the state and the decline of individualism.[2] Peikoff largely reflects the general philosophy of Ayn Rand, but he puts Randian thought into a historical perspective that has a powerful intellectual impact. Basically, Peikoff's book contrasts Plato and his idealistic philosophy with Aristotle (Peikoff and Rand's hero), who is against the "supernaturalism" of Plato. Aristotle's specifics are contrasted with Plato's abstractions.

It should be stressed that in the present book I am synthesizing many of the ideas of Plato and Aristotle, as well as of many of their followers. This is not a Platonist book; neither is it Aristotelian. It is a dialectical book that

2 Leonard Peikoff, *The Ominous Parallels* (New York, 1982).

seeks to harmonize many of the ideas stemming from both orientations. For example, I am taking a general Platonist (or, perhaps more accurately, a non-Aristotelian) stance in epistemology, but—and it should be noted— I am not at all with Plato in his political philosophy.

Plato's emphasis in political philosophy—reflected later by Hegel and others—on duty to the state and on sublimating the individual to society is not my emphasis.[3] However, I must say that this Platonic emphasis is important and is a needed corrective to the excesses of individual freedom. And it is this merger of Platonic social responsibility with Aristotelian political individualism (the latter is exemplified even better by Socrates) that is the underlying theme of this book. It forms the critical dialectic in press-government relations and in the general symbiosis between journalism and society.

Plato does, indeed, symbolize a kind of collectivistic philosophy in which elites control the masses. For Plato the masses, as contrasted to their rulers, the philosophers, are slaves to the daily, personal concerns of life, bogged down in routine and unable to plug into mystic enlightenment through intuition or revelation. Therefore, their purpose is to obey orders, and their virtue is in submitting themselves to the state.

Aristotle, by and large, opposed Plato's supernaturalism, intuition, revelation, and mysticism. He denied the existence of a "World of Forms" and maintained the reality of a "world of particulars" that we can perceive through our physical senses. Aristotle says that reality is composed, not of Platonic abstractions but of concrete entities. His is the world of science, a world that is orderly, intelligible, and knowable to the human mind.

Aristotle denied the mystical elements of Plato's epistemology. There- fore it might be said that he is the Father of Logic and the proponent of *reason* (rather than intuition) as a way to achieve knowledge. Aristotle, then, was the real founder of empiricism and a proponent of absolutes and objectivity, whereas Plato can be thought of as representing mysticism, intuitivism, relativism, and subjectivity.

In the area of ethics Plato saw the good life as largely one of selflessness, of submerging the self in the ongoing collective, of placing society first and

3 Many writers on Plato have placed him in the authoritarian or elitist political camp. Often he is referred to as the Father of Authoritarianism. Perhaps the modern philosopher who has done most to point out the authoritarian aspects of Plato's political (and moral) philosophy is Karl Popper. See his *The Open Society and Its Enemies* (4th ed.; 2 vols.; New York, 1963), and his many articles on Plato reflecting the same theme.

self second. It is basically an altruistic, even utilitarian morality that Plato espoused. It is a kind of pre-Christian morality of renunciation and self-denial. As Leonard Peikoff has said, Plato would have us negate our own individuality in the name of "union with the collective."[4] Aristotle, on the other hand, places more emphasis on the individual—on a kind of rational self-pride and on the development and definition of the individual's moral character.

History, as well as the individual human being, reflects this clash between Platonism and Aristotelianism. The concepts exemplified by the two philosophers buffeted each other during the classical period; then in the Middle Ages Platonism dominated, under the influence of such philosophers as Plotinus and Augustine. But Aristotelianism emerged as a powerful force in the thirteenth century, largely through the efforts of Thomas Aquinas. And in the Renaissance there was the rebirth of the Aristotelian spirit, which in Western civilization helped lead to the Age of Reason or the Enlightenment of the eighteenth century. Individualistic political philosophy arose in the thought of John Locke and others, and the concept of freedom spread rapidly, culminating with the birth of the United States, a country of individualism and freedom.[5]

Then Platonism struck hard at Aristotelianism in the late eighteenth century, and the Age of Reason began to give way to Idealism and Romanticism. Immanuel Kant had much to do with it. He was determined to bring an altered form of Platonism back into the mainstream of Western culture. Sounding much like Plato, he maintained that things in themselves are not knowable and that reason cannot discover anything about reality. Faith, he held, is the real key to reality. So Kant denied rational method; in a sense he denied knowledge to make room for faith. He also denied happiness to make room for duty. For Kant, the essence of moral virtue is selflessness, obedience to duty without thought of consequences.[6]

Heraclitus and Flux

Journalism and journalistic concepts—in whatever system—grow and change and render absolute categorization unsatisfactory and often meaningless. Paradoxes abound in journalism. But conflicts and disagreements

---

4 Peikoff, *The Ominous Parallels*, 33.
5 See *ibid.*, 30–33, for a good brief account of this cyclic development of Platonism and Aristotelianism.
6 *Ibid.*, 33.

4

in journalism are healthy, not unhealthy. Contraries contend and clash, and that is good. For, as Heraclitus contended as far back as the sixth century B.C., "Opposition brings concord," and "Out of discord comes the fairest harmony."[7] Certainly Heraclitus was an ancient precursor of Hegel's thought concerning dialectics and change.

As Heraclitus said in another place, "Into the same rivers we step and we do not step." He stressed coalescence and the sense of "otherness." Nothing, he said, is exclusively this or that. Mergers are important; essences and concepts are distilled into new essences that continue to change. "It is one and the same thing," he said, "to be awake or asleep, young or old. Always the former aspect becomes the latter, and the latter again the former, by sudden unexpected reversal."[8]

Heraclitus, like the General Semanticists of the twentieth century, urged people to transcend the "either-or" type of thinking and to recognize in each phase of experience a "both-and" relationship.[9] Certainly, the ideas of this ancient Greek thinker presaged the later dialectical philosophy of Hegel and the "non-Aristotelian" or "multivalued" orientation of the followers of Alfred Korzybski (1879–1950). Relativism has clashed with absolutism, flux with permanence; for, as Heraclitus says, "Everything flows and nothing abides; everything gives way and nothing stays fixed."[10]

No journalist steps into the same journalistic river twice, as Heraclitus would say. Not only the river—not only the reality of the event—but also the journalist is constantly a different being. A new "core" or essence is always in the process of emerging. When it is reported, an event is not the same event it was. Into this world of change comes conflict, perhaps more precisely, conflict brings about this change. Contraries clash and merge. Change, for Heraclitus, is friction between two ontological opposites or contraries. This conflict is the ultimate condition of everything, Heraclitus tells us. Tension is the ultimate, and strife, which often follows tension, is necessary for progress and is not to be avoided.[11]

7 Heraclitus, Frags. 98, 110, quoted in Philip Wheelwright, *Heraclitus* (New York, 1968), 90–91.

8 Heraclitus, Frags. 98, 113, quoted in Wheelwright, *Heraclitus,* 90–91.

9 See Wheelwright, *Heraclitus,* for an extensive explication of Heraclitus' view that all is constantly changing.

10 Heraclitus, Frag. 20, in Wheelwright, *Heraclitus,* 29.

11 For a good discussion of the importance of conflict and strife in the philosophy of Heraclitus, see Wheelwright, *Heraclitus,* 35–38. For a strong anti-Heraclitean position, see Peikoff, *The Ominous Parallels,* and any of Ayn Rand's books.

So Heraclitus' thought supports the underlying theme of this book: that reality (the world of things) is changing constantly—as are concepts and ideas—and that nothing can be absolutely this or that. The thought of this Greek philosopher merges with, and forms a foundation for, a much later philosopher—Hegel (1770–1831), a German follower of Kant's idealism who resurrected the Heraclitean spirit of flux, combined it with a sophisticated concept of dialectical logic, and propelled it in many directions into the twentieth century.

The Hegelian Dialectic

Dialectical thinking was not invented by Hegel. From Heraclitus on, philosophers from time to time had stressed the clash-and-fusion concept of ideas and reality. Immanuel Kant (1724–1804) dealt peripherally with the dialectic, and followers of Kant such as fellow Germans Johann Fichte (1762–1814) and Friedrich von Schelling (1775–1854) added their own ideas about it. Then came Hegel, who synthesized the previous thinking on the dialectic, expanded it, and refined it. In short, Hegel's dialectical method represented the culmination of German classical philosophy and built substantially on many of the great Greek philosophers of antiquity, from Heraclitus onward.

Reality, according to Hegel, is filled with contradictions (or paradoxes, as Heraclitus called them). Dialectical logic is needed to deal with this reality. Such a logic, according to George Novack, is the opposite of Aristotle's formal logic; it is the logic of movement, of evolution, of change. Reality is too elusive, too multisided, and too dynamic "to be snared in any single form or formula or set of formulas," Novack has written.[12]

The Hegelian dialectic states that every condition of thought, every idea, and every world situation leads to its opposite and then, united with it, forms a higher and more complex whole. In a sense, every idea and thing has within it the seeds of its own destruction. This dialectical movement infuses everything that Hegel wrote. Basically, according to Hegel, the

12 George Novack, *An Introduction to the Logic of Marxism* (New York, 1971), 71. Novack's book discusses the differences in formal logic (Aristotle) and dialectical logic (Hegel, Marx). See especially Chapter 5, which succinctly explicates the dialectical method and Hegel's contribution to it. *Cf.* Robert C. Tucker, *Philosophy and Myth in Karl Marx* (London, 1969), Part I, for a discussion of Hegel's dialectic.

truth is an organic unification of opposites or, as I call them in this book, antinomies. There is a continuous fusion or synthesis of opposites or oppositions, brought about by merging and reconciliation, and from this clash comes a new idea or creation.

As the German dialectical philosophers put it, this process of thesis, antithesis, and synthesis is the formula and secret of all development and all reality. The reasonable person, believed Hegel and his followers, is one who is not welded to an extreme or absolute position but recognizes that a new truth will emerge from a clash of positions. This concept, it is interesting to note, is found—as it relates to "truth"—in John Milton's ideas of the "self-righting" process and the "free marketplace of ideas" as far back as 1644 and is further reflected about a century later by such "libertarians" as John Stuart Mill and Thomas Jefferson.

No condition in journalism is permanent. At every stage of journalistic practice and conceptual concern a contradiction arises, and this clash of opposites results in a synthesis or moderated idea or state. It has been said that the deepest law of society—of politics and all social institutions—is freedom, which Will Durant has called "an open avenue to change."[13] Human history is the story of the lessening of freedom, the story of increasing societal controls on freedom, of the shift from emphasis on the individual to emphasis on the society, of the imposition of increasing discipline on the person as concern for the collective and its harmonious functioning grows.

So we can see that the thesis (freedom) is presently being attacked by the antithesis (social control). From this dialectical cauldron is emerging a synthesis of social responsibility—a moderated and socially concerned use of journalistic freedom. And in the future the dialectic will continue. The new thesis, social responsibility, will be buffeted by new antithetical winds—either from the anarchistic direction or from the totalitarian direction—and that will result in a new hybrid, a new journalistic Weltanschauung, the precise nature of which is impossible to foresee at this moment.

Instead of trying to eliminate contradiction, Hegel made it the keystone of his concept of reality and his system of logic. A thing is not only itself, but something else. A is not merely equal to A; it is also equal to non-A. Alfred Korzybski, the founder of General Semantics, stressed the same

13 Will Durant, *The Story of Philosophy* (New York, 1961), 297.

idea in the twentieth century, just as Heraclitus had stressed it in the sixth century B.C. This view, as a logic, is counterposed against the formal logic of Aristotle and its basic law of identity: A is A.

In a sense the Hegelian dialectic says that everything is opposite. The either-or is not realistic; everything has opposition within it. Processes are always contradicting themselves as they develop, and contradictions are what move the world. Dialectics is the process of moving out of and into contradictions or oppositions. Development, according to Hegel, is inherently self-contradictory, and everything generates within itself a force that leads to its demise, to its negation—its passing away into another (and higher) form.

Hegel, however, emphasized ideas. For him, ideas constituted the essence of all reality, and as ideas developed, the rest of reality was moved forward.[14] Marxists, who accept much of Hegel's dialectical thought, are critical of it for stopping society's evolution with its capitalistic mode. One wonders if the Marxists' dialectical materialism does not do much the same thing by assuming that society's development will stop in the communist mode.

Dialectics and Journalism

Journalism itself—in its ideas and outward manifestations—is subject to the Hegelian dialectic. Absolutes and extremes are unproductive in journalism if they are honored as static values. They must be looked upon as *means*—as instruments of opposition and friction—that lead to a new and better journalistic idea or essence. Principles, issues, and traditional wisdom, expressed in dogmatic and self-perpetuating ways, do little to enhance journalistic endeavor; in fact, such dogmatism or absolutism only bogs journalism and the journalist down in a mire of static intellectual sludge.

The thrust of this book, prompted largely by Heraclitus and Hegel, is that reality in journalism, as well as in journalistic concepts, combines and changes. No journalist can afford to push aside the awareness that ideas and events have complex and contradictory natures and that all is constantly changing. Flux is king in journalism. Dynamic thinking and dialogue is essential to journalistic progress. Conservatives must become

14 See Novack, *Introduction to the Logic of Marxism.*

more liberal; liberals must become more conservative. Progressives must become more careful and less precipitous in their advocacy of "progress"; cautious journalists must be bolder.

Journalistic libertarians must be more disciplined and have more respect for authority, and authoritarians must be more sympathetic to the rights of others. Freedom lovers must be more ethical and thereby more controlled; ethicists must strive for increased freedom. That is a large part of the message found in the following pages, as they bring together the flux philosophy of Heraclitus, the dialectical philosophy of Hegel, the philosophy of moderation of Aristotle, and the multivalued orientation of the Korzybskian semanticists.[15]

Aristotle is out of step, in many ways, with Heraclitus, Hegel, and Korzybski. Certainly his "two-valued," or strict-category philosophy contradicts their philosophy of flux and merger. But here again the dialectic is at work, moving toward a synthesis of the ideas of the two main contraries.

It is widely felt that the journalistic world is filled with contradictions, with theses and antitheses. And unfortunately, too often these theses and antitheses are kept separate by communications scholars and communications practitioners, and worshipped idolatrously as discrete values. This is this, and that is that, and never the twain shall meet. Such is the antidialectical propensity found so often among journalists, academics, and politicians. They take a position and defend it, always making it more or less unchanging and discrete. The either-or temptation is great: either objectivity or subjectivity, either authoritarianism or libertarianism, either absolutism or relativism, either freedom or control.

But in spite of this gravitational pull toward either-or thinking, the journalist is really more dialectical than I am indicating. Journalistic liber-

15 The General Semanticists, led by Korzybski, have commented extensively on the weaknesses and dangers of an Aristotelian "two-valued" orientation. The Korzybskians basically subscribe to the philosophy of Heraclitus, Hegel, and their supporters throughout the history of philosophy. For a firsthand look at this non-Aristotelian thought system, see Alfred Korzybski, *Science and Sanity: An Introduction to Non-Aristotelian Systems and General Semantics* (Lakeville, Conn., 1933). Revised editions were published in 1941, 1948, 1958. See also J. Samuel Bois, *The Art of Awareness: A Textbook on General Semantics and Epistemics* (Dubuque, Iowa, 1973), Wendell Johnson, *People in Quandaries* (New York, 1946), Stuart Chase, *The Tyranny of Words* (New York, 1938), and S. I. Hayakawa, *Language in Thought and Action* (New York, 1941), for good modern interpretations of Korzybskian thought.

als are also—or are becoming—conservatives; conservatives are also—or are becoming—liberals. Both groups are constantly conserving and changing their ideas. They are changing what they value, however slowly, and they are in the process of conserving what they value, albeit unsuccessfully. The subjective reporter writes about objects; the objective reporter strains his report through his or her own subjectivity. Most journalists talk about moral imperatives or principles and often think in absolutes while making exceptions every day. Journalists are both relativists and absolutists.

It might be said that journalists are, really, absolute believers in relativism—or relativistic believers in absolutism. They are both egoists and altruists, in spite of affirming a certain emphasis at any one time or in any particular situation. Journalists are not really "either-or" persons; they are all mergers—creatures of the clash between inflexibility and flexibility and between all the other contraries that impinge on their lives. They are, whether they realize it or not, dialectical journalists. Some, of course, are more dialectical than others, or, to say it another way, some are more purposely or more intentionally dialectical than others.

Those in journalism who know the value of dialectics and who are determined to exercise dialecticism to the maximum will be more in tune with reality than those who cling tenaciously to extreme positions. Dialectical journalism is perfectly consistent with the philosophy of pluralism; it is consistent with the philosophy of the libertarian clash of ideas in the marketplace; it is consistent with the liberal orientation toward change and with the historicism and individualism of the conservative. In short, dialectical thinking is perfectly consistent with the spirit of relativity, with multidimensional empiricism, with constant change, with continual dying and rebirth, and with a whole host of cyclic theories. But the dialectical stance is often overlooked or underemphasized and thus journalists cling to their favorite concepts and perspectives, doggedly defend them, and persistently treat them as if they are eternal and unchanging.

It is hoped that the following pages will awaken in journalists and students of journalism the dialectical spirit, especially in the area of freedom and responsibility. A widespread recognition that journalists are not ever absolutely free or perfectly ethical, but that they are *somewhat* free and *somewhat* ethical—that would certainly be a dialectical step forward. Freedom and responsibility are, in a real sense, contraries of great importance in journalism; they are the tension agents that bring conflict into the dialectic. Freedom clashes with ethics to gain more flexibility and individualism. Ethics conflicts with freedom to supplant personal licentiousness with social concern. Neither ever completely wins the battle, and neither falls completely vanquished. Instead, a reconciliation, a hybridization, a mediation—a *dialectical synthesis*—results.

There is here a paradox implied by the dialectic itself. A fundamental paradox of journalistic endeavor lies in the fact that we can realize our freedom, our individualism, only as members of communities and only as we are forced to interact with others. Society, as Nicola Chiaromonte points out, must set limits on human freedom in the interest of justice for all.[16]

Journalists evidently want neither anarchy nor nihilism, though they say they prize freedom. Neither do they want complete control and collective harmony, though they say they prize social responsibility and institutional and professional discipline. What they really want is a moderated version—a synthesis—of both extremes, a synthesis that combines the admirable and helpful characteristics of the contraries. Some journalists may not know this is what they want; certainly they may not *say* this is what they want. But it seems to me that this is a deep psychological yearning always—to have the best of *many* (not just both) worlds.

A main intent of this book is to show how freedom relates to ethics in journalism and at the same time to discuss how a number of other contraries or antinomies are unsuitable in the real world of journalism.[17] I also hope to demonstrate how a synthesis—a position near the Aristotelian Golden Mean—is the best solution to many of the problems of mass communication. We need to form the habit of thinking dialectically about many of our journalistic problems, realizing that a clash of opposing positions is not harmful but useful in the constantly changing world of journalism.

---

16 Nicola Chiaromonte, *The Paradox of History* (Philadelphia, 1985). *Cf.* Sidney Hook, *The Paradoxes of Freedom* (Berkeley, 1967) for a discussion in even more detail of this paradox.

17 *Antinomies* is perhaps not the perfect word in this context; however, over the years it has been imbued with a special significance, roughly, expressing the extremes of a dialectic, *e.g.,* the thesis and the antithesis, which clash and result in a mutation or synthesis. *Antinomies* has been used in this sense by many others. For instance, Henry E. Allison deals with antinomies in his *Kant's Transcendental Idealism* (New Haven, 1983), 30–50, 310–15.

The Author's Confession

This book has simmered in my mind for many years. It was simmering even before I wrote *The Imperative of Freedom*. As the years have gone by, I have realized that absolute positions and ideologies are not realistic or helpful; nor do they provide an adequate way of getting the best (most useful) information and concepts from opposite and often extreme positions. So I have come to see the usefulness of moderation in conceptual thinking; by moderation I mean separating the wheat from the chaff in the case of each of the main opposing positions and combining compatible strains of the wheat into new but similar hybrids. Theoretically, such a combining procedure should lead to a better variety of wheat.

The basic principle of the dialectic is to let the opposites clash and watch the stronger portions of each merge to combine in a new concept that is stronger than either of the original concepts. This principle is usually associated with Hegel, but it was probably developed in this three-stage form by Fichte. It is the principle that permeates this book, a principle that in theory can prevent journalists in general, and me in particular, from becoming too attached to any one position. It is a way to remain ideological without becoming an ideologue.

I recall when I could see no virtue whatsoever in collectivistic concepts of the press. To me, only libertarian perspectives were valid, worth discussing, and applicable to a press system that was vital, progressive, and moral. No more. Although I still support the basic concept of a libertarian (capitalistic, pluralistic, and competitive) press system, I am no longer so certain of its unquestionable moral—or even its socially pragmatic—advantages over other systems. Perhaps it is time for journalists to recognize that freedom must pay its way to somebody, regardless of its journalistic context, and that responsibility often blindly stumbles along hand in hand with political ideology.

At one time American-style press freedom in its extreme manifestation ("The people be damned; *I* am the editor!") had a great appeal for me. Now I am surprised that I was stuck in that dark corner of the dialectical thesis. I am presently moving away from it, being nudged less than gently by colleagues in recent years who have a more humane and populist orientation. Also, what might be called People Power, an antithesis resulting from a combination of populism and collectivism, rapped me more than lightly on the head as it evidenced the sterility of my earlier conviction that it was proper for the press to have power (freedom) without any concomitant obligations to the people.

Various intellectual forces have shaped my new—but ever-changing—journalistic philosophy. One of them has been a longtime interest in process philosophy, an interest that stemmed largely from Heraclitus. Hegel, of course, had an impact.[18] So did many of the concepts and ideas of the General Semanticists, who have a most eclectic orientation, but one that reemphasizes the importance of flux and the need to demolish rigid, two-valued perspectives for a more dynamic, multivalued linguistic (and conceptual) world of change and merger.

Good and bad journalism, objective and subjective reporting, personal and impersonal journalism, hard and soft news, news and commentary, ethical and unethical reporting, people's rights and press rights—and on and on could go the antinomies of journalism. It is easy to get stuck on one side or the other of all these antinomies. And probably even worse is the proclivity of a person, in getting so stuck, to justify this intransigent position by appealing to clichés of virtue such as steadfastness, loyalty, courage, and tenacity. After all, one is prone to think, only the weak-willed, the fearful, and the uncommitted will refuse to take a stand for a principle, an absolute, for one of the sacred antinomies of American journalism.

For years I took such positions. I thought that by taking stands I was being courageous, when often I was being foolhardy. I saw my convictions as necessary, when in fact they were often no more than biased sophistry. I saw my iconoclasm as helpful, when often it was simply confusing and debilitating. Not that I now have forsaken all obstinance or contentiousness—far from it. And I still believe in taking definite positions when my feeling, as well as my intellect, tells me that they are warranted and helpful. I have not retreated into a relativistic world where all values are equal, where choosing and acting are not incumbent on the person, and where the self is depreciated and authenticity cowers in some shadowy corner. But I am now willing to break loose from antinomies more than in earlier times and to merge useful insights and concepts into new syntheses that can enrich journalism and push it forward.

18 For a readable and refreshing look at Hegel's philosophy, see Robert C. Solomon, *In the Spirit of Hegel* (New York, 1983). What I propose in this book is in the spirit of Hegel, especially as it relates to the dialectic, though not as it relates to some of the other aspects of his philosophy. I pay little attention, for example, to his political philosophy or to his ethics.

A Shift to the Middle

One can say with considerable truth that there is nothing new about my account of the dialectic, my shift from extremes to the middle. But it is a new orientation for me, and it may also be for great numbers of journalists who daily wrestle with important philosophical concepts. There is nothing wrong, I realize after a long attachment to antinomies, with the more flexible middle ground of conceptual synthesizing that often forces one to give equivocal answers ever more frequently and, often, to say simply, "I don't know."

This stance is not one that many journalists—or, for that matter, many nonjournalists—find appealing. Definite positions, specific allegiances, and inerrant loyalties tend to dominate in our society. It is thought that there is something fuzzy, something inauthentic, something weak and indecisive about this great middle area of synthesis formation. It is an area of paradoxes, constant change, ideological conflict, and conceptual seepage; it is an area where even our language seems incapable of stating just where we are, what we believe, and what we are doing.

The Imperative of Freedom, published in 1974, was indicative of my younger self, the "antinomies period" of my journalistic thinking. I am not repudiating that book here, but I am revising it, updating it, and, I believe, lifting it to another (and higher) plane of discourse. In 1974 I defended and argued for a strong Jeffersonian position. Setting journalistic autonomy on a throne, I was the consummate press libertarian. I placed individualism astride a white horse and had this valiant warrior ride triumphantly (and often roughshod) over collectivism. I deprecated social adjustment and gloried in existential or personal maverickism. I repudiated all kinds of conformity, especially in the newsroom and in journalism schools, and urged a free-wheeling, courageous existentialist position.

Since 1974 I have not noticed journalism becoming more individualistic, more Jeffersonian, or more existential. On the contrary, journalism is increasingly adjusting itself to its capitalistic context, wallowing in conformist muck and mire, veering in the direction of "the people's" interaction in editorial affairs, and accepting ever more controls—all in the name of social responsibility and moral considerations. In other words, American journalism, as I see it, has struck at the individualistic Jeffersonian thesis with the antithesis of social adjustment or Marxist collectivism, and we are now trying to find a firm footing in the still-soggy middle ground of individualized social consciousness.

There are at least two ways to deal dialectically with journalistic concepts and issues. The first way is the way I tried in 1974: to make the whole book an antithesis to what I saw as the dominant, or at least a rising, press philosophy—collectivism. I decided to present *only* the antithesis; at the time others were presenting the thesis in numerous books and articles.

The second way to handle the dialectic is the way I have chosen for this book: to present theses, antitheses, and syntheses all in the same work. Such a book may suffer, of course, from less vigorous rhetoric and a lack of focus and emphasis, compared with the book written from a single position, but it has what is perhaps the offsetting advantage of providing the reader with the entire dialectical process, including the synthesis.

Hegel had a lot to say. Much of it (largely his conception of the dialectic) can be related to the problems of the modern journalist. This influential German philosopher exemplifies the dialectic in his own writings. He has been claimed by fascists, Nazis, and other groups on the authoritarian Right, and at the same time, his ideas have been appropriated by socialists, communists, and Marxists of the authoritarian Left. And he has been claimed, in part, by many people in the middle who would not, by any stretch of the imagination, be called fascists or communists. So just as there are "Hegelians" of the Left and Hegelians of the Right, there are also Hegelians of the Center. And that is as it should be, given the fact that we are talking about the greatest thinker of modern times.

Many will say that it is too bad that one cannot pigeonhole Hegel. If he is an authoritarian, as he is generally considered to be, he must be only a temporary one—if his process philosophy is correct. What people want to know is what political label to apply to him. They seem to want a static Hegel who can be captured by one label, a Hegel without movement, without paradox. Such a rigid description of Hegel will not be forthcoming. For whatever he is, is what he is not; whatever he became and what his ideas become is what he was and is. The preceding sentence is not esoteric verbalizing or playing with words; it is the very essence of the dialectic. And it is a stance that the journalist facing an increasingly complex world might do well to adopt. I have tried to adopt it in the following pages, and I hope that—as with Hegel—it will be difficult, or impossible, for the reader to pigeonhole me.

Part I

THE DIALECTICAL APPROACH

One

THE SEARCH FOR FREEDOM

Freedom is a big word. It covers a vast territory—psychological, political, philosophical, economic, and sociological. And certainly, it is easily applied to communication and journalistic activities. Although there are many meanings of freedom, varying among individuals as well as nations, there is no doubt but that the concept is universally considered of some importance and has, throughout history, received considerable attention.

Since this book is concerned with the problems of the journalist, a broad but relatively neutral definition of freedom is adopted: freedom is the condition of being able to select and to carry out purposes. This definition, of course, retains the basic dictionary meaning—the idea of the absence of external constraints on one hand and on the other the concept of practicable purposes, the effective capacity to do what one wishes. In other words, this short definition includes both *negative* freedom (freedom from) and *positive* freedom (freedom to).

Freedom is a state in which a journalist (or media director, whether private or governmental) can determine what to do in his or her situation, what kind of self or journalist unit to become. Freedom, in other words, implies self-determination of what is right and good, and that is where the ethical or moral dimension enters the picture.[1]

---

1 Naturally the main perspective on journalistic freedom in this book is derived from the American experience.

Freedom: Its Ambiguity

An initial problem, of course, in dealing with freedom is its many meanings, nuances, and general impreciseness. In short, the term is ambiguous; it is filled with semantic "noise" that gives rise to innumerable arguments about its nature, especially among persons coming from different ideological or political contexts. We hear of people making distinctions between freedom and liberty, between negative freedom and positive freedom, between freedom and license, and on and on.

There are as many meanings or understandings of *press freedom* as of freedom itself. One would expect the concept of press freedom to differ widely from one ideological or political context to another, but it also should be noted that even in the misty middle zones between capitalism and socialism there are strange, ambiguous meanings assigned to the term. For instance, in 1986, an incident involving Dileep Padgaonkar, the Indian-born director of the Division of Free Flow of Information and Communications at Paris' UNESCO headquarters, indicated what a wide range of interpretations the concept of journalistic freedom may have. Padgaonkar demanded that journalists who covered a conference in Copenhagen on the international flow of information obtain permission from participants before quoting from their speeches or papers. Indignant journalists were told that this procedure was necessary in order to assure "correct coverage of the meeting" and to bring about a freer debate among delegates.[2]

Naturally there has been a multitude of interpretations of, and perspectives on, freedom. Quite often these interpretations or emphases have stemmed from the political and social philosophies of the writers. Freedom, for example, is variously,—in summary fashion—natural, acquired, and circumstantial (according to Mortimer J. Adler); the ability to choose (Herbert Muller); the possibility of meaningful choice (P. D. Partridge); choosing and acting (Jean-Paul Sartre); personal growth (John Dewey); spontaneity (Erich Fromm); the right to rebel (Harold Laski); living in an unplanned society (F. A. Hayek); living in a socialist planned society (Richard Tawney); being able to pursue one's rational self-interest (Ayn Rand); a result of tradition and order (Russell Kirk); practically impossible in today's technological society (Herbert Marcuse); and possible only

2 *IPI Report* (May, 1986), 1.

through the dictatorship of the people (Mao Tse-Tung). There are about as many views on freedom as there are people.

Immanuel Kant had a rather interesting one. He believed that "inner-bondage, self-constraint, [and] compulsion" were necessary to give a person freedom. Only when one is morally driven to do something, feeling it to be compulsory and feeling oneself a slave to the self-imposed command to do it, is that person really free. In other words, one must rule the self well in order to be free. It is a dictatorship of the moral "ought." Kant called it a type of autocracy—an autocracy of one. Man is free, Kant contends, "in so far as he identifies himself with the internal autocratic authority and compels himself to obey all its perfectionist dictates."[3]

Robert Tucker, summarizing Kant's concept of freedom, maintains that a person is free "in so far as he submits willingly to the internal autocratic order, unfree in so far as he acts in accordance with mere impulses or desires." Tucker also makes the interesting observation that there is an analogy between Kant's position and that of the political authoritarian or dictator who claims that his restrictive rule is the "higher form of freedom" and that there is "no real freedom in a democracy, where everyone does as he pleases."[4]

John Stuart Mill defended freedom on utilitarian grounds. Freedom would make it possible for the maximum happiness (or good) to accrue to society. He saw capitalism as the system best suited to bring the most happiness to the public, though he also saw that capitalism was based on the desire for selfish profit. But according to Mill, the individual must be as free from government regulation as possible—not because he has an inalienable right to freedom, but simply on the grounds of social utility.[5]

Herbert Spencer defended freedom (from government) on the basis of a social Darwinian principle, believing that as time goes by, the weak will be weeded out and only the strong will survive. That would guarantee mankind's happiness. So as not to interfere with this evolutionary principle, the government, Spencer thought, should not seek, by controlling the economy or through undue charity, to hinder the strong or nourish the weak. Thus, Spencer believed in a policy of strict laissez-faire.[6] Like Mill,

---

3 Tucker, *Philosophy and Myth in Karl Marx*, 36.
4 *Ibid.*
5 Peikoff, *The Ominous Parallels*, 119–20.
6 *Ibid.*, 121.

he accepted the principle of individual rights for the utilitarian reason that the freedom it gave rise to would result in social benefits.

Closer to the present, Alfred North Whitehead conceived of freedom in its negative sense, that is, as a state of being unrestricted, able to act according to one's own disposition. Whitehead said in 1933 that for a human being, the impulse to be free is the desire not to be hampered in purposive action. His definition applied, he said, not only to freedom of expression, (which includes freedom of the press) but also to all the main pursuits of living.[7]

Like Whitehead, Alexander Solzhenitsyn values a "sense of the worth of life," and this entails a deep love for freedom. Also like Whitehead, he believes that freedom and harmony are inseparable. According to Solzhenitsyn, when maximum freedom which gives sanctity to every being, exists, then the people can play a significant part in a harmonious world. In perhaps his best work, *The Gulag Archipelago,* Solzhenitsyn shows the relationship between freedom and harmony. Although the book's main theme is the inhuman conditions in Soviet labor camps, the underlying message is that true freedom must be achieved on a spiritual level: to be able to contemplate, to be able to perceive the truth, to have no unnecessary physical needs—this is the path to real contentment, he maintains. Freedom, to Solzhenitsyn, is thus a kind of spiritual, internal freedom, somewhat as it is for Kant. But for Solzhenitsyn, in order to be authentic or genuine, this freedom must break out and be expressed.[8] In this demand for the active expression of freedom Solzhenitsyn evidences a strong existentialist inclination. First an inner sense of freedom and harmony permeates one's being; then one speaks freely, thereby externalizing this inner freedom.

Two Main Types of Freedom

The words *freedom* and *liberty* are usually used interchangeably. Seldom, in common parlance, is a distinction made between the two terms. However, many authors and speakers have, in recent years, equated *liberty* with what is generally called *negative freedom*—the capacity not to be

7 Alfred North Whitehead, *Adventures of Ideas* (New York, 1967), 66.
8 Leopold Labedz (ed.), *Solzhenitsyn: A Documentary Record* (Bloomington, 1973), 300–305.

coerced or enslaved. The word *freedom* is then often reserved for what is usually called *positive freedom*—freedom to be a doer or to achieve something. Although in this book the term *freedom* will be used instead of *liberty,* such a distinction can be, and often is, made today.[9] When necessary—and that will be seldom—the terms *negative freedom* and *positive freedom* will be used to express the main emphasis given to the concept of freedom. Personal journalistic freedom—the emphasis on *existential* freedom—really revolves around positive freedom—the freedom to act, to choose, to make one's self through choices and actions.

Positive freedom (usually attributed to Rousseau or Hegel), then, is freedom to achieve some good, whereas negative freedom (generally attributed to Hobbes or Locke) is freedom from restraint.[10] Many commentators on these two kinds of freedom have implied that negative freedom is irresponsible and that positive freedom is responsible. This positive-negative dualism is troublesome, however. For, as I pointed out in *The Imperative of Freedom,* it appears that if a person were not free of restraint, he or she would not have the freedom to achieve some good of his or her choice. Therefore, it seems that the heart of the concept of freedom is a synthesis of the two varieties.[11]

Certainly a journalist concerned with freedom will be desirous of both eliminating restrictions on his or her autonomous activities *and* determining to do something with this "freedom from restrictions." What can I *do*? This is a basic existential question, and it propels the journalist into the future, making him or her a person of action. For surely one can be free to do, without doing; one can have the freedom to act, without acting. A journalist, for instance, can have the freedom to write a particular government exposé without ever getting around to it. In other words, negative freedom almost always exceeds positive freedom—even in so-called controlled or totalitarian societies. Some choices in journalism can always be made that are not made. People do not ever really live up to their potential. Possibilities exceed achievement. Choosing and acting on one's own initiative is positive freedom; absence of obstructions, interference,

---

9 I have decided to use the term *freedom* because it is more commonly used in the context of the press, and besides, it has an adjectival form (*free*) to go along with it, and *liberty* does not.

10 See Isaiah Berlin, *Two Concepts of Liberty* (Oxford, 1958).

11 John C. Merrill, *The Imperative of Freedom: A Philosophy of Journalistic Autonomy* (New York, 1974), 32.

coercion and control is negative freedom. So if journalists do not *do* when they are not restrained by others, they are not truly free in the positive sense.

It appears that we are all caught somewhere between the extremes of human freedom and human bondage. As Richard Taylor writes, "Virtually all men are to *some* extent free; their conduct is to some extent subject to their own will." He continues, "Similarly, all are to some extent in bondage: their conduct is to some extent involuntarily subject to the will of others."[12] The journalist is never completely free, either in the negative or the positive sense. Caught in the twilight zone between compulsion and inertia, he or she stumbles along through the shadows of dialectic journalism. Unfortunately, not all journalists can do; even more unfortunately, those who can do, often do not do.

Existential Freedom

The journalist, when considering freedom on the personal or individual level, is thrust into the existential dimension. The journalist senses the difficulty of personal freedom in the workaday world. The so-called "realities" of working for a newspaper or some other news medium dominate, and the journalist cannot simply do his or her "own things," but must follow directions, conform to editorial policy, and sublimate self to others.

Existentialists would say that this rationalization is always standing by, ready to be used by journalists who live largely in a state of Sartrean "bad faith"—a kind of inauthentic existence—in their work. From existentialism's early days in the time of Kierkegaard, through the era of Nietzsche, and into the period of the more recent existentialists, such as Karl Jaspers, Albert Camus, and Jean-Paul Sartre, these philosophers have made us aware of the difficulty of being free. But according to the existentialists, each journalist, in spite of such difficulties and dangers, has the inescapable responsibility to accomplish his or her ends—or at least the journalist must *try* to. As Sartre points out, it would be absurd to argue that a prisoner is always free to get out of prison, but one can say that "he is always free to try to escape." And as Sartre says in another place, "The formula 'to be free' does not mean 'to obtain what one has wished' but

12 Richard Taylor, *Freedom, Anarchy, and the Law* (Englewood Cliffs, N.J., 1973), 9.

rather 'by oneself to determine oneself to wish' (in the broad sense of choosing)."[13]

Furthermore, if the journalist does not will himself or herself to be free (even if he or she fails), the choice is for an inauthentic life. For such a journalist must, as Karl Jaspers says, "on his initiative independently gain possession of the mechanism of his life, or else, himself degraded to become a machine, surrender to the apparatus."[14]

As I wrote in my book *Existential Journalism* (1977), the existential journalist prizes free acts. Such acts, of course, have consequences, and the existential journalist must take these into consideration when making decisions. The journalist is responsible for the consequences of these freely determined acts, whether anticipated or not. The journalist can always say no to orders; there is never an absolute necessity to act. A person, according to Peter Koestenbaum, chooses and must live with these choices— must accept personal responsibility for them. He continues: "My involvement with the consequences of my actions is neither a moral relation in the traditional sense, nor a sociological convention, nor a divine edict. That I am responsible for the consequences of my acts, because I initiated these and could have chosen otherwise—whether the consequences could have been foreseen or not—is merely the recognition of a fundamental and irrefutable *fact* of my nature and a *fact* about my experience of being human, disclosed by introspective phenomenological analysis."[15]

Many journalists therefore fear freedom because they fear to assume responsibility for decisions. For when a journalist acts freely, there is a necessity to throw off inertia, cut loose from tradition, and—what is more important—slip into a position of accepting moral responsibility for actions taken. From time to time, from place to place, some journalists rise to the defense of freedom (not just press freedom, but also *personal* freedom), speaking out against limitations of the prevailing system. But more often, it seems, a journalist in such a situation will call in an organization of journalists for support, instead of choosing to make a stand alone.

This struggle for freedom and authenticity in journalism is a personal fight fought in the face of a dark future in which it appears that conformity

13 Quoted in Robert C. Solomon (ed.), *Phenomenology and Existentialism* (New York, 1972), 462. See also Jean-Paul Sartre, *Being and Nothingness* (New York, 1956).
14 Karl Jaspers, *Man in the Modern Age* (Garden City, N.Y., 1957), 195.
15 Peter Koestenbaum, *Philosophy: A General Introduction* (New York, 1963), 324.

and depersonalization will increase and freedom diminish. Existential freedom is pitted against pressures to conform. The journalist, if an existentialist, is committed to protecting and expanding his or her individuality and to *acting* in the face of personal risk. It is only in this way that the forces of enslavement and depersonalization can be frustrated.

Stalwarts of Freedom

In the course of history, freedom of the press has had many stalwarts.[16] John Milton (1608–1674) in his *Areopagitica* (1644) argued that licensing of the press was impractical and impaired the search for truth, which could arise only from the free and open encounter of ideas. Later in the seventeenth century, John Locke (1632–1704) extolled man's rationality and postulated that free expression was a natural right.

In the eighteenth century, Voltaire (1694–1778), one of the best-known defenders of freedom of expressions at that time, affirmed the biblical dictum that "The truth shall make you free" even while recognizing a related problem: one had to be free to know the truth. Adam Smith (1723–1790), at about the same time, was proposing his famous concept of laissez faire—that government should keep hands off and let the various business enterprises, including the press, make their own way in the marketplace.

In America, Thomas Jefferson (1743–1826), following Locke in England, expressed strong faith in man's rationality and advocated a minimum of government interference in everyday affairs. For Jefferson, a free and autonomous press was essential for public enlightenment and as a safeguard for personal liberties. Another great American spokesman for press freedom was John Adams (1735–1826), who advised journalists in 1765 that they should not "suffer themselves to be wheedled out of their liberty by any pretences of politeness, delicacy, or decency." These, said Adams, were simply different names for "hypocrisy, chicanery, and cowardice."[17]

16 For a good discussion of the landmarks of press freedom see Carl L. Becker, *Freedom and Responsibility in the American Way of Life* (New York, 1960), chapter 2, and William L. Rivers, Wilbur Schramm, and C. G. Christians, *Responsibility in Mass Communication* (New York, 1980), Chapter 2.
17 Reuven Frank, "The First Amendment Includes Television," *Nieman Reports* (December 1971), 8.

Back in England there was Jeremy Bentham (1748–1832), who believed that every law was a restriction of freedom and urged that laws be minimized. For him, society was composed of atomistic individuals pursuing their own happiness, and a realization of individual self-interest (of which the best judge was the individual) must occur in an atmosphere of freedom. Press freedom he defended on the grounds that publicity was necessary to good government and that it was the best way to get and keep public confidence in government.

Bentham's close associate James Mill (1773–1836) thought the "middle rank" of society was the wisest and most virtuous. He advocated freedom of the press because it publicized individuals who were elected to wield power in government, and unless information about their activities was made public, the officials might serve only their own interests.[18] James's son John Stuart Mill (1806–1873) built on his father's ideas, and his famous tract *On Liberty* justified free expression on utilitarian principles. He maintained that liberty was the right of a *mature* person and that for the good of society, individuals must be restrained. He insisted that intelligence atrophies and initiative dies from overzealous direction by government.

Until the twentieth century, discussions of press freedom and freedom of expression generally centered on laissez faire, on government separation from the press, on personal and media autonomy, on the elimination of licensing, and on the "free marketplace of ideas." But early in this century that began to change. Oliver Wendell Holmes (1841–1935) set the stage for the new trend toward limited freedom with his "clear and present danger" concept and his implication that the government should be allowed to protect itself. Entering the scene were the new "moral guides," who were determined to give a different direction to the press and lead it into more ethical and responsible pathways.

Enter the Moral Guides

These new moral guides prescribed what the press should do to keep its freedom. Their impact has been great, as evidenced by the recent trend toward such pressure groups and media arbiters as press councils, critics, and ombudsmen. The broadcast media, of course, have from the begin-

18 E. M. Zashin, *Civil Disobedience and Democracy* (New York, 1972), 25.

ning operated under the "responsibility doctrine" instead of the "freedom doctrine," and though many broadcasters are agitating for equal freedom with the print media, they are likely to get nowhere as long as the trend continues toward responsibility.

Although moral guides for the press have always been with us, the twentieth century has spawned a new breed of articulate and very vocal ones who claim to know what the press should do to be responsible to society. They have shifted, and are continuing to shift, the concept of press freedom from an emphasis on individual media freedom to a stress on a kind of social freedom to have a responsible press.

This new emphasis has been on positive freedom, or on what the press must do. Put another way, the implication is that the state and the press must somehow cooperate to give society or the people what they need or what they *should have the freedom to get*. A Canadian journalist has articulated this new idea of press freedom as the people's freedom in these words: "The truth about freedom of the press is that it stands for freedom of the people. . . . It is not a special right or cloistered virtue. . . . To deserve its freedom a press should strive daily to be reasonably responsible. . . . Freedom of the press is not a press freedom but a public freedom, a public possession and right, and in some ways its stoutest weapon."[19]

Walter Lippmann, one of the foremost of the modern guides for the media, has best expressed his feelings on press freedom (though he is actually referring to freedom of speech) in *The Public Philosophy*. He stresses what he calls dialectic as the prerequisite for such freedom of expression. As Lippmann sees it, the press should "confront ideas with opposing ideas," so that people will get "true ideas," and if this is not done, freedom cannot be defended. For him, when communication is silly or filled with deception, it cannot be "preserved against the demand for a restoration of order or of decency." He goes on: "For in the absence of debate unrestricted utterance leads to the degradation of opinion. By a kind of Gresham's law the more rational is overcome by the less rational, and the opinions that will prevail will be those which are held most ardently by those with the most passionate will. For that reason the freedom to speak can never be maintained merely by objecting to interference with the liberty of the press, of printing, of broadcasting, of the screen. It can be maintained only by promoting debate."[20]

19 Norman Smith, "Freedom Is a Public Freedom, not Just a Press Freedom," *Seminar Quarterly* (September, 1972), 21–22.
20 Walter Lippmann, *The Public Philosophy* (New York, 1955), 100.

Another person who would guide the press is Walter Berns, a political scientist who is an apologist for censorship on the grounds that virtue is a higher good than freedom. Of course, like any good guide, he is certain that he knows virtue when he sees it. In his *Freedom, Virtue, and the First Amendment* he maintains that the public interest requires the law to take a hand in guarding us from "bad" messages, and that First Amendment freedoms are privileges rather than rights. He sums up his position, and evidently the position of most of the new moral guides, with this statement: "Freedom ideally is extended to those we can trust not to misuse the privilege."[21]

It is easy to confuse democracy and even responsibility in journalism with the idea of "giving the people what they want." But that concept may be an erroneous application of the democratic principle, for journalism is something more than a mere public utility that produces a physical staple such as gas or electricity. It is at least partly an art, a creative enterprise; individual talents go into its production. Journalism—at least free journalism—is something other than a fountain that pours forth a predictable and consistent product at the beck and call of consumers.[22]

So in spite of a few voices here and there trying to lure us back to the pristine libertarian days of Locke, Mill, and Jefferson, today there is a disposition to redefine freedom of the press, to divorce it from independent editorial determination by the media and infuse it with increased "guidance" of one type or another. But this is the dialectic at work in journalism, and it cannot be stopped. This redefining, whether it comes from politicians or from intellectuals in nonpolitical situations, is limiting (or perhaps expanding?) and changing the concept of American press freedom. The attempt to make the press "responsible" or "accountable" is the synthesis of freedom and control, and the time for such a synthesis is at hand.

American Press Freedom in Flux

Let us now turn more specifically to the area of journalism, especially the traditional concept of press freedom in the United States. What follows, of course, is but the broad outlines of the American concept, minus the myriads of esoteric interpretations, eccentric deviations, and minority perspectives.

21 Walter Berns, *Freedom, Virtue, and the First Amendment* (Baton Rouge, 1957).
22 See Sydney J. Harris, *The Authentic Person* (Niles, Ill., 1972), esp. Chapters 3 and 4.

It is difficult to discuss freedom of the press in the American context because there is no single American viewpoint. But there are some common emphases and perspectives. One of them is what might be called "journalistic autonomy."[23] Journalistic autonomy means a kind of separation of press and state, an independence of press (print media units) from government—a form of "institutional freedom." It implies that there is no direction, interference, or control of content from outside the media themselves—at least none from the state. That is the core meaning of press freedom that is rather generally accepted in the United States. But it is being slowly changed, and there are other aspects of, and graftings onto, the concept.

One can look at press freedom as determination of the content of mass communications by the media or as determination of it by the public (in a kind of people's lobby or majority desire). The relevant freedom can be considered mainly as belonging to the press or as belonging to the people. The latter view of press freedom (really a pseudoview, in my opinion) appears to be in its ascendancy, and the future journalism of the United States will likely be a journalism of social adjustment.

At any rate, the older concept of press autonomy is being challenged, and this challenge has arisen primarily since World War II. The well-known Hutchins Commission report of the 1940s and the development of the "social responsibility theory" of the press have done much to bring about the shift in thinking toward a stress on the press's responsibility, duties, and obligations.[24]

Although the First Amendment to the Constitution, which more or less protects press freedom in the United States, is still intact, subtle changes are taking place. They have been brought about by the many press excesses of recent years and by a rising suspicion and fear of the press and its power on the part of the American public at large.[25]

The public has come to see the press as arrogant, careless, and in many

23 See Merrill, *The Imperative of Freedom.*

24 See Commission on Freedom of the Press, *A Free and Responsible Press* (Chicago, 1947). The book that did most to conceptualize the theory of social responsibility was Fred S. Siebert, Theodore Peterson, and Wilbur Schramm, *Four Theories of the Press* (Urbana, 1956), esp. 73–103.

25 Among many recent books dealing with press power and the public's growing concern about it, two excellent ones are Robert Stein, *Media Power* (Boston, 1972), and J. Herbert Altschull, *Agents of Power: The Role of the News Media in Human Affairs* (New York, 1984).

ways unethical in its pursuit of the news. *Irresponsible* is an epithet increasingly hurled at the American press. There is no need to enumerate here the many sins of the press that have been pointed out in the last decade or so. The fact is that the American public is becoming ever more aware of these press flaws, and the image of the press becomes darker all the while.

Therefore, pressures are mounting on the press to become more responsible. Of course, among the significant questions are, What is meant by *responsible,* and who (or what agency) will be the definer? And if the answer is, as it has been traditionally, that the determination of socially responsible journalism will be left strictly to the media themselves, then the question is closed and the debate is over. For this is exactly what we already have in our libertarian, laissez-faire, self-determining media system. But since more and more people are questioning the right and power of the press to make such independent determinations, the debate is far from over.

The Trend Toward Professionalization

Other approbative theories of press responsibility are being considered as alternatives to the old theory.[26] Perhaps the most popular one in the United States—and the one most likely to succeed—is the "professionally defined" concept. Rather than see the courts or the government take steps to define and enforce responsibility in journalism, American journalists are ever more willing to control journalism through their own organization—through professionalization. Under the professionally defined concept, professional journalists as a body would control each individual journalist and enforce his or her responsibility. The individual journalist would no longer regulate himself or herself. The Profession of Journalism would define and approve the actions of all members of the press.

Many journalists in the United States see this trend toward professionalization as a good move, one that will assure a certain degree of journalistic freedom while increasing responsibility. It is a way, they say, of making sure that only well-educated and ethical journalists practice journalism—*i.e.,* are admitted to the Profession. The idea of the Profes-

---

26 These approbative theories of journalistic responsibility have been discussed in John C. Merrill, "Three Theories of Press Responsibility and the Advantages of Pluralistic Individualism" (Paper presented at the Annual Conference of the International Communication Association, Honolulu, Hawaii, May 23–27, 1985).

sion of Journalism has many supporters, but it also has detractors. Its foes see the move to further professionalization as dangerous to press pluralism; they see it as excluding many "eccentric" journalists from practicing journalism; they see it as a trend toward conformity in journalism; they see it as a tendency toward a journalism of "self-interest" rather than public interest; they see it as essentially bringing about licensing of journalists with all that would entail; and they see it as basically contrary to the whole idea of open journalism in an open society.

In any event, whether from the "professionalizers" in American society or from other places, pressures are mounting on the press to become more responsible. Newspapers are pulling their punches more and more. Editors are making fewer editorial decisions in touchy cases; lawyers are playing an ever greater role. The standard joke among journalists in the United States is that lawyers now edit American newspapers.

People's Freedom: A New Notion

The shift in emphasis from press freedom to press responsibility has resulted in a change in the meaning of the term *press freedom*. Whereas traditionally the "freedom" belonged to the press, nowadays one can hear many people talking about press freedom as belonging to the people, however illogical that might sound. Press freedom is becoming the people's freedom.

This shift from the press's freedom to the people's freedom (the people's right to use the press as they see fit) is a definite departure from the older core meaning of press freedom in America. The press libertarian wants to retain the traditional or pure nature of press freedom. He is radical—in the sense of desiring to stay with the *roots* of the concept—in wanting individual journalists, or at least the media managers, to be able to act in accordance with their own rational self-determination. This concept, coming to America out of the Age of Reason in Europe, implies *rationalism* (thoughtful use of freedom) on the part of the journalist and thereby circumscribes individual freedom to the extent that it does not degenerate into nihilism or unprincipled license. In other words, reason circumscribes freedom.

Jerome Tuccille, in his little book *Radical Libertarianism,* sees Lockean-Jeffersonian libertarianism being endangered in today's world. He writes: "The American heritage, our birthright as a society of free individuals, is being trampled by an army of bureaucratic politicians who have been nurtured in the miasma of a philosophical swampland. Relativistic values have displaced absolutes; relativistic ethical codes have displaced moral conviction; pragmatism has displaced objective reasoning as the motive power for human activity. All this must be stopped before we destroy ourselves and the remnant of liberty that remains to us today."[27]

With the recent trends toward "public access" to the press and other deviations from pure libertarianism in American journalism, the pendulum is swinging away from the press and its freedom. And coinciding with this trend is a public demand for more authority to make the press more "responsible" and socially oriented. Here again is the inevitable dialectic at work. Friedrich Hayek, not worrying much about any dialectic that might give balance to the journalistic situation, has added his warning to that of Tuccille: "Perhaps the most alarming fact is that contempt for intellectual liberty is not a thing which arises only once the totalitarian system is established but one which can be found everywhere among intellectuals who have embraced a collectivist faith and who are acclaimed as intellectual leaders even in countries still under a liberal regime."[28]

It is perhaps natural for us to hear much talk of late about "public access to the press" and how necessary it is that minorities and others be able to get their information, ideas, and opinions into the press. The well-known Tornillo case brought this issue to the public's attention. Although the case was finally decided in favor of the traditional concept of editorial self-determination, the ideas of public access are now firmly ingrained in American discourse. No doubt the issue will arise again, and in time public access will be legalized. For there are many Americans—Jerome Barron being an early spokesman—who doubt that press managers should have the right to make editorial decisions.[29] So even in this one small area, further erosion of the concept of press freedom in the United States is taking place, and in the future the American editor will forfeit much of his decision-making power, presumably to some judge.

27 Jerome Tuccille, *Radical Libertarianism* (New York, 1970), 113.
28 Friedrich Hayek, *The Road to Serfdom* (Chicago, 1944), 163.
29 See Jerome A. Barron, "Access to the Press—A New First Amendment Right," *Harvard Law Review,* (Spring, 1967), 1641–78. See also Barron, *Freedom of the Press for Whom? The Right of Access to Mass Media* (Bloomington, 1973); Ben Bagdikian, "Right of Access: A Modest Proposal," *Columbia Journalism Review,* Spring, 1969), 10–13; Benno C. Schmidt, Jr., *Freedom of the Press vs. Public Access* (New York, 1976).

The new stress on people's freedom as opposed to the press's freedom in the dialectic can also be seen in the growing popularity in the United States of the concept of "the people's right to know."[30] Rather strangely, this concept is being pushed even by journalists themselves—most of them seemingly not realizing what such a concept does to the old media-centered idea of press freedom. If the people have a right to know, then the press has an obligation to tell them. And of course, the traditional concept of press freedom has held that the press can determine independently whether to print a story. In other words, the press has always accepted the basic notion that the people would know what the press wanted the people to know.

Many things are not printed. Wastebaskets filled with unpublished stories attest to the fact that journalists do not really believe in the public's right to know. Editors and reporters determine that some stories are not suitable, or fit, to print. The people are not informed of many important things that happen, and the press, as well as the government, is responsible for this state of affairs. But after all, freedom of the press has always meant that editors had the freedom *not* to let the people know. Now many of them say they believe in the people's right to know. Every time they proclaim this so-called right (and it may well be one, even if it is not in the Bill of Rights), they are burying a little deeper their own prized concept of editorial self-determination. They may never get around to realizing this until it is too late. It may well be that they have had their editorial self-determination long enough, that the antithesis of people's rights has at last clashed with it, and that it will never again be the same. The dialectic continues to do its work, and the whole concept, along with the entire system of American journalism, is seeking the middle ground.

Press Freedom and Journalistic Freedom

A distinction should be made between *press freedom* and *journalistic freedom*. In the United States today there seems to be much more press freedom than journalistic freedom. Both types of freedom are important, of course. Press freedom concerns a relationship between the press and the government. Journalistic freedom concerns a relationship between the

30 Kent Cooper, *The Right to Know* (New York, 1956). *Cf.* Charles W. Whalen, Jr., *Your Right to Know* (New York, 1973).

journalists working for a news medium and the executives and editors of that news medium. In other words, journalistic freedom *individualizes,* or brings down to the personal level, press freedom. The press is to a large degree free of direction and interference from the government, but reporters are certainly not free from direction and interference from editors and publishers. The national press as a whole has much freedom (independence and permission to be critical), but there is really not much room within American journalism for eccentricity, deviance, or independence on the part of journalists; managers hold tight control in newsrooms across the country.

When we talk of press freedom in the United States, then, we are really talking about institutional press freedom from government control. We are *not* talking about freedom *within* the press itself. We are talking about legalized institutional freedom, not about existential journalistic freedom.[31] This is a distinction worth making, for it reveals that press freedom is really in the hands of a very few press people. Press freedom is not a democratic concept at all. It is an institutional concept tied in with economic control and power, and it lies in the hands of a press power elite. In spite of the value that can be ascribed to the American type of press freedom, it has a very narrow base and is a purely capitalistic, institutionalized freedom that excludes at least 90 percent of all journalists.

What is needed in the United States is more, not less, respect for the individual journalist. Individualism is disdained in the average news operation. The eccentric, the person with a mind of his own, is being squeezed out of journalism—or shoved over in some safe corner. This person is looked upon increasingly, by his superiors and his co-workers, as a poor "team player," one who does not fit nicely into the corporate journalistic system. The journalist with his own ideas, sense of moral values, strict standards of language usage, and personal journalistic philosophy—if you will—is looked on with suspicion or even hostility.[32]

This chapter makes several main points that are worth reconsidering. First, the basic concept of press freedom in the United States is changing from the traditional emphasis on the press to a new emphasis on the people. The old institution of the press and press freedom is giving way to a

31 See John C. Merrill, *Existential Journalism* (New York, 1977), for the concept of individual journalistic freedom in the context of an existentialist philosophy.

32 For further insights to the problem of the individual in today's society, see William Barrett, *Irrational Man* (New York, 1962), and Jaspers, *Man in the Modern Age.*

new conception that would provide the *people* with more power over the press. And of course, this is leading to a situation in which the governmental and legal establishment has an ever-growing power over the press, because it is only through such an establishment that "the people" can get more power.

Second, the concept of journalistic freedom (as distinct from press freedom) hardly exists in the United States. It should be given much more attention. What we need is more thought about how the individual journalist can get (and use) more freedom vis-à-vis the publisher, how the journalist can operate in an environment of freedom within his own institution. Hardly any attention is given to this aspect of editorial freedom.

In addition, traditional press freedom is being upstaged by admonitions for press responsibility. We see the rise of press councils, journalism reviews and journals, ombudsmen, and codes of ethics for journalists. And journalists in the lower echelons are going about their duties not as professionals who deal with their clients directly and independently, but as functionaries who fashion their work in accordance to supervision and direction by their editors, publishers, and news directors. They are little more than cogs in the corporate wheel. The main freedom they have is the freedom to quit and seek another job.

Journalism is losing more and more of its personal touch. It is becoming more institutionalized all the time, more mechanized, more formalized, more predictable, more timid—albeit often more lurid and sensational in some areas.

The press's recent proclivity to become a "profession" has increased its sameness and flatness. As journalism becomes even more professionalized (and there is no doubt that it will), it will become more conformist, more monolithic, more of a closed system—an elite club. And as a profession, it is likely to exclude eccentrics and become less innovative, less courageous, less interesting, less pluralistic, and, yes, even less concerned with the personal journalistic freedom of its individual members.

Two

IN SEARCH OF RESPONSIBILITY

"Ought" implies "can." Freedom is a prerequisite for ethics. In this book, as in *The Imperative of Freedom*, I insist on the essentiality of freedom, while counterposing responsibility as a natural limiting factor. The fundamental dialectical theme of this book is freedom and ethics in a critical tension that results in a higher synthesis—the ethical use of freedom.

Freedom, or at least a large measure of it, is guaranteed by nature; responsibility in the use of this freedom is a human enterprise and, of necessity, limits or restricts natural freedom. Therefore, the desire for responsibility (which naturally arises out of social relationships) places demands on individual freedom, disciplines it, and narrows it in the name of public responsibility or social ethics.

In the realm of journalism and mass communication, the potentially limitless expanse of individual freedom, at least in the United States, is necessarily reduced by a consideration of the effects of media messages and by the techniques involved in producing journalism. Point and counterpoint in journalism, thesis and antithesis in mass communication, freedom and control, freedom with good motive, freedom with a social conscience—such tensions make up the essence of dialectical journalism, my underlying theme.

Growth of Social Concern

The journalist who thinks, feels, and cares, who is sensitive, empathic, and socially concerned, deliberately sheds the egocentric, often selfish cocoon of unrestricted freedom and imposes from within himself or herself a discipline, a code of conduct, that channels freedom into responsible action. The journalist concerned with freedom must also be concerned with ethics. Moral duty is important, but to have ethical significance, it must be freely assumed by oneself. Kant believed that moral duty is the same as moral obligation, in that it must be freely accepted. It is binding on the individual, not by external force or threat of external punishment, but only because, as Ernest van den Haag has said, "the person obligated feels bound without coercion."[1] An uninhibited *choosing to be ethical* is the operative concept.

It is important for the journalist to recognize that ethics is contingent on freedom. If the reporter must write a story a certain way, if the reporter is told what to put into the story or what to leave out, how to handle quotations, etc., then this reporter (if he or she chooses to follow orders) is really *beyond* ethics. Ethics assumes free will, voluntary and independent choosing. Aristotle asserted in Book III of his *Nicomachean Ethics* that a person is responsible for his actions except for reasons of either ignorance or compulsion. Richard Taylor, a contemporary philosopher, puts it this way: "Only a will that is free . . . that is, not in subjugation to another . . . can be morally good. The will of a slave is neither morally good nor bad, for indeed such a will has for all practical purposes ceased to exist. . . . Only a free man can be morally estimable or, for that matter, morally reprehensible. Such freedom, or command over oneself and responsibility to oneself, is the precondition of a man's life that has any moral significance at all."[2]

Ethics in journalism, then, rests on the assumption that the journalist can choose among alternative courses of action. This possibility of choosing implies the existence of considerable journalistic freedom. If the journalist is *forced* to act a certain way, for example, to write certain types of stories in certain ways and to subscribe to a set of standards, then this journalist is amoral, and his endeavors must be considered a result of a forced or external morality. Freedom is an essential foundation of morality. But it must be stressed that freedom is a valid foundation only when an edifice of morality and social responsibility is built upon it.

1   Robert Paul Wolff, *Philosophy: A Modern Encounter* (Englewood Cliffs, N.J., 1971), 291; Ernest van den Haag, *Political Violence and Civil Disobedience* (New York, 1972), 108.
2   Taylor, *Freedom, Anarchy, and the Law*, 9. Cf. Sidney Hook (ed.), *Determinism and Freedom in the Age of Modern Science* (New York, 1961), 177.

The journalist must recognize this fact. Freedom used thoughtlessly or viciously will ultimately bring a justifiable reaction against its user and against freedom itself. The intelligent journalist who wants to retain a maximum degree of freedom will voluntarily circumscribe this freedom by considering the feelings and rights of others. Forces within the journalist and the various social forces outside him or her constantly are at work to curb excesses in the use of freedom and to continue the essential dialectical ferment permeating all journalistic activity.

In spite of these internal and external forces, there is still a strong pragmatic, Machiavellian magnet pulling the journalist toward journalistic action that does not temper freedom with a sense of responsibility. Too often, the end justifies the means for the journalist. Too often, the journalist does not consider the feelings and rights of others. "The story, the story at all costs!" cries the journalist, and persons and institutions are pushed aside in the mad race to meet deadlines and scoop competitors.

Journalistic media are, by and large, unloved and distrusted in the United States today. Ever-increasing barrages of criticism are being fired at journalists, journalism, and the press by irate citizens. For example, in 1984 a Gallup survey for *Newsweek* magazine showed that the public believed "only some" of what was read or heard in the news media. Only 46 percent of those polled said the media get the facts straight. A Louis Harris poll, taken later that same year, found that only 17 percent of the public had "a great deal of confidence in the press"—down from 19 percent a year earlier.

Tom Goldstein, an experienced journalist who has worked for the *Wall Street Journal,* the New York *Times,* and other newspapers, has thoroughly documented the reasons behind this distrust of the press in an excellent book. He places much of the blame directly on the press itself. Concerning today's journalists he writes: "They are almost inarticulate on the subject of what they do and why they do it. They are often careless or incompetent, and they acknowledge mistakes reluctantly."[3]

Dialectical Possibilities

As society becomes more complex and populations explode and wash over one another, the moral obligations of the journalist increase. The days

3 Tom Goldstein, *The News at Any Cost: How Journalists Compromise Their Ethics to Shape the News* (New York, 1985), 18.

when careless journalism did little harm are gone. Martin E. Marty has written that in a simpler age—"in the days of little village newspapers"— editors and publishers could say almost anything they liked. But not to- day. What we now need, says Marty, are journalists concerned with the "larger moral community."[4] The implication is that, in the early stages of social development, individualist ethics is rather easily accommodated, but as societies grow and become more complicated, this individualism must give way to a more sensitive morality built on a social ethics.

Here is the dialectic at work again. Individualist or existential ethics confronts group opinion in the area of morality. It is a case of the person against the collective. Compromises must result. Thesis batters antithesis, and a synthesis emerges. The journalist then retains—or moderates—his or her personal integrity by seeking the social good. The journalist merges self with society—at least to a large degree—in a new sense of morality that considers both egoism and altruism. What is good for the society is good for the journalist, and what is good for the journalist is good for the society. Such a frame of mind is not always easy to develop, but it is the dynamic and natural waltzing of the dialectic in the field of journalism as antinomies resolve themselves in a synthesizing moderation.

The individualist institutions of the press that developed and thrived in the United States during the nineteenth century and into the twentieth solidified their power and, in the eyes of many critics, operated in ex- tremely selfish, callous, and irresponsible ways. But in the mid-twentieth century—though it was anticipated earlier—a reaction set in, and it quickly developed into a force battering against the private-sector liber- tarianism that had heretofore been supreme. This new force, another challenging antithesis in the ongoing dialectic in journalism, was the theory of social responsibility. In the years after World War II it probably became the dominant theory about the role of the press in America, and it was not losing its power as the closing decades of the century began.[5] The emphasis was shifting from the press to the people, from private and individual rights to public and social rights, from the press's freedom to the press's responsibility to society.

4 Martin Marty, "Ethics and the Mass Media," in Lee Thayer (ed.), *Communication: Ethical and Moral Issues* (New York, 1973), 193.
5 The social responsibility concept has been discussed in many books and articles, chief among them being Commission on Freedom of the Press, *A Free and Responsible Press*, and Siebert, Peterson, and Schramm, *Four Theories of the Press.*

Responsibility: The New Emphasis

Today one hears frequent reference to the responsibility of the press and less about the freedom of the press to react independently in a democratic society. This is perhaps a natural reaction to the excesses of press freedom. Contrary to the general view, such a reaction started early in the United States, perhaps with Thomas Jefferson, the Great Libertarian himself. Jefferson, in spite of his oft-expressed dedication to press freedom, was also concerned about the excesses of the press. To him the First Amendment, however valuable it was, also posed a danger. Jefferson knew instinctively that freedom must be restrained in the interests of the people. He saw that the First Amendment, as important as it was to him, could well turn into a kind of threat to society, since great social damage could be done by irresponsible journalism. To Jefferson, Tory lies, for example, could not possibly be valuable to the general citizenry.[6] It was a troublesome problem for Jefferson, and it remains one for us today. Our theoretical respect for press freedom conflicts with our pragmatic wish to develop a moral society.

It should be remembered that though Jefferson said, in effect, that he would prefer the press without a government to a government without a press, he also qualified that statement with the remark that "Every man should receive those papers, and be capable of reading them." And though he evidently had high regard for the press as an institution, he did not think too highly of newspapers individually; in fact, he decried their lack of responsibility on many occasions. He once said, though it is seldom recalled, that "Nothing can now be believed which is seen in a newspaper." Toward the end of his life, Jefferson said he read only one newspaper and that one chiefly for the advertising, which he believed contained "the only truths to be relied on in a newspaper." In short, Thomas Jefferson, long before the Hutchins Commission of the 1940s, recognized the poor quality of the press. He summed up his opinion of newspapers in strong words: "I rarely think them worth reading, and almost never worth notice."[7]

6 Thomas Jefferson to Thomas McKean, February 9, 1803, in Leonard Levy (ed.), *Freedom of the Press from Zenger to Jefferson* (Indianapolis, 1966), 364.
7 For Jefferson's criticisms of the press of his day, see Saul K. Padover (ed.), *The Complete Jefferson* (New York, 1943), especially his letters to John Norvell (June 11, 1807) and to Adamantios Coray (October 31, 1823) and a selection from the second inaugural address. *Cf.* Levy (ed.), *Freedom of the Press,* for many Jefferson letters dealing with the press.

In spite of some reservations by Jefferson and others who debated the First Amendment, the press was considered a useful social instrument. Why? Because it was produced and read by the social and educational elite of the day. As Herbert Altschull stated in an insightful book, the press "was seen as an instrument of social control, an agency for the improvement and benefit of society."[8] The implication of Altschull's observation is that the Founding Fathers saw the press as a pragmatic instrument for the elite to control the masses. One wonders if this were really a worthy purpose for the nation's founders, who were supposedly concerned with creating a democratic society. At any rate, a concern for press responsibility manifested itself quite early in American history—at the same time that freedom was first extolled.

In the years since the Age of Jefferson not much has been said about press responsibility; the persistent emphasis has been on press freedom. But even when freedom was stressed by freedom lovers such as James Mill and John Stuart Mill, the emphasis was always accompanied by a kind of schizophrenia. James Mill, who may have been the one who conceived of the "watchdog" function of the press, advocated liberty of the press for utilitarian reasons, that is, out of a concern for responsibility. Press freedom, he thought, made "known the conduct of the individuals who have been chosen to wield the powers of government." His son John Stuart Mill wanted to hold the individual to a high standard of responsibility to his fellow men. He embraced freedom to the extent that he preferred that "the conscience of the agent [person] himself" enforce that person's responsibility and that society put few restrictions on its members' behavior.[9]

In the nineteenth century, many speakers and writers began to question the excesses of press freedom in the United States and pointed the way to more responsible journalism. It was not until after World War II, however, that the trend toward responsibility began to be deeply felt, probably at the time of the so-called Hutchins Commission (the Commission on Freedom of the Press), chaired by Robert Hutchins, chancellor of the University of Chicago. The commission studied the American press during the war and reported its findings in several books immediately after the war. Its main report, *A Free and Responsible Press,* was published in 1947. It hit the journalistic community like a bombshell and has had fallout ever since. Before the Hutchins Commission, responsibility was assumed to be

8 Altschull, *Agents of Power,* 30.
9 E. M. Zashin, *Civil Disobedience and Democracy* (New York, 1972), 25, 49.

a personal concept or something that was somehow automatically built into a libertarian press. At least it was generally felt in the Western world that a "free press" was by its very nature responsible to its social system.

The Hutchins Commission thought differently. After seeing great danger in the decreasing number of media outlets and the decline of widespread press responsibility and the concentration of so much power in the hands of a few, the commission offered an ominous warning: "If they [the agencies of mass communication] are irresponsible, not even the First Amendment will protect their freedom from governmental control. The amendment will be amended."[10]

Two basic assumptions (and conclusions) stand out in the Hutchins Commission report: first, that the press has a responsibility to society; second, that the American press of that day was not meeting its responsibility and that therefore a new press theory emphasizing responsibility needed to be given wide circulation. And such a new theory was being circulated, with increasing frequency. Such press stalwarts as Walter Lippmann were becoming concerned, and in 1955 he maintained that free expression was often taken too far and used irresponsibly and that the only real justification for free expression was to provide a clash of opposing ideas.[11]

In 1956 a little book was published that helped set the Hutchins Commission's concept of press responsibility in concrete. *Four Theories of the Press,* by Fred Siebert, Theodore Peterson, and Wilbur Schramm, attempted to put in intelligible language this new theory that had been slowly developing in the United States. The authors put the theory of social responsibility alongside three others—communism, authoritarianism, and libertarianism. From that book the theory has made its way, largely unchallenged, into innumerable books, articles, speeches, and academic dissertations.[12]

10 Commission on Freedom of the Press, *A Free and Responsible Press,* 80. For a good discussion of the Hutchins Commission's philosophy, especially its resemblance to the ideas of Reinhold Niebuhr, see Michael McClellan, "Social Responsibility and the New Technology," XI *Mass Comm Review* (Fall, 1983), 13–22. See also Altschull, *Agents of Power,* Chapter 8.

11 Walter Lippmann, *The Public Philosophy* (New York, 1955).

12 Siebert, Peterson, and Schramm, *Four Theories of the Press.* The theory has been challenged and criticized by many persons, but it has been generally accepted, often with modifications and some attempts at clarification. See Robert C. Picard, *The Press and the Decline of Democracy: The Democratic Socialist Response to Public Policy* (Westport, Conn., 1985), for a criticism from the left, and Merrill, *The Imperative of Freedom,* for a criticism from the right.

Different Roads to Responsibility

Journalists are putting increasing emphasis on various theories of ethics or responsibility as they manifest a deepening concern about their moral obligations to society. Perhaps the earliest ethical road cut through the social forests was that of Aristotle. He considered the key to ethics to be the concept of "virtue," which he equated with acting according to rational principles. His argument was based on what he saw as natural for man, but he focused his moral concern on only a small group of persons.

Crucial distinctions exist between ancient and modern perspectives of goodness or moral action. The most significant, perhaps, is the difference in the scope of their applicability. Aristotle considered only an elite—the small class of Greek male citizens—to be capable of true happiness through moral contemplation and action. Others, such as slaves and noncitizens, might be comfortable enough and do their chores efficiently, but they could not be called truly happy. Only the elite were capable of such excellence—if they lived up to their potential in terms of personal achievements, intelligence, wit, and other rewards stemming from an aristocratic upbringing.[13]

Kant's moral philosophy, unlike Aristotle's, judged all rational people by the same standards—the standards of duty. No elites existed for Kant. What applied to one person applied to everyone. Judgments of moral worth were made strictly on the basis of good intentions. For Kant, a "good" person, with the best intentions, can still make errors and perhaps even cause unhappiness all around him. Yet the fact remains that this person is, according to Kant's conception, still a good person. Aristotle would find this absurd. He would ask: How can a person be virtuous only because of his intentions? How can one who fails exemplify ideal goodness?[14]

For Kant, the morally responsible person operates from a sense of duty. For Aristotle, only women and servants follow a morality of duty, because only people who are incapable of true goodness and happiness depend on a morality of duty. Kant's morality consists of proscriptions and prescriptions; Aristotle's consists mainly of personal desires and ambitions. Robert Solomon has contrasted the two philosophers: "The key element

13 Robert C. Solomon, *Introducing Philosophy* (New York, 1985), 524.
14 *Ibid.,* 535.

of Kant's philosophy, duty, is treated minimally in Aristotle, where the emphasis is on personal growth and achievement. But, on the other side, the image of the well-rounded, successful man, excellent in all things and the envy of his fellow men, plays only a secondary role in Kant's philosophy. . . . For him, what is important is the person who does what he or she is supposed to do. For Aristotle, the ideal is to strive for personal excellence."[15]

Later there were philosophers, such as David Hume and Jean Jacques Rousseau, who argued that morality is really based on certain feelings or sentiments. Hume said, "Reason is and ought to be the slave of the passions," and Rousseau, who believed that people were naturally good, agreed.[16] Kant's thought was quite different. He insisted that ethical behavior is strictly social and devoid of all interests, desires, or "inclinations."

Thomas Hobbes's *Leviathan*, published in 1651, presented the first egoistic ethics that is systematic, outright, and secular—egoistic through and through. His ethical theory defines the good in terms that are ultimately individualistic. People pursue gain, safety, and reputation, he said. Jeremy Bentham, more than a century later, developed this Hobbesian egoism into a social philosophy. "In Bentham's hedonism," according to Abraham Edel, "a man inevitably pursues his own pleasure and avoids his own pain. . . . The social standard—the greatest happiness of the greatest number—emerges from each man's pursuit of his own gain."[17] Bentham and the utilitarians who followed him, especially John Stuart Mill, shifted morality away from egoism and the individual and turned it increasingly toward the collective and the consideration of consequences for the majority of persons in society.

And then came Friedrich Nietzsche (1844–1900), who urged a return to Aristotelian virtues. He was fundamentally opposed to modern moral philosophy of the Kantian and Christian type. He also attacked J. S. Mill and utilitarian morality, which he saw as a weak, vulgar philosophy that evidenced no respect for the person acting. Nietzsche believed that Kant's concept of duty was fit only for servants and not for those who respected

15   *Ibid.,* 525.
16   For a good discussion of Rousseau's thought on freedom and authority and on other ethical considerations, see Fred Weinstein and Gerald M. Platt, *The Wish to Be Free* (Berkeley, 1969), chapter 3.
17   Abraham Edel, *Ethical Judgment* (New York, 1955), 24.

personal excellence and achievement. In many ways Nietzsche was, like Aristotle, an unabashed elitist. Although he is often considered an ethical egoist, that interpretation is deceptive. He did say that a person must develop his own virtues, but this is not the same as saying that a person must act in his or her own interests. For Nietzsche saw, as did Aristotle, that individual excellence is part of, and contributes to, the total excellence of society.

Thus, the maverick Nietzsche rejected both the Kantian and the utilitarian roads and urged a return to Aristotelian elitism and individualism as the proper moral path. He argued that we individually create our values and must not have them placed upon us by others. Stimulated by the thought of Nietzsche—though their roots are found much further back in history—the existentialists, led by Jean-Paul Sartre, have built a new moral road emphasizing freely and individually chosen values and insisting that there·is no one "true" morality—only personal commitments to self-selected standards.

Also in the twentieth century, American pragmatists, such as John Dewey, have constructed another relativistic road of morality that rejects the distinct boundaries between "is" and "ought" and considers the concept of progress as moral.[18] In addition, going off in all directions from these main ethical roads laid out by thinkers from Aristotle to the present, and forming networks of roads between them, have been numerous smaller paths and byways of ethical thought.

Thus, the subject of ethics is a complex, extremely nebulous one in which no general agreement has been reached by even the greatest philosophers. That does not mean, however, that journalists should despair of growing in their moral sophistication. Nor does it mean that all roads are equally good and reliable. What it does mean is that in this wide and ongoing ethical discourse there is a constant dialectic of ideational confrontation. And from this multidimensional clash and synthesis of concepts will come to the sincere and studious journalist new and meaningful moral insights to serve as reliable guides for daily action.

John Rawls (b. 1921), a contemporary Harvard philosopher who takes issue with the elitism of Aristotle and Nietzsche, is probably the leading advocate today of egalitarianism. His chief work in ethics is *A Theory of*

18   See Richard J. Bernstein, *John Dewey* (New York, 1966), for a readable summary of the pragmatists' ethical ideas.

Justice, published in 1971. Rawls is a kind of social contract philosopher in the tradition of Hobbes, Locke, and Rousseau, though he is more egalitarian then they were. He believes that the ultimate basis of society is a set of agreements. Unlike Aristotle, Rawls has little sympathy for the able or successful in society; they are, he says, merely lucky, having been blessed by good social environments or by superior natural attributes, and having them with us acting in a laissez-faire manner leads to social injustice.

To remedy this basic injustice in society, Rawls introduces the concept of an *ideal observer* who would operate behind a "veil of ignorance," paying no attention to persons' special talents, social status, politics, or any other accidental aspects of their lives. All participants in a moral situation would act as ideal observers—as free and rational persons with all facts of inequality eliminated from their moral thinking. Considering ethics from behind this veil of ignorance, from this neutral position, we should then be able to strive to achieve Rawls's two basic principles: first, to provide everyone with an equal right to maximum freedom, and second, to permit inequality only to the extent that it serves everyone's advantage and only as it comes about under conditions of equal opportunity. This is the core of Rawls's concept of social justice.[19]

Taking exception to Rawls's moral philosophy is his Harvard colleague Robert Nozick. Writing from a scholarly libertarian perspective, Nozick has developed another theory of justice, which he calls "the entitlement theory." Nozick rejects Rawls's call for a more extensive state, and he is critical of theories of "distributive justice," such as that of Rawls. His is a more individualistic ethics, and in many ways it is reminiscent of the philosophy of Nietzsche. Certainly Nozick feels that striving for social equality in making ethical decisions will not necessarily lead to a higher moral level socially. Morality, for Nozick, is something beyond egalitarianism.[20]

Another critic of Rawls's moral philosophy, and one who is far more virulent in his comments, is Leonard Peikoff, a follower of Ayn Rand. Taking an Aristotelian position, Peikoff writes of Rawls's moral philoso-

19 John Rawls, *A Theory of Justice* (Cambridge, Mass., 1971). See also Bernard Williams, *Ethics and the Limits of Philosophy* (Cambridge, Mass., 1985), 78–79.
20 See Nozick's *Anarchy, State, and Utopia* (New York, 1974), for a complete exposition of his ethical theory. *Cf.* his *Philosophical Explanations* (Cambridge, Mass., 1981) for a clearer version, or at least a shorter one.

phy: "In a philosophy of sacrifice, the top duty is the negating of values; the top virtue, their nonpossession. Hence the new social conclusion: values properly belong to those who have reached the eminence of *not* having achieved them."[21] In other words, for Peikoff, Rawls's theory is absurdly altruistic and a devaluation of the ethical actor's intelligence. It is a philosophy of self-sacrifice, and Peikoff and Rand have little patience with anything other than what they call "rational self-interest."

Rawls and Nozick exemplify antinomies in political philosophy as well as in ethics. Each follows one of two mainstreams of political thought that Bertrand Russell saw as basic: Rawls follows that of Rousseau, and Nozick, that of Locke. Such a schema is perfectly consistent with my position, for I would lump Plato with Rousseau, and Aristotle with Locke. The first pair put great stock in the state, in society as a collectivity, and they would have individuals sublimate themselves, in politics and in ethics, to the state. The second pair are more individualistic, placing the person rather than the state in the primary position.

The Plato-Rousseau axis would find support from "statist" philosophers such as Hegel, Marx, and Rawls. On the other hand, the Aristotle-Locke axis would be resonated in such philosophers as Voltaire, Kierkegaard, Ayn Rand, and Nozick.

In contemporary journalistic thought the first perspective would be represented by socialist media people and also by "fascist" media people, who generally find Rousseau's ideas compatible. The second would be represented by capitalist media people, who typically identify with Locke's position. With the exception of the right-wing dictatorships, the First World is with Locke, and the Second World is with Rousseau. The developing nations of the Third World are sitting on the fence, but they are, without a doubt, gravitating in Rousseau's direction.

Of course, the divisions are not absolute. In the United States, certainly a representative of the First World, there are disciples of Rousseau who stress the group, the society, and the national polity over the individual; many of them are not Marxists or extreme collectivists. Instead they are idealists, democrats, or as some of them refer to themselves, "majoritarians." Many of their beliefs are ambiguous. For example, many of them say that they are opposed to the government, but they nevertheless support what they call "the society." Yet they are descendants of Plato,

---

21   Peikoff, *The Ominous Parallels*, 292.

Hegel, and Rousseau, even though they live in a country that basically enthrones the virtues of Locke—the individual, meritocracy, and laissez-faire competition.

Representing this Rousseauean perspective among today's North American theoreticians of communication and the press are such persons as Dallas Smythe, Herbert Gans, Denis McQuail, Heather Hudson, William Melody, Herbert Schiller, George Gerbner, Clifford Christians, and Theodore Glasser. They are joined by many articulate spokespersons in other countries, such as Robert White, James Halloran, and Jeremy Tunstall of the United Kingdom, Cees Hamelink of the Netherlands, Roberto Grandi of Italy, Wimal Dissanayake of Sri Lanka, Karl Erik Rosengren of Sweden, Kaarle Nordenstreng of Finland, and Yassen Zassoursky of the Soviet Union.

And representing the Lockean perspective would be such Americans as Leonard Sussman, Wilson Dizard, Ithiel de Sola Pool, William F. Buckley, Jr., Robert Stevenson, Robert Lindsay, and Jeane Kirkpatrick. It must be admitted that among the main-line members of the academic community, Lockean proponents are not nearly so numerous as are those of Rousseau. A few Lockean, or Lockean-tending theoreticians among non-Americans should be mentioned also—Osmo Wiio of Finland, Elisabeth Noelle-Neumann of West Germany, Elihu Katz of Israel, Jean-François Revel of France, and Tomás McHale of Chile.

The two camps may be overdrawn here, and many of these persons might challenge their being put into one or the other. But the two groupings serve to show that even today these two traditions go on: the Aristotelian-Lockean and the Platonist Rousseauean. The first is geared to the individual, emphasizing maximum journalistic autonomy, for example. The second is geared to the needs of society, placing social obligations on the press, for example. The first would enthrone the person and stress self-enhancement; the second would enthrone the society or the state and sublimate self-enhancement.

Locke put his emphasis on liberty, whereas Rousseau stressed equality. Locke enthroned personal autonomy; Rousseau, cooperation and merger with the state. Locke placed his faith in *individual* liberty; Rousseau, liberty *for all*. Locke was primarily interested in what is now called "negative freedom"—freedom from outside restraints. Rousseau thought more about "positive freedom"—utilitarian or pragmatic freedom, freedom to achieve social goals.

These two political orientations are seemingly clear-cut and mutually exclusive, with ideologues and "true believers" on either side. But in dealing with real people it is seldom that simple. Although politically Hegel may have inclined toward the statism of Rousseau, he was certainly not a "static thinker"; he recognized that ideas clash and new hybridized ones emerge. That is the nature of the dialectic. So it may well be that many of the persons named above as representing one of the two camps are not firmly in either one of them but are only caught in the dialectic in a way that they are now somewhat in one, now somewhat in the other. Pure Lockeans are hard to find, and perhaps most people are libertarian statists, individualist collectivists, and the like. Some might call such positions ineffectual, even cowardly. But if Aristotelian moderation is taken seriously and Hegelian dialectic is recognized as useful, then there is reason to believe that such a position of change and merger is a good one for reasonable people.

Journalistic Implications

Why should a journalist lean toward Locke or Rousseau, toward Nozick or Rawls, toward Kant's Neoplatonism or toward Aristotle? How should the journalist merge the idea of personal freedom with social responsibility, of individualistic ethics with collectivist ethics? He or she can, for instance, determine to minimize outside restrictions on personal freedom but also determine to use this freedom, not just protect it, and to use it for the social good; prize self-enhancement and ethical autonomy, but recognize the society that makes this individualistic potential possible; acknowledge the value of duty to guiding moral principles, while at the same time not devaluing other people or minimizing consequences to them; use journalism to seek justice in the sense of recognizing social inequities, and even try to eliminate some of them, while not falling into the trap of naïve egalitarianism, which negates meritocracy; and ultimately, understand the Aristotelian ideal of character building, while not abdicating an appreciation of normative ethics.

Aristotle, then, provides a philosophy that emphasizes the positive, the development of a full vision of a virtuous and happy existence, with stress on full personal development, appreciation of self-worth and personal progress, and suspicion of an egalitarian society or morality. In other words, Aristotle would tell the journalist that what he or she *is* is more important than what he or she *does* in specific cases. Nietzsche supports and even enhances self-respect and individual moral determination; such a philosophy serves to modify a journalist's ethical inflexibility and legalistic stance and makes suspect "institutional" or "herd" morality legislated by some elite at the top.

Mill and Rawls certainly enter into the journalist's formula with their respect for people and for the importance of consequences. In such thinkers the journalist will find a deep social concern that will take precedence often over absolute a priori moral rules. With such an orientation merging into his or her overall moral philosophy, the journalist can have a social consciousness that is both flexible and rational.

But Kant, with his formalistic deontology, should not be abandoned by the ethically concerned journalist. The concept of duty to principle, which Kant championed, should have an appeal for the journalist. It will help imbue him or her with a sense that the moral journalist will have to go beyond simply a concern for consequences, that a certain steadfastness and predictability in ethics is important, and that an inculcation of such traits helps define a principled person. And Mill and other utilitarians, and even the modern Rawlsian egalitarians, will have value for the journalist trying to produce responsible journalism. Other people are important, and attempting to maximize good and human happiness is, indeed, important for the journalist trying to act ethically. The thoughtful journalist should not simply attempt to develop a kind of personal or elite virtue, but instead realize that the idea of producing social justice must be grafted onto a healthy respect for the self and the need to develop a personal morality.

So, the yea-saying of Nietzsche and Aristotle, with its overtones of personal growth, independence, and virtue, will be merged with the strict social consciousness of Kant, Mill, and Rawls for a journalistic orientation that is dialectical in nature: a conception of press responsibility that emphasizes both the individual journalist and the public or society that he or she is influencing.

It is easy for the journalist to stray too far over into egoism. And it not difficult at all for the journalist to demean his or her own person and to become a puppet of "social forces" by falling into the trap of altruism or of a kind of majoritarianism. One must remember that "society" is not always right in its expectations or desires, and sometimes the journalist must make decisions based on his or her own values, not on what society seems to want or demand. The journalist must use both egoistic and altruistic yardsticks for measuring or determining moral action.

So what does the rational journalist do? He or she, developing a moral sense, will rein in the expansive concept of freedom that has been instilled from childhood, and will use such freedom through the press in the service of society. This is *responsible* journalistic freedom—a merger of egoism and collectivist philosophy. It is, in short, the result of dialectical thinking in journalism.

The rational journalist who reins in excessive freedom is certainly on the road to responsibility. But at that point the search is just begun. Becoming aware of what *not* to do in order to be responsible is the first step, but then the journalist must consider *what to do* in order to be responsible. Where will the journalist find guideposts to lead him to responsible journalism? Does some kind of absolute, timeless "responsibility" exist out there somewhere, just waiting to be discovered by the caring journalist? If so, how does the journalist go about finding either the guideposts or the responsibility?

It might be noted that there are differing responsibilities, depending on the locus of the expectations among various segments of the society. A journalist might have certain responsibilities to the publisher of his newspaper, to various segments of the audience, to his government, and to society at large. Just what these expectations should be and how conflicts among them (and thus among responsibilities) will be resolved is a big problem. It must be resolved ultimately by the journalist through rational consideration of the various expectations—or, to add another dimension, perhaps through a decision not to consider expectations at all but rather to ignore external promptings and provide what the individual journalist thinks is responsible journalism.

This last path, however, is strewn with pitfalls, for there is a basic distrust by social ethicists of individual self-determination of ethical standards. Responsibility, it is said ever more frequently, does not come from autonomous persons, each determining what is best to do; that is the road to irresponsibility, license, and anarchy. The message gets ever louder and clearer: there must be *social adjustment* in ethics. The individual journalist, for instance, simply cannot operate by following his or her own ethical predilections; rather, a social consciousness must be plugged into by each journalist, so that the path followed will be in harmony with the best interests of the group and will lead to collective objectives and social stability.

In spite of the virtual triumph of social ethics over individual ethics in the last few decades, there seems to be some justification for the individual journalist to hold on to as much ethical autonomy as possible while cooperating with other journalists (and with the public) in determining an ethical stance that best meets the needs of as many people as possible. The advent of the concept of *social* responsibility of the press shifts the emphasis significantly. Selfish or self-serving interests must more and more be curbed or sublimated, to be replaced by a spirit of public concern and enlightened social-consciousness. This is not always easy for the individual journalist to achieve, given the power of the media managers, the pressures of economic factors in the capitalistic system, and the great peer pressure for social adjustment. In other words, too often the socially responsible journalist finds it difficult, if not impossible, to put this responsibility into action, because of media-wide policy that forces an institutional ethic to take precedence over a social ethic.

The typical journalist recognizes that a certain amount of adjustment to the group is necessary in today's journalistic world. There is really very little room for the Nietzschean Overman, who is able to transcend common ethical standards or media policy and "do his own thing." The corporate world of journalism is simply not set up for that; there must be common goals and common action so that efficiency can be maximized. Internally, institutional efficiency is often a synonym for journalistic responsibility. This, of course, evades the subject of social responsibility, for a journalist can be responsible to his newspaper, following its policies assiduously, and still not be responsible to the public out there that reads the newspaper.

Certainly a problem of responsibility lies in trying to serve more than one master at once. The journalist finds it a perplexing task. How to be responsible to self, to employer, to fellow journalists, to the public, and to one's government? And surely each journalist has many other loyalties or constituencies that deserve consideration in the responsibility department. The journalist must decide on priorities of responsibility. For often when the journalist is "responsible" to one constituency, he or she finds that another constituency is neglected or treated irresponsibly. Responsibility, then, may well be a relative concept, and undoubtedly it is always a matter of degree. Total responsibility, presumably, would be responsibility to everyone, often an impossible objective. So the journalist must determine who has priority, or which responsibility is most urgent, in particular cases. This, of course, is a subjective exercise seen daily in American journalism in the various decisions and actions manifest throughout the media.

One way, and a satisfying way for many journalists, that the problem of responsibility can be overcome is simply to follow orders, ask advice and conform to it, read and adhere to the newspaper's policy statements, do what colleagues are doing, and rely on some professional code of ethics. To act in such a way is strictly an "other-directed" sense of responsibility and relieves the individual journalist from agonizing over many ethical quandaries that come up each day. It is, however, more of an institutional stance of responsibility than a stance of social responsibility. What about society? What about one's responsibility to that nonpress constituency—the public "out there"? One basic reason—perhaps the most important reason—that this is such a difficult question for the journalist to answer is that, in American society, there is no clear-cut conception of what the public wants, needs, or expects from the press in the way of responsibility.

How can a journalist be responsible to society if he or she does not know what being responsible means? There are, of course, certain obvious, commonsense guidelines that more or less give the journalist a sense of direction. For example, the journalist "senses" that society needs reliable information, intelligent analysis, a broad and balanced perspective of the world, and a myriad of useful tidbits to make life easier. But the problem comes in determining reliability of information, differentiating intelligent analysis from faulty analysis, finding a proper balance of perspectives, and knowing just what will be useful or beneficial and what will be useless or harmful.

What the journalist can do, and what he or she must do, is to have an attitude of serious concern about these matters, to care about being responsible, to think about priorities of responsibility, and to try to reconcile personal, institutional, and social responsibilities in a rational but socially sensitive manner. It is not easy. In fact, no one really has a nice, firm answer for the journalist who faces this problem of responsibility. But the attitude, the concern, is important; the journalist who has a will to be responsible will find a way to be responsible. Or at least such a journalist will be much more responsible than if he or she had no desire or determination to be responsible. Responsibility is elusive; often it remains hidden. But the search must go on, and the journalist must persist.

Three

THE POWER OF ANTINOMIES

Journalistic concerns are, like all complex theoretical and practical considerations, filled with contradictory perspectives. Opposites abound in journalistic dialogue; contraries, or antinomies, take over and, like ideological magnets, pull us toward their poles. Antinomies are potent; they tend to enslave us and our thinking. They direct our fundamental orientations by clarifying or simplifying and by presenting alternatives in "either-or" terms.

The individual journalist is usually dualistically oriented. Gravitating naturally to one extreme or the other, the journalist normally neglects or overlooks the many possible positions between the contraries. Clustering at the extremes, journalists tend to be either scientifically or artistically oriented; they are normally dedicated either to objectivity or to subjectivity, to theory or to practice, to conservatism or to liberalism, to rationalism or to intuitivism, to involvement or to neutralism, to individualism or to groupism, to egoism or to altruism, and so on. All journalists, then, are to a large degree enslaved or trapped in this two-valued orientation that stems from the antinomic nature of language as well as from basic psychological proclivities.

Often such a dualistic entrapment, with a dedication to one extreme, is looked upon by journalists as an indication of courage, commitment, integrity, or dedication—in short, as a sign of "standing for something," of being willing to take a position. It is seldom considered that this "dedication" might be the stance of absolutism, dogmatism, or rigidity. It is certainly not the position of Heraclitus' philosophy of change, the dialectic of Hegel, or the "both-and," multivalued orientation of the Korzybskian semanticists.

Journalism's Either-Or Prison

The world of antinomies is a prison world. Journalists, enslaved in it in great numbers, must constantly try to escape. To bring a greater sophistication to their reports and commentaries, journalists must recognize that reality is more complicated than words usually make it and that it changes constantly, making the static language used to describe it unsatisfactory. It is, of course, impossible for a journalist to escape completely from the world of the either-or, but escape should be the goal. No absolute, single key unlocks this prison, so the journalist must seek various keys. One key is the Hegelian dialectic, merged as it is with the concept of moderation represented by the Aristotelian Golden Mean. Such a new orientation will give the journalist a glimpse of a new world of multi-dimensionality and dynamism necessary both to reporting and interpreting events and to philosophizing about ideas and concepts in the field of journalism.

Antinomies—or the "dialectical extremes," as Kant termed them—abound in journalism. A great bulk of the rhetoric and polemic found in journalistic and communications literature today deals with powerful antinomies that seek to pull students and journalists in one or the other direction and make "true believers" of them. What follows is a partial list of antinomies in journalism that are frequently discussed and debated in lectures, speeches, articles, and books.

- Responsible journalism vs. irresponsible journalism
- Free journalism vs. controlled journalism
- Objective journalism vs. subjective journalism
- Absolute journalistic ethics vs. relative journalistic ethics
- Egoistic journalism vs. altruistic journalism
- Conservative journalism vs. liberal journalism
- Individualist journalism vs. collectivist journalism
- Professional journalism vs. nonprofessional journalism
- Hard news vs. soft news
- Neutral reporting vs. involved reporting

Innumerable antinomies such as these exert their pull on every part of the journalist's work in both very abstract and very concrete areas. It is not easy to escape them. They have a potent attraction, calling journalists to polar positions that usually have deep psychological and intellectual appeal. There is a natural tendency to embrace an antinomy, become dedicated to it, and to close one's mind to other conceptual and realistic possibilities.

Most journalists like to label themselves. They find it comfortable to think of themselves as conservatives or liberals, as objectivists or subjectivists, as egoists or altruists, as reporters or analysts, or even as reporters or investigative reporters. A single journalist appropriates a great number and variety of such labels in the course of a career. Either out of personal conviction or out of a social instinct to follow the crowd or to follow respected peers, the journalist repeatedly seeks an antinomy and becomes dedicated to it.

The longer the journalist pays allegiance to an antinomy, the more the enslavement deepens and the more difficult it is for him or her to break to the middle and seek a more moderate position in the personally created zone of the dialectical synthesis. Difficult as it is to escape antinomies, the attempt can prove intellectually stimulating and pragmatically rewarding; for the journalist becomes involved in the fascinating enterprise of gathering values from the extremes and of creating from them a new value or set of values in the middle area between the two old antinomies.

There are several simple models that are helpful in analyzing journalistic antinomies. Four basic models and the basic questions raised by each of them are: 1) The Loyalty Model: To whom or what is the journalist obligated or loyal? 2) The Self-Relatedness Model: How does the journalist consider freedom and control? 3) The Ethical Model: How does the journalist relate to the concept of responsibilities? Or, what are the moral orientations of the journalist? 4) The Work-oriented Model: How does the journalist relate to his journalistic work?

In the case of the Loyalty Model, two sets of antinomies are these: journalistic personalists versus journalistic institutionalists, and journalistic ideologists versus journalistic neutralists. For the second construct, the Self-Relatedness Model, two sets of antinomies involved are freedom lovers versus authority lovers and journalistic individualists versus journalistic collectivists. Two sets of antinomies suggested by the Ethical Model are journalistic absolutists versus journalistic relativists and journalistic egoists versus journalistic altruists. Finally, under the Work-oriented Model two sets of antinomies are journalistic rationalists (who cultivate an aloof scientism) versus journalistic existentialists (who embrace an involved personalism) and journalistic objectivists versus journalistic subjectivists.

The antinomies, or dialectical opposites, found in these four models are extremely important to the journalist. They mold, in fact, the kind of journalism produced and in a real sense help to determine the character of the journalist involved in this production. Antinomies determine basic orientations in journalism, and there are many of these orientations. Before considering in detail some of these antinomies, especially freedom versus authority from the Self-Relatedness Model and absolutism versus relativism from the Ethical Model, I will present several antinomic journalistic orientations or stances.

Journalistic Orientations

Journalists are complex, and it is difficult to generalize about their orientations. Affecting their work is a wide variety of interests, ideologies, educational levels, cultural backgrounds, and other factors. This is true even in societies where conformity and institutionalism have led to highly monolithic press systems. In any society—but especially in a libertarian or quasi-libertarian society—the journalist is a many-sided person with several strong traits and tendencies, dominant psychological and ideological orientations that manifest themselves in his or her journalistic thinking and action.

A journalist normally writes the way he or she thinks, and this varies according to basic orientations. A journalist, of course, may have a mixture of orientations, but one side from each set of antinomies will usually dominate. The problem comes when one tries to classify orientations, but it can be done. And though there are many possible classification systems, the tendency is for all such systems to gravitate into two types—the *scientific* journalist and the *artistic* journalist. This dichotomy may not satisfy everybody, of course, but it is a highly significant dualism. A particular journalist is almost always either predominantly scientific or predominantly artistic.

Perhaps the greatest problem with dichotomizing orientations is that we do injustice to reality, as the either-or typology leads to distorted and simplistic thinking about the nature of the subject. However, it must be noted that *any* system of classification (or of language usage in any form) distorts reality and is unsatisfactory in some sense. In spite of the weaknesses of typologies, failure or refusal to classify—even dualistically—might well lead to more problems of understanding than the typologies do. General semanticists and other linguistic philosophers have not really helped much in this respect. The Hegelian dialectic may assist somewhat to alleviate the problem—this polarized view of orientations—by projecting us into a kind of synthesis thinking.

So in the absence of a better alternative to classification, let us look briefly at five journalistic orientations as parts of sets of antinomies, dualistic though this may be. They should at least serve as catalysts for disagreement.

1. *Involved or aloof.* This is a basic and common way of classifying journalists. The "involved" journalist is one who is oriented to participation, to activism, to being personally and emotionally involved in the events of the day. This journalist does not believe in neutrality, thinking it desirable that personal ideological beliefs, preferences, and biases be brought to bear on journalism. This person is often referred to as the "subjective" journalist, one who, as J. K. Hvistendahl says, "looks at traditional reporting as being sterile and . . . considers reporters who refuse to commit themselves to a point of view as being cynical or hypocritical."[1] Hvistendahl goes on to say that "truth-as-I-see-it" reporting might be a more accurate description of this orientation in journalism. These journalists believe that reporters who are seeking the truth should report the truth *as they see it.* The "involved" journalists desire to bring their intelligence, sensitivities, and judgments to bear on the news; they are not satisfied to be bystanders, observers, or recorders.

The journalist with the "aloof" orientation, on the other hand, maintains that journalism is a disinterested activity in which audiences are not to be encumbered by the journalist's biases, prejudices, judgments, feelings, or opinions. This journalist is often called the "objective" journalist, subscribing to the neutralist position, the one that is still the dominant orientation in the United States.

2. *Dionysian or Apollonian.* This is another pair of antinomies that can describe a journalist's orientation. These are the dichotomous tendencies toward emotion on one hand and reason on the other. This dualism was first analyzed using these terms by Nietzsche. He observed two antinomic

---

1 J. K. Hvistendahl, "The Reporter as Activist: Fourth Revolution in Journalism," *Quill* (February, 1970), 8.

elements in the ancient Greek tragedies and came to believe that they are fundamental metaphysical principles. Nietzsche named them for two Greek gods—Apollo and Dionysus. In brief, the Dionysian journalist would be the "feeling, sensitive" journalist, akin to the artistic or literary "New Journalists" of the 1960s. The Apollonian journalist would be more prosaic, more neutral, more dispassionate—more akin to the scientist than to the artist.

3. *Poetic or prosaic.* This dualistic classification of journalists is constructed on the basis of their stylistic proclivities. Some journalists, of the Dionysian type, tend to subjectivize their journalism in an attempt to get beneath the surface of reality and present a fuller and more authentic picture. These are the poetic journalists. Other journalists, largely Apollonian, are content with the more traditional style of expression common among journalists who have adopted what might be termed the "wire-service" or mechanistic style—a more scientific or prosaic one.

This basic difference in communicative expression stems from the dominant orientation accepted by the journalists: poetic (a kind of "open" or flexible style) or prosaic (a kind of "closed" or mechanistic style). The poetic journalist is willing to experiment with journalism, especially in story form and style. Not as hemmed in by normal or traditional practices as the prosaic journalist, the poetic journalist delights in giving journalism the stamp of individual personality, placing great importance on self-expression and freedom.

On the other hand, the prosaic journalist is a believer in facts, stressing literalness and explicit statements, praising objectivity as basically the same as reliability and truthfulness. The prosaic mind, according to George W. Morgan, considers the objective as identical with the factual. "In addition, and most important," Morgan writes, "it is believed that to be objective means to withhold the feelings and to be detached and impersonal."[2]

As Morgan rightly points out, facts are important to a person (and especially to a journalist), but they can be overstressed to the detriment of other things that are equally important. For example, Morgan says that persons with prosaic minds tend to have little respect for interpretation "because it appears incompatible with fact: fact is what *is*, they think, while interpretation is whatever one makes it; facts are believed to be

2 George W. Morgan, *The Human Predicament* (New York, 1970), 83.

objective, and interpretation, subjective." And he notes that for prosaic persons, knowledge of facts—no matter how isolated, irrelevant, or minuscule—becomes genuine knowledge and interpretation becomes prejudice. For the journalist with a prosaic orientation, "sticking to the facts" is the height of responsibility, and anything else is "irresponsible fancy."[3]

4. *Personalist or factualist*. These orientations are similar to the poetic and prosaic but they relate more to the total outlook on journalism and its purpose, going beyond the simple style of presentation of the message. The personalist is the "people-oriented" journalist who makes most decisions on the basis of the way people most probably will be affected. The main concern is with people—their feelings and the consequences that might follow as a result of the story. People are always at journalism's center for these journalists, and in an important way the personalist is a utilitarian because of his or her concern with consequences. In other words, the personalist is largely controlled by sensitivity to people connected with the story. Personalism is very much an "involved" or "subjective" stance, and it differs strongly from factualism—the orientation of dispassionate neutralism that focuses on what was said or done.

The factualist is aloof or neutral, taking a prosaic position, concentrating on the facts, the events themselves, on what happened, on what people said, and the like. The what of the story is more important than the why, even if the what is simply an accurate accounting of someone else's version of what happened, or someone else's opinion. Although the factualist recognizes that people are important in news stories, there is little or no concern about the consequences to the people involved. The facts simply fall where they will, with consequences taking care of themselves. The factualist is usually considered an objective journalist, with varying degrees of suspicion of, or hostility to, evaluative or subjective journalism.

5. *Existentialist or rationalist*. The last set of antinomies that I will mention here poses these questions: How do we best know what we want to know? How involved and committed should we be? What is reality, and how should we get at it? Finally, how should we pass on such information about reality? We can refer to the existential orientation as romantic and the rational orientation as scientific. In addition, the old conflict between emotion and reason is with us again.

The existentialist position insists that the journalist be involved, com-

---

3 *Ibid.*, 88.

mitted, moving, choosing, changing. "Man is nothing else but what he makes of himself," Sartre has said, calling this the first principle of existentialism.[4] Certainly the existential journalist, in the serious business of "becoming," would not be devoid of rationality. It is a matter of emphasis: the existential journalist would stress intuition, feeling, and any other aspects of subjectivism that might help in the acquisition of a more complete and realistic picture of the event or personality being described.

Existentialism does not exclude rationalism, but it gives great emphasis to mystical, emotional, and intuitive concerns. It also gives extraordinary attention to personal freedom. As Hazel Barnes has said, the existentialist's "one certainty is his own freedom."[5] The existentialist believes that one cannot be ethical without freedom. I *ought* implies I *can, i.e.,* that I have a choice. Therefore, it is easy to see why the existentialist believes that B. F. Skinner and other determinists are "beyond ethics," since they think that people are enslaved to forces over which they have no control, forces that cause them to act in certain ways regardless of their desires.

The rationalist, in contrast to the existentialist, has a tendency to be more scientific than artistic, more prosaic than poetic, and more Apollonian than Dionysian. William Barrett has compared the rationalists with Jonathan Swift's Laputans in *Gulliver's Travels*. The rationalist would be one of the cerebral people, powerful but dreary, and scientifically oriented. And as Barrett says, the whole Romantic movement was an attempt to escape from Laputa—a protest of feeling against reason. This Romantic protest was furthered by the early existentialists such as Kierkegaard, who called for a kind of subjective thinking, the kind he claimed for himself.[6] It is this subjective thinking—a sort of harmonious marriage of emotion and intelligence—that marks the existentialist in journalism and differentiates him or her from the rationalist, who is determined to exclude emotion and make every decision—ethical and otherwise—on the basis of reason and reason alone.

These five sets of antinomies go a long way toward describing the dominant orientations among journalists today. Every journalist tends toward either one or the other antinomy in each of the pairs. However, it should be noted that such either-or orientations are not really mutually

---

4 Jean-Paul Sartre, *Existentialism and Human Emotions* (New York, 1957), 15.
5 Hazel Barnes, *An Existentialist Ethics* (New York, 1971), 51.
6 Barrett, *Irrational Man,* 122–23, 150.

exclusive, nor is it desirable that they be. For instance, we have existentially inclined New Journalists with us today, who are escaping from the Laputa of conformist and traditional journalism. But these New Journalists are not exclusively subjective and emotional; they manage to merge their artistic instincts with considerable scientific technique. All thoughtful and sensitive journalists make the effort to transcend powerful antinomies and create a new position, a synthesis on which to stand. This is the spirit of the dialectic—the tendency to merge useful aspects from the clash of opposites, to evolve a new and superior stance or orientation in the form of the journalistic synthesis.

Basic Allegiances: The Loyalty Model

In the Loyalty Model, four principal allegiances suggest themselves in two sets of antinomies: allegiance to people versus allegiance to institutions and allegiance to ideologies versus allegiance to events and facts. Again, as is true with all classification systems or typologies, in a real situation it is never entirely an either-or thing, but at any time there is the tendency for one of these allegiances to dominate. And, of course, the basic journalistic allegiance ties in with the general orientation a person has, and it has a direct bearing on the journalistic philosophy (especially in the area of ethics) that is embraced. The four allegiances suggested by these two sets of antinomies may be referred to, following the Loyalty Model, as loyalties of personalism, institutionalism, ideologism, and neutralism (factualism).

The personalists, mentioned earlier in the dichotomous classifications, are the people-oriented journalists, those who have strong loyalties to people—either to themselves or others. They are egoists or altruists, sensitive to the consequences of their journalism. They have, therefore, mainly a utilitarian motivation in their activities. Because of this basic allegiance to people, they tend to be more personal, polemical, opinionated, subjective, and humanistic in their journalism.

Second are the institutionalists, whose main loyalty or allegiance is to their journalistic organization or to some other group or institution. They differ from the personalists in that they are directed mainly, not by their own self-interest or the interests of other persons, but by an institutional loyalty. Theirs is more of a collectivist orientation than an individualist one. Loyalty to their body of colleagues, to their institution—that is the motivating factor for them. The institutionalists are either oriented toward their own journalistic media or toward some other entity, such as a political party or a religious group. It is obvious that if their prime allegiance is to some institution, their overall philosophical stance in journalism will be quite different from the personalists, who shape their activities to persons and their needs.

Next come the ideologists, journalists who are mainly loyal to a cause, to a social ideal, or to a particular philosophical or political concept. Often, though not always, these journalists also tend strongly toward institutionalism, since their espoused ideology is often reflected in some institution or organization to which they belong. These journalists enthrone philosophies, causes, programs, movements, and concepts, and they find their loyalties tied to potent ideas rather than to persons or organizations. A journalist oriented in this way may have an allegiance to a political or nationalistic philosophy or movement, such as Marxism or Zionism, or a special ideological movement, such as the women's liberation movement or the peace movement. In any case, for the ideologist it is the ideology or the philosophical idea that is the dominant catalyst for journalistic action.

Finally, there are the neutralists—the fact lovers, the event-oriented journalists, or the objectivists, as they are often called. Their loyalty is to events and situations "out there," not to persons, ideologies, or groups. The neutralist is mainly reportive, not judgmental or polemical; his or her main allegiance is to the objective event or to the facts surrounding the event. Little concerned with consequences or ramifications, or with any group or institution, the neutralist's loyalty is really to the story and the event and nothing more.

Rousseau's Quandary

In the case of the second model—the Self-Relatedness Model—the binary journalistic orientations are freedom lovers and authority lovers. Philosophers have always been concerned with this freedom-authority problem, most of them having been stuck (as good philosophers should be) somewhere between these two antinomies. Jean Jacques Rousseau (1712–1778) is a good example of a thinker who valued autonomy and personal independence while at the same time recognizing the basic inclination to dependency on an authority. Throughout his writings, Rousseau worried with these antithetic attitudes, and this paradox helps illustrate one of the main concerns of the French Enlightenment of the eighteenth century and, for that matter, of the government of the new United States after the American Revolution.

Rousseau, like Jefferson, believed in personal autonomy but was uncertain of his and his fellow men's capacity for freedom. He was determined to be free, but he was also unsure of such a possibility in the real world. He wanted freedom for himself and for others, but at the same time, he desired security in his society. At one point he wrote, "How forcibly I would have exposed all the abuses of our institutions; how simply I would have demonstrated that man is good naturally and that it is by their institutions alone that men have become wicked." Man may have seemed naturally good to Rousseau, and he may have seen society and institutions as causing men to become wicked. He may have desired to see a person "wholly sufficient to oneself," but he was never comfortable with such freedom, for it meant a kind of isolation that autonomous people must experience and it meant consequences that he could not completely accept.[7] Many journalists today are like that.

Rousseau felt that the journalist is good (moral, responsible, well-intentioned) *naturally,* but is corrupted by the institution of the press. The expectations of the newspaper, for example, often cause journalists to put aside personal standards and succumb to institutional standards and objectives. Editors' desires too often, Rousseau would say, take precedence over the journalists' desires. This, of course, shows the deterministic streak in Rousseau—the same streak that manifests itself constantly in the practice of journalism.

Every day journalists shift responsibility for certain of their actions to others—to a source, to the editor, to a colleague, to somebody—and refuse to do what Rousseau's natural or inner voice demands of them. The pressures of pragmatic journalism in a competitive society, the power exercised by press authorities—plus other deterministic pressures of the daily routine—undoubtedly afflict Rousseau's naturally responsible journalist. But as Kant would say, this is simply an excuse or rationalization, not a valid reason for failing to accept personal responsibility; the journalist could, in Kant's view, act responsibly out of a sense of duty to principle, not out of a consideration of consequences.

Today's journalists have much to say about freedom, and they usually

7   Fred Weinstein and Gerald M. Platt, *The Wish to be Free* (Berkeley, 1969), 84, 87.

pay allegiance to it. They talk also about authority—about press control and editorial direction—and pay a certain respect to it, also. American journalists usually stress press freedom from government authority. Marxist-Leninist journalists usually stress press freedom from capitalist exploiters. Other statist press systems stress freedom of the press to serve national interests and to preserve national security. Few journalists say much, however, about personal journalistic freedom.

Whether journalists are talking about freedom of the press from government control, freedom of the press from capitalist propagandists and profiteers, or freedom of the individual journalists vis-à-vis their media superiors, the basic issue of the discussion is always the nature and limits of freedom. Some of us are trying to justify our favorite concepts of press freedom as we try to disengage ourselves and our press systems from any taint of authoritarianism. We are, in a real way, caught in Rousseau's quandary—not only semantically, but practically. We are usually gravitating toward one of the extremes—toward either authority or liberty—when, perhaps, we should be trying to escape from these powerful antinomies into some middle zone of conceptual thinking.

We should at least try to escape from this quandary by seeking to break out of the simplistic and stultifying limitations of this freedom-authority dichotomy and recognize that all journalists and all press systems are at the same time both libertarian and authoritarian. All press systems are somewhat free, and all are under some authority. And when we locate the authority, we locate the holder of the freedom.

Freedom and Authority: Three Levels

A certain trinary classification of freedom and authority might be applied nationally or internationally to get beyond simple antinomies. And why not emphasize the necessary symbiosis of freedom and authority, thereby eliminating many problems stemming from this dualism? Freedom and authority can be considered as inseparable, with the locus of authority determining the source of the freedom, and with authoritarianism always merging with libertarianism.

First, freedom can be analyzed as having three levels: authoritarianism, libertarianism, and existentialism. In the Soviet Union, under what journalists in the United States call an *authoritarian* system of the press, there is what can be termed "state freedom"—freedom applied to the state authorities (the government-party apparatus), a kind of centralized freedom. The state has the freedom to develop and control journalism as it sees fit. There is freedom on the part of the state to see that the press is used as an instrument of social stability and national progress and development. The authoritarian level of freedom is, most likely, not even thought of as freedom by journalists in the United States. But the authoritarian level, like the other two levels, implies freedom for *someone*.

Next is what is usually called the *libertarian* level. Here the freedom rests with the press itself. The freedom, instead of being government-centered, is consolidated in an institution and takes on a corporate identity. The freedom really belongs to the press units and basically is a negative freedom—freedom of the institutions of the press from outside interference or control. Freedom at the libertarian level is in the hands of the media owners and managers, with only sporadic bits of freedom filtering down to the lower ranks of the journalists.

Finally, there is the *existential* level of freedom, which is applied to the individual journalist and not to the institution or to the state. There is, in any press system, a considerable latitude of personal freedom; at any rate, there is always more freedom available to the journalist than he or she actually uses. The concern at this level is with how much journalistic autonomy can be found among individual journalists.

The other antinomy is, of course, authority. It is important to think of authority simultaneously with freedom, for there is a tight relationship between the two concepts. One can just as reasonably refer to each of the three levels of freedom as levels of authority also. Thus, the three levels of authority are state authoritarianism, institutional (or press) authoritarianism, and individual (or existential) authoritarianism. The key question is, Where is the authority centered? The location of the authority determines who has the freedom, just as who has the freedom determines who has the authority. If there is an authority or several authorities in a system, one can realistically call the system "authoritarian." But in the United States we normally call *only* state authoritarianism by this name. Perhaps this is unfortunate; certainly it is unrealistic.

In the society of the United States today, there is little that resembles classical liberalism, according to Noam Chomsky—a man who is interested in power as well as linguistics. He sees private power centers other than the state appearing and growing ever stronger. Chomsky believes this new situation highly authoritarian. It is a system, he says, "which accepts a number of centres of authority and control—the State on one hand, agglomerations of private power on the other—all interacting." And he continues, "Individuals are malleable cogs in this highly constrained machine."[8]

What is the significance of Chomsky's observation for American journalism? For one thing, it indicates that, contrary to popular belief, the American press is really quite authoritarian—in the sense of having a number of centers of authority and control. These power centers, such as newspaper groups, corporations, and conglomerates, are authorities directing journalism and public opinion.

Such a system, Chomsky would say, might still be called democratic or open or pluralistic by many, but really it is not. The individual is depreciated in such a system; the journalists—and perhaps also their audience—are simply as Chomsky puts it, "malleable cogs" in the machine. On the societal level, the press centers of power combine with government to keep journalism as a whole from being truly libertarian. And on the microcosmic level of the press (where the individual works within the institutional context), journalists are not free either and find themselves controlled by directors and supervisors. In addition, as press power centers grow and pluralism constricts, the individual journalist has less and less freedom and voice in determining the direction of American journalism.

Authoritarianism—or direction by an authority—at the *individual,* or existential, level is, of course, centered on the person, on the individual journalist. Contrary to general belief, the journalist has a certain degree of authority not only in personal decisions and in terms of integrity, but also over others in the workplace. At least, this is the existentialist credo. Personal influence through example, persuasion, and pressure is always present in all political and press systems, and through such influence the determined journalist can have considerable impact on journalistic and even institutional directions.[9] Some individual journalists, just as some governments and some publishers, do not use the authority they have to the maximum. But they still have it, and it is potentially powerful.

Authority, as well as freedom, therefore exists on three levels. When we talk of freedom, we are talking of authority, and when we talk of author-

8 Quoted in Bryan Magee (ed.), *Men of Ideas* (New York, 1982), 193.
9 One work in which this personal or existential impact is discussed at some length is Merrill, *Existential Journalism.*

ity, we are talking of freedom. The dialectic leads to a merger, the hyphenated synthesis "freedom-authority." The publisher of an American newspaper has much authority and therefore much freedom. It is at this media-manager level that the locus of freedom-authority exists in a so-called "libertarian" country, such as the United States. The state (or the state-party apparatus) or national leader in a so-called "authoritarian" country, such as the Soviet Union, Paraguay, or Iran, is really the locus of freedom-authority. And on the existential or individual level, the person—the journalist—is the locus of freedom-authority. So everywhere in the world there are three kinds of freedom related to journalism: state freedom, press freedom, and individual freedom. These freedoms relate also to authority, since authority is necessary for the exercise of freedom. Therefore, there are also state authority, press authority, and individual authority.

In the journalistic context, then, all systems are finally both free and authoritarian. If journalists will think in these terms, perhaps some of the profession's divisive rhetoric, much of which stems from semantic confusion caused by the use of certain labels, will disappear. A consideration of this dialectical fusion of freedom and authority should help journalists escape from this potent prison of either-or, this enslavement to antinomic thinking, and break out into the sunlight of a more realistic view of free and controlled journalism.

Absolutism and Relativism: The Ethical Model

Another antinomic problem for journalists arises out of the issue of absolutism versus relativism. This dualistic monster often raises its head, since journalists, especially in the area of ethics, tend to be absolutist or relativist in their outlooks. This set of antinomies is part of the Ethical Model.

Journalists, like everyone else, have many problems with this dualism. Ethics concerns doing what is right, and there are absolute and relative concepts of "right." Relativists generally believe that contexts and circumstances determine what is right; absolutists say that right is right regardless of situations and circumstances. Kant said that morality involves autonomy—the ability to decide independently what is right and wrong, whom to obey and whom to ignore. For Kant, if ethics is in any way relative, it is relative to the person making the ethical decision. If ethics is tied too tightly to social mores, there is little room left for autonomy. If the journalist, for instance, simply subscribes to institutional ethical codes, then this is nothing more than a form of relativism. The journalist alone, must, for Kant, determine the laws and maxims to abide by, and these will be absolute, universal laws for that journalist to follow in every situation and context.

Unlike Kant, most journalists view ethics as relative, varying from press system to press system, ideology to ideology, culture to culture, and country to country. In fact, many journalists see ethics as relative to news medium, time, and situation even within the United States. But it is easy to succumb to what has been called in philosophy the "naturalistic fallacy"—the idea that whatever is, should be. The fact that journalistic ethics vary from place to place and time to time does not prove that such ethics *should* so vary.

It seems that morality is by its very nature supposed to be a set of universal standards or principles that do not differ between persons, lifestyles, or cultures. Are not lying, misrepresentation, falsifying information, and harming reputations unethical in all societies, in all press systems? Cannot, for example, Soviet journalists be justified in criticizing the journalistic morality of the United States? And cannot the American journalist question ethical practices among Soviet journalists?

These are difficult questions. But if one does not take a strict either-or position on them, they can be answered effectively. The general answer is that there are *some* absolutes in journalism (even in vastly different political systems, such as those of the Soviet Union and the United States) and there are other principles that are relative, *i.e.*, contingent on the particular society and its own values. Many journalists, of course, will not be satisfied with "splitting" morality in this way. The ethical relativist will say that, even if one assumes that two moralities are fundamentally different, it is possible that each is as correct as the other. It can, therefore, be just as right to falsify a report in Country A as it is to be accurate in a report in Country B. The ethical absolutist will also be dissatisfied, for the absolutist sees ethics as being all or nothing. If something is an ethical action here, it is ethical over there and everywhere else. The absolutist journalist of Country A would project his or her personal morality, not only to other journalists in country A, but even to journalists in Country B.

Journalists, then, who believe that there is but one set of ethical principles or one truth are *absolutists;* those who believe there are varying rules or principles of morality for different people (and therefore different truths) are *relativists*.[10] Both ethically and epistemologically these anti-nomies are extremely important. Journalists should come to terms with them and try to reconcile them through intelligent synthesizing.

Since the days of Kant, the war between relativism and absolutism has heated up—not only in ethics and epistemology but also in politics and the arts. Kant's idealist and romantic followers generally embraced relativism, though, especially in ethics, Kant himself is often considered more of an absolutist. A good example of a post-Kantian relativist was Friedrich von Schelling, who came up with at least one relativistic system every year as the eighteenth century drew to a close. But the best known of these rela-tivistic or romantic philosophers was Schelling's contemporary and schoolmate, Hegel. He provided many alternative ways of looking at, and living in, the world; his idea was that there are various orientations or world views—all valid—and that we move constantly from one to another.

According to Hegel, humankind should cease talking about "true" or "false" philosophies—about good or bad political systems, morality, and anything else—and consider the fact that there are only "different" sys-tems, concepts, and values. None is wholly true or false. Here was a supreme relativist expressing himself. Reality, said Hegel, is no more than the sum total of all the various ways people view it, and these ways are constantly changing, clashing, and merging. Although Hegel was, in many significant ways a romantic, he opposed individualism and supported a community spirit—a belief that exerted strong influence on Karl Marx and, it might be added, on persons such as Mussolini and Hitler.

Hegel came up with the idea of the dialectic, in which he suggested that the "forms of consciousness" are linked to one another in a logical way. One evolves—flows into and out of—another, and in this flowing there is no placid or smooth progression. Rather there is a violent battle of op-posites and then a reconciliation, followed by further clashes and more reconciliations.

This is the essence of the famous Hegelian dialectic, which he describes in his *Logic* and assumed in his better-known book *The Phenomenology of Mind*. These reconciliations, or syntheses, have been considered by a variety of philosophers as quite valuable. D. Elton Trueblood's remarks

10   Robert C. Solomon, *Introducing Philosophy* (New York, 1985), 186.

typify philosophers' general satisfaction with the dialectic: "The synthesis, in human thought, tends to re-establish the thesis, but with the advantage of the criticism which the antithesis has provided. Then the synthesis becomes a new thesis and the process continues, if thought continues."[11] Marx developed his notion of historical class conflict from Hegel's ideational or conceptual dialectic. He replaced Hegel's abstract theory with his own more important battles over jobs, wages, exploitation, profits, and class differences.

By the second half of the nineteenth century, relativism was becoming well entrenched. Nietzsche presented a powerful attack on traditional ideas of truth, saying there can be many equally true (or false) views. For Nietzsche, not only was truth thrown out, but all traditional wisdom was challenged. The creative, courageous person can, according to Nietzsche, determine his or her (though Nietzsche, given his views toward women, might not have said "her") own morality, which transcends that of the society. This was a moral philosophy completely relative in nature, fully individualistic, and made for the transcending person—the heroic Overman (*Übermensch*).[12]

Relativism is still very much with us. Absolutists are found here and there, but it seems that—in spite of protestations of many persons in favor of the rationality and desirability of absolutism—most people, including journalists, are relativists in their daily lives. Journalists, for example, are forever making exceptions, considering the situation and the special circumstances, and using double standards in their treatment of events and persons.[13]

The position most consistent with the dialectic and a flexible orientation, of course, is relativism. But though relativism is often practiced by journalists, especially in the United States, it is usually done so in a kind of accidental, *ad hoc,* unthinking manner. Inconsistency in journalism is far too often a kind of irrational inconsistency, one that cannot be explained or justified logically. The dialectic of absolutism and relativism is a healthy

11   D. Elton Trueblood, *General Philosophy* (Grand Rapids, Mich., 1963), 81.

12   For Nietzsche's main discussion of the *Übermensch* see any edition of his *Thus Spake Zarathustra,* Part I: Prologue. See also Crane Brinton, *Nietzsche* (New York, 1965) for a good description of the *Übermensch*.

13   For a defense of moral relativism, see Gilbert Harman, "Moral Relativism Defended," in Michael Krausz and J. W. Meiland (eds.), *Relativism, Cognitive and Moral* (Notre Dame, 1982), 63–78.

one that the rational journalist must recognize and use every day. The absolutist should be a relativistic absolutist, and the relativist must be an absolutist in the practice of relativism. A composite journalist—the relativist-absolutist—will result, one who may have inclinations toward general truths or standards but is also ready to deviate from them on occasion.

Hermeneutics is an attempt to span the gap between dogmatism (or absolutism) and relativism. *Hermeneutics* is an old name for interpretation—a way of seeking the truth. For many centuries the term was used only for biblical interpretation, the goal of which was to get to the Truth of God. Today the term has a broader meaning and applies generally in philosophy to the business of analyzing or interpreting (trying to understand) the world.

Contemporary hermeneutics is an attempt to comprehend perspectives other than one's own. Many believe it is dogmatic to insist that the structures of the human mind are the same everywhere and that, as Kant and others have insisted, all people have a common basis of knowledge. But it is also wrong to insist that we are all different and have varying truths, since obviously all people hold to many common truths. It has been said that hermeneutics is an attempt to be empathic—to get into the shoes of others. It is an effort to understand other points of view without giving up one's own.

Many modern hermeneuticists insist that their orientation is more than simply another method; they see it rather as trying to overcome all methods and as de-emphasizing the stress on proof and certainty. Their stress is on shared understandings that they believe people already have. This orientation is, in short, a search for commonalities. The emphasis is on dialogue—on sharing and uncovering similarities and syntheses—rather than getting stuck in a search for differing and absolute solutions and proofs.[14]

It should be apparent that absolutism and relativism can be merged, resulting in a third stance in ethics—a synthesis. C. David Jones has called this the "rationalist stance."[15] It takes into account both of the other orientations. The rationalist recognizes the validity of some aspects of both the absolutist and the relativist (or situational) theories. This new

14 Solomon, *Introducing Philosophy*, 189–90.
15 See C. David Jones, *Hominology: Psychiatry's Newest Frontier* (Springfield, Ill., 1975).

stance is almost identical to what I will call "deontelic ethics" in Chapter 9.

The rationalist, or synthesis, theory would begin with certain specific and absolute maxims or principles (*e.g.,* the journalist should not lie, or the journalist should always seek the truth), but would recognize that there are times when such an absolute maxim must be modified or broken, that there are occasions when it is more *rational* to keep the truth or part of it from the audience.

This ethics of synthesis realizes that absolutes are not necessarily rational, that changes take place, reasons differ, and situations alter decisions in morality. The synthesis theory also recognizes that relativist ethics is basically pragmatic and easily turned into a rationale for doing almost anything the journalist wants to do; relativism can simply become a way to act out of selfish motivation. So it is evident that the dialectic is at work on this issue, that absolutism and relativism have collided and a middle way, or synthesis, has evolved—one that is more useful and meaningful to the modern journalist, than either of the old ways. It should be noted, however, that this is a synthesis based on the assumption that the journalist has a considerable amount of freedom to determine his or her own dialectical resolution.

The dialectical position is, of course, that the journalist's ethical duties may be absolute in some respects and relative in others. Henry Hazlitt has noted that Herbert Spencer was one of the few moral philosophers who dealt extensively with this problem. To Spencer, we should not think in terms of absolutes, for there is not in every case a right and a wrong. In a multitude of situations there is no definite right but only a "least wrong." For Spencer, as for most of us in our daily decision making, an ethical choice is often not in favor of the right, but in favor of the least of several wrongs.[16]

The journalist recognizes that. A common case: The reporter knows that the source of the quotes in a story *should* be given in the story. But the source will speak only anonymously; so the reporter promises not to reveal the source's name. The best "right" would be to use both the quotes and the name of the source. But the reporter has chosen a lesser "right"— the use of the quotes with no source. The poorest choice, of course, would have been to refrain from publishing the story at all. In other words, if the

16 Henry Hazlitt, *The Foundations of Morality* (Los Angeles, 1964), 150.

story is to be published, the reporter must resort not to the best, or ideal, practice (giving both the source and the quotes), but to a lesser good— giving the quotes only. This is a kind of relativism; it is certainly not the absolutist position, which is to always give the source of a quote.

What is important in this situation is that the reporter thoughtfully and carefully decide whether the sourceless quote is worth enough to the readers to keep the reporter from choosing to ignore the quotation al- together. This is where rationality forces itself upon the journalist. It is not simply a matter of following some Kantian rule or principle of duty auto- matically; it is a matter of choosing among options in the context of the specific situation.

The rational journalist, then, cannot really be an absolutist, for abso- lutism constrains reason and leads to only a kind of mechanistic decision making. A journalist, concerned with ethics and not simply with epis- temology, finds that there are times when it is more rational to withhold the truth or part of it from the audience. In short, there are times when ethical ends might justify the abandonment of epistemological means.

Also, it should be noted that the journalist who is a rationalist in ethics realizes that relativism, or situationalism, is fundamentally pragmatic, and thus, a person can easily rationalize away a principle or act out of purely selfish motives with little or no thought to ethics. So the rational journalist sees, on occasion, that the relativist position is untenable. This rational journalist will not blindly follow either antinomy, realizing that there are components other than self and situation that are important, such as change and human capacity. At the very least, basic values (maxims), the capacity of the person to act rationally and morally, and the specific situation must all be taken into consideration in making journalistic decisions.

All the antinomies that have been discussed in this chapter are ex- tremely powerful. They insistently pull the journalist to the extremes. But the intelligent, rational, and sensitive journalist refuses to fall prey to the either-or of the dialectic without seeking the new position that arises out of the synthesis. The nature of the synthesis may differ somewhat among journalists—just as Aristotle's Golden Mean may differ for various of its seekers—but the synthesis will at least drag the journalist away from the powerful pull of the extreme positions toward a more rational ground in the middle. Escaping the power of antinomies is, for the journalist, diffi- cult and sometimes debilitating but with cautious and intelligent effort, it can be achieved, with great rewards in personal satisfaction.

Four

A NIETZSCHEAN DIALECTIC

Friedrich Nietzsche is usually considered to be far out on the fringes of philosophy—a kind of antithesis to the generally accepted virtues of social consciousness, altruism, and collective loyalties. He is often excoriated as arrogant, emotional, egotistical, and autocratic. Some scholars, however, see him differently. Here, they say, is a thinker of an Aristotelian (as well as existential) bent who does, indeed, value the individual person. And like Aristotle, he is a firm believer in saying yes to life, affirming life to the fullest. Just where Nietzsche falls on various spectra is an open question; the fact remains that he exhibited in his work (even if not always in his life) many uplifting and challenging ideas that portray individual life as rich and valuable. In this day of negativism and self-depreciation, such a stance is rather invigorating, at least to persons with existentialist inclinations.

Nietzsche's concepts of "master morality" and "slave morality" (he championed the former) are rather difficult to understand. Another of his major concepts was that of the *Übermensch,* the Overman or Superman, whom he saw as a kind of evolutionary result of master morality, a person who has risen above morality, has transvalued values. The Superman, for Nietzsche, is one who will develop as people learn to transcend themselves, and clearly only the noble few and those with a "Will to Power" will aspire beyond themselves in this way.

At some indeterminate point, then, there will be this higher person, a total aristocrat in whom virtue resides and who is a law unto himself. This person will be of a type that Nietzsche called the Dionysian, a figure of great energy and vitality, tremendous power, and exuberant self-expression. The Superman will be strong, self-confident, alert, self-disciplined, independent, authentic, and freedom loving. He will not scorn emotion; in fact, he will take great pride in subjectivity, sensitivity, and passion. He will be lifted above the humdrum multitude who spend their prosaic days thoughtlessly and emotionlessly in mundane affairs.

This picture of the ideal person contradicts that of Karl Marx, who saw the heroic coming master of the earth in the person of the proletarian who would rise from anonymity among the masses to rule society. Exactly what Nietzsche meant by the *Übermensch* is not certain, but the portrayal surely contains overtones of superiority, meritocracy, and authoritarianism, and a great stress on self-respect, even self-love. And there is resemblance to Aristotle in Nietzsche's emphasis on "yea-saying." Hazel Barnes has thrown some light on the meaning of this "saying yes to life" that was at the center of Nietzsche's moral philosophy: "Learning to comprehend the full meaning of one's own growth and to find the process interesting even when painful is one of the prime sources of human satisfaction and quite legitimately so. To experience one's self as both creator and created, to welcome the playing of one's own part, even if the play proves to be a tragedy—this is to me the profound meaning of Nietzsche's Yea-saying."[1]

The Dionysian becomes for Nietzsche a kind of tragic (but courageous) attitude to life that scorns any wish that things were other than they are; the attitude of the hero is so strong and self-reliant that he welcomes the buffetings of life and would go to seek them if they did not come to him. It is this Dionysian person that Nietzsche projects into his yea-saying Superman who is able to transcend the slave morality of average people.

Usually Nietzsche is thought of as an ethical egoist (perhaps akin to Ayn Rand), but actually, like Aristotle, he saw the excellence of the individual as part of, and a contributing factor to, the excellence of the whole society. And though he talks much about creating values, the values he asserts are very old. Like Aristotle, he takes ethics to be based on human nature, and so it is not really a question of creating values so much as finding them in oneself. What Nietzsche did was to rebel against the usual Kantian style of thinking; this anti-Kantian tone makes Nietzsche's writing take on a harsh note compared with Aristotle's gentlemanly rhetoric. Although he was similar to Aristotle in many ways, Nietzsche did not

---

1 Barnes, *An Existentialist Ethics*, 315.

think that each person's nature was the same. He thought that everyone should discover and follow different values, different standards of excellence; thus, each person would have a distinct morality.

In rejecting the morality of obedience for a more personal set of principles, Nietzsche gave rise to successors—often called existentialists—who carried on his emphasis on individual choosing, on creating the self. Sartre, for example, rejects the idea of a uniform morality and urges all people to create their own values and become personally committed to them. In answer to any question about ethics, the only ultimate answer for the existentialist is: "I do this because I choose to accept these values." But Sartre does not really abandon general principles, as Nietzsche does; he adopts an almost Kantian stance about the need to choose principles for all mankind, not just for oneself. However, he claims no correctness for these principles; he says only that this or that is what he chooses mankind to be. Thus, Sartre's moral philosophy is a curious mixture of the most radical relativism and the most traditional (*i.e.,* legalistic or Kantian) moralizing. The dialectic is seen at work again.

Nietzsche's Thesis and Antithesis

Nietzsche had much to say about the antinomies of reason and emotion, which he expressed as the Apollonian and the Dionysian. These are dichotomous tendencies in all persons, and they form a dualism that Nietzsche first highlighted in these terms in *The Birth of Tragedy* (1872). He observed two opposing elements in Greek tragedies and believed them to be basic metaphysical principles of reality. And he named them for two Greek gods—Apollo, the god of light, and Dionysus, the god of wine.

Dionysus can be thought of as a symbol of passion, mysticism, subjectivism, free and unfettered spirit, intuition, irrationality, and darkness. On the other hand, Apollo is symbolic of reason, beauty, order, discipline, wisdom, and light. Nietzsche thought of Apollo's reason and other qualities as necessary but unrealizable elements and thus an inferior guide to existence, since he saw man as more of a feeling animal than a thinking animal. Nietzsche believed that it is through sensitivity, passionate involvement, feeling, intuition, and mystical experiences that a person comprehends reality. He would have us dig beneath the surface of facts, of the rational world around us, and try to get to the pulsating spiritual world of reality.

In many ways Nietzsche might be considered the real father of the New Journalism that swept onto the American journalistic scene in the early 1960s and to a large extent is still with us. Nietzsche would probably say to modern journalists that the Dionysian inclination would help unravel reality better than a purely Apollonian stance; he saw the Dionysian orientation as superior, for it is the free spirit that offers man, through some kind of mysterious sensitivity or intuition, a more valid and profound vision of the world around him.

E. L. Allen, in his perceptive little book *From Plato to Nietzsche,* adds his perspective on Nietzsche's yea-saying and the Superman. In Allen's view, Nietzsche would have us return to Greek culture before the rationalism of Socrates vitiated it somewhat and to the virtues of the aristocracy "that does not conceal its contempt for the many and needs no law but its own inherent nobility." Allen points out that in Nietzsche's later works, Dionysus absorbs Apollo, and if this is a synthesis, certainly it is an unbalanced one. Dionysus is made to symbolize Nietzsche's affirmation of life, whereas Apollo increasingly stands for an escape from life into a realm of calm cogitation.[2]

These human tendencies that Nietzsche calls by the names of Dionysus and Apollo are closely akin to what Karl Jaspers has called "the law of day" and "the passion of night." One is Dionysian urge: dynamic, creative, ecstatic, and even frenzied at times. The other is Apollonian order: reason and discipline.

Although Nietzsche may have tended to submerge Apollo, he did not throw him out; he simply hid him under a more encompassing Dionysus. Reason, though not dominant for Nietzsche, is part of a person. It has value, but this value must be held in check if a person is to reach greatness and is not be controlled by the dictates of society and its political leaders.

It is interesting to note that Carl Jung, a modern psychoanalyst, came to a psychological conclusion about human beings that has similarities to Nietzsche's more philosophical one. Jung contends, in his essay "Wotan" (1936), that various gods are really personifications of basic psychic forces. One of the main Teutonic deities, Wotan, personifies certain attributes of a person's psyche: He is the god of storm and frenzy, the

---

2 E. L. Allen, *From Plato to Nietzsche* (New York, 1964), 176, 172. On Nietzsche's *Übermensch* and his Apollo-Dionysus dichotomy, see also R. I. Hollingdale, *Nietzsche: The Man and His Philosophy* (Baton Rouge, 1965).

unleasher of passions and the lust for war; he is the restless wanderer who creates unrest and stirs up strife wherever he goes. He is a magician and an artist of disguises; he is versed in the secrets of the occult. In other words, he is quite similar to Nietzsche's Dionysus. It seems that, for Jung, Wotan (or Odin) is the dominant force in people, for another god (in place of Apollo) is not juxtaposed against Wotan. Wotan has a more positive side also. He is the god of inspiration, poetry, and wisdom.[3]

The Journalistic Clash

Journalists should understand this binary classification of Nietzsche's. They are constantly pulled in one or the other direction, toward Apollo or toward Dionysus. Surely they pay lip service to reason; they want to think, to make serious decisions in their journalism, to act only out of thoughtful consideration of alternatives. Their education, their dedication to truth and the presentation of fact, and their recognition of the advantages of the scientific method propel them in the direction of Apollo. But their natural instincts, their biases, their values, their selfish motivations, their altruistic ones, and their passion for social impact and public service often carry them headlong into the halls of Dionysus.

How often do we hear journalists talking about what they "feel" to be the right procedure, the right action? How often do we see journalists making fast, whimsical decisions based on nothing more than the instinct of the moment? Why did they quote this person instead of that one? Why did they select this piece of data instead of that one? Why did they use a direct quote here and an indirect quote there? Why, in fact, did they choose to write this story instead of that one? Their answer, when it is given, is, "Just because." This is the Dionysian in them; they are motivated by feeling, not by reason. This is not to say they are not justified in such action; Nietzsche would certainly support their stress on feeling, emotion, and instinct in doing their stories.

But the Apollonian urge is too strong for the journalist to be happy with a mystical approach to journalism. The urge to think, to research, to compare, to verify, and to appraise is so fundamental in journalism that

3 V: W. Odajnyk, *Jung and Politics: The Political and Social Ideas of C. G. Jung* (New York, 1976), 88–89.

the reporter, for example, is ill at ease departing very far from it. Whim, emotion, and passion are fine, but the journalist knows that much more is expected. So the journalist tries to bend in the direction of reason, research, and logic. But he or she does not bend very far, usually. The journalist's rationale for not leaning further toward reason is insufficient time, the urgency of the story, competition, or the fleeting nature of journalistic endeavor. So in spite of the journalist's basic Dionysian proclivities, there is a strong pull toward Apollo.

Apollo and his antithesis, Dionysus, form the basic framework of the vocation of journalism. In effect, journalism is an activity that is caught somewhere between the antinomies of Apollo and Dionysus, between reason and emotion, between precision and abstruseness. Here, again, is the dialectic at work.

The Nietzschean distinction between the Apollonian and the Dionysian—between reason and feeling—is an interesting and perhaps valid way to consider extremes among orientations. But as Ayn Rand has suggested, it is not necessary for reason and emotion to be irreconcilable antagonists. Nor, for her, must emotion be this kind of wild, unknowable element raging somewhere within a person. She does state, however, that if a person tries to subordinate reason to emotion—as she believed Nietzsche tried to do—that is what emotion is likely to become. "This much is true," she said. "Reason *is* the faculty of an individual, to be exercised individually; and it is only dark, irrational emotions, obliterating his mind, that can enable a man to melt, merge and dissolve into a mob or a tribe. We may accept Nietzsche's symbols, but *not* his estimate of their respective values nor the metaphysical necessity of a reason-emotion dichotomy."[4] Rand believes that the attempt on the part of many philosophers to divorce reason from reality (in line with the Dionysian emphasis on a "deeper" and more complete view of reality) has pushed much contemporary thinking to extremes, far over in the darker corners of existentialism where reason is abandoned and intuition is enthroned.

Too many existentialists, according to Rand, have looked at modern philosophy and equated it with reason and as a result have been alienated from, and disgusted with, the rational philosophies of pragmatism and logical positivism, with their overemphasis on scientism, linguistic analy-

4 Ayn Rand, *The New Left: The Anti-Industrial Revolution* (New York, 1971), 58.

81

sis, and relativism.[5] As Rand points out, however, pragmatism and positivism should not be confused with rationalistic philosophy, for these pragmatists and positivists have all but obliterated reason. The existentialists, however, have generally held them up as examples of rationality, rebelled against them (as they should have) and then, unfortunately, proceeded to all but reject reason itself.

Looking for a Synthesis

The journalist, to fulfill his or her potential, must synthesize or harmonize these tendencies of rationality and passionate commitment. This will lead to a kind of journalistic scientist-artist, part Apollo and part Dionysus, as the person merges the perspectives of objective reason and existential subjectivity. Elsewhere I have called this synthesis or merger of journalistic orientations the "Apollonysian" stance.[6]

Such a synthesis will produce a journalist who both thinks *and* feels, who is both rational and sensitive, who is concerned both with facts and with interpretation, and who is dedicated both to the objective world "out there" and to the subjective world "in here." Such a journalist is, in essence, the complete journalist—one who intends to develop a journalistic philosophy that merges the strains or stances of freedom, rationality, and duty. The journalist, then, is Sartrean, Aristotelian, and Kantian at the same time. And that is a big order. But the merging strains of these perspectives combine to give the journalist the ingredients essential to the kind of reportorial and analytical work required of a systematic and conscientious press worker.

I should note that responsibility or ethics is considered implicit. The rational, free, and committed journalist who constrains his activities with a Kantian duty to principle will be a responsible journalist. At least such a journalist will desire to be responsible, and that is a significant step.

A journalist is inclined toward subjectivity and emotion. But the op-

---

5 Pragmatism teaches that truth is to be judged by consequences—by how well it works. Logical positivism teaches that ethical propositions have no cognitive meaning and are merely reports on our feelings. Linguistic analysis is concerned with showing people what they really mean when they use language and with showing that knowledge consists of nothing more than linguistic manipulation.

6 Merrill, *The Imperative of Freedom*, Chapter 9.

posite inclination is also strong, pulling the journalist in more rational directions. So the journalist is caught right in the middle of the dialectic. Some journalists succumb to one of the antinomies and become extremists; others, fortunately, are able to merge or synthesize the orientations and become Apollonysian. They are part scientist and part artist, part poetic and part prosaic, part logical and part intuitive, part realist and part idealist, part rationalist and part existentialist.

In short, the Apollonysian journalist is one who manages to combine the stances of the two main Nietzschean deities, a feat that gives this journalist at various times and in various situations the necessary ingredients of the two dichotomous orientations: 1) The Dionysian is the involved or artistic orientation—existentialist, romantic, poetic, mystical, intuitive, emotional, subjective, personal, informal, persuasive, humanistic, judgmental, directive, idealistic, propagandistic. 2) The Apollonian is the aloof or scientific orientation—rationalist, neutralist, prosaic, scientific, objectivist, impersonal, formal, reportive, disinterested, nonjudgmental, calm, dispassionate, realistic, unemotional.

Every journalist is to some degree an amalgam of these two main tendencies. But there is no doubt that every journalist evidences significantly more of one than of the other. In fact, an interesting hypothesis might be formulated: That journalists with the aloof, scientific orientation are those whose education and interests were more prosaic than poetic, more scientific than artistic. On the other hand, the involved, artistic journalists are frequently persons with a prejournalism background inclined toward imaginative literature, philosophy, and the humanities generally. It is probable that the artistic journalists are more emotional, more sensitive, more convinced of their own rightness, more desirous to proselytize and propagandize, and more dogmatic than are the scientific or uninvolved journalists.

In journalism these two tendencies in the Nietzschean dialectic are best illustrated by so-called "objective" and "subjective" journalism. The first, of course, reflects what was just called the aloof, scientific orientation; the second, the artistic, involved orientation. One could maintain that the objective and the subjective are the antinomies in the Nietzschean dialectic, but it might be more productive to look at the two sides *of objectivity* (the scientific and the artistic), since all journalists claim that what they are seeking to do is to present an objective story, even if some of them are using subjective techniques.

Apollonian Objectivity

A new way to consider objective journalism is to consider its scientific and artistic antinomies as representations of Nietzsche's Apollo and Dionysus respectively. People generally think of objective journalism as either being 1) factual and accurate, composed of verifiable bits of information, or 2) something far more complex and sophisticated—something that goes beyond the mere reporting of acts and statements and brings to the story another dimension that might be called reportorial discernment and sensitivity. The first may be called the Apollonian road to objectivity, and the second, the Dionysian road. What may be somewhat troublesome is that they are both often thought of as approaches to, or conceptions of, objective journalism. But they illustrate well the Nietzschean dialectic.

The first of objective journalism's two antinomies—the Apollonian, or the detached, dispassionate one—tends to dominate today in American journalism. It insists on reportorial detachment and neutralism and glorifies the separation of fact and opinion. Longtime Senator Barry Goldwater has described this approach clearly: "I am a great believer in the device, practiced by most responsible American newspapers, of separating the news developments and the newspapers' editorial opinion. The first should be a flat, unembroidered account of the facts surrounding the item of news. It should be, so far as is humanly possible, free from the writer's or the commentator's personal interpretation or views."[7]

Kent Cooper, when he was general manager of the Associated Press in the 1940s and 1950s, defined this kind of objectivity as "true and unbiased news." Wes Gallagher, a successor to Cooper in that job, also subscribed to what might be called the "AP concept of objectivity." In 1965, speaking at Indiana University, he said: "It seems to me that all men and women must have a Holy Grail of some kind, something to strive for, something always just beyond our fingertips even with the best of efforts. To the journalist that Holy Grail should be objectivity. To have anything less would be demeaning and would result in the destruction of the profession."[8]

Gallagher and many others who extol the value of Apollonian objectivity see it as an unreachable goal, but something that good journalists can come close to. Be that as it may, it should be noted that even those who

7 Barry Goldwater, *The Conscience of a Majority* (New York, 1971), 157.
8 Quoted in Altschull, *Agents of Power,* 130.

84

do not agree with Gallagher's core concept of objectivity are also seekers after objectivity. But these persons are still in the minority in the United States and are looked on by most mainstream journalists as eccentrics.

Everette Dennis, director of the Gannett Center for Media Studies in New York City, has made the point that Apollonian objectivity (though he did not call it that) in journalism "is merely a method and style of presenting information." He was referring to the factual concept of objectivity, the perspective presented by Goldwater. Dennis has noted that the defenders of this perspective say that it has three main characteristics: 1) separation of fact from opinion, 2) emotional detachment in presenting the news, and 3) a constant attempt at fairness and balance.[9]

Many persons, perhaps most of them academics, are skeptical of the Apollonian perspective on objectivity. They think that objectivity can be sought (and approached ever more closely) by infusing emotions and feelings, along with interpretation, analysis, and other subjective elements, into the story. But it may not be fair to compare journalists' concepts of objectivity with those of sociologists and other academics. For Paul Radin's characterization of the social scientist as a "thinker" and the newsperson as a "doer" contains a large portion of truth. The social scientist (and the philosopher) can engage in epistemological examination, whereas the practicing journalist does not have the time and seldom has the inclination.[10]

So a host of practicing journalists and many journalism professors, as well as a number of concerned politicians, such as Goldwater, take a more mundane or Apollonian position on objectivity. While recognizing limitations, they stress strategies of journalism that they identify with "objective" stories and "precision" journalism. As sociologist Gaye Tuchman has said in her perceptive discussion of journalistic objectivity, such persons "assume that, if every reporter gathers and structures 'facts' in a detached, unbiased, impersonal manner, deadlines will be met and libel suits avoided."[11] This is a very realistic, pragmatic way to consider journalistic objectivity.

Most newspeople identify objectivity with "facts" that they observe,

9 Everette E. Dennis and John C. Merrill, *Basic Issues in Mass Communication* (New York, 1984), 111.
10 Paul Radin, *Primitive Man as Philosopher* (New York, 1957); Gaye Tuchman, "Objectivity as Strategic Ritual: An Examination of Newsmen's Notions of Objectivity," *American Journal of Sociology*, LXXVII (January, 1972), 662.
11 Tuchman, "Objectivity as a Strategic Ritual," 664.

hear about, read about, and verify. But according to Tuchman, there are several other ways the journalist can claim objectivity for a story: 1) by presenting conflicting possibilities, 2) by presenting supporting evidence, 3) by the judicious use of quotations, and 4) by arranging facts in an appropriate sequence. In putting these four strategies into practice, the journalist first collects and presents "facts." For example, "X said A" can be considered a fact, even if A is false. Then the journalist locates and cites supporting "facts" that are commonly accepted as true. The journalist uses direct quotes from other persons to remove himself or herself from the story—thus letting the facts "speak for themselves." Finally, the journalist structures the story in an inverted pyramid, by which the most important "facts" come first and the least important come last, thereby achieving objectivity.[12]

In all this seeking of objectivity, the neutralist journalist, a Nietzschean Apollo, visualizes a dispassionate, neutral and rational journalism that, by and large, can somehow succeed in being genuinely objective. For this Apollonian journalist, the world "out there" can be adequately appropriated, substantially intact, and passed on to the audience. This is the antinomy of neutralism, which has been challenged and is increasingly being challenged, by the rising voice of the Dionysian journalist, who is counterposing the more mystical, personal, and existential dimension of the dialectic.

Dionysian Objectivity

The views expressed by Goldwater, Cooper, and Gallagher highlight the Apollonian perspective on objective journalism. Seldom, if ever, would proponents of such journalism concede that more interpretative and personal journalism, such as that of Tom Wolfe, Norman Mailer, and other "New Journalists," could be designated as objective. However, this personal journalism is seen by many as more objective than the Goldwater type. Michael Novak, writing about objectivity in journalism, has succinctly described what is meant by the personal or subjectivist view of objectivity. The passage sounds as if Plato or Kant might have written it, given its strong idealist epistemological flavor.

12 *Ibid.*, 665–70 *passim.*

The myth of objectivity leads to . . . misunderstandings in American journalism. There are no facts "out there" apart from human observers. And human observers become not more, but less astute when they try to be neutral. . . .

Reporters and newscasters know that if they aim at objectivity, at presenting "the facts" without editorializing, they run the risk of giving dignity to nonsense, drivel, and outright lies. What really happened in an event is not, they know, discovered by some neutral observation machine, not even by a camera. Events are not events until they are interpreted by human beings. . . . To list statistics, or outwardly observable happenings, or quotations from witnesses, is to give a very narrow view of the human world. It is to offer interpretation and editorial comment of a very misleading sort. Reality does not come divided into "facts" and "interpretation."[13]

Novak's remarks are in the tradition of such thinkers as Jaspers, Sartre, Martin Buber, Paul Tillich and Martin Heidegger, thinkers who in their writings have shown great respect for subjectivity and great suspicion of the empirical and pragmatic objectivity so beloved by American journalists. Back in the 1940s the noted journalist H. L. Mencken put this Novakian concept of objectivity quite bluntly: "We talk of objective reporting. There is no such thing. I have been a reporter for many years, and I can tell you that no reporter worth a hoot ever wrote a purely objective story. You get a point of view in it. . . . You can't escape it. A man that is worth reading at all has opinions. He has ideas. And you are not going to improve him by trying to choke him."[14] So Novak and Mencken—without using the label, of course—provide a glimpse of Dionysian objectivity—the subjective, artistic, existential, and personal stance of Nietzsche's Dionysus.

Nietzsche himself clearly saw the Dionysian person as one who was able to probe objectivity with a nonscientific perspective. In *The Twilight of the Idols* he wrote of this artistic and mystical individual: "He possesses to the highest degree the instinct for understanding and divining, just as he

---

13 Michael Novak, *The Experience of Nothingness* (New York, 1971), 39.
14 Quoted in Theo Lippman, Jr. (ed.), *A Gang of Pecksniffs* (New Rochelle, N.Y., 1975), 203.

possesses the art of communication to the highest degree. He enters into every skin, into every emotion; he is continually transforming himself."[15]

As Donald McDonald has written in a seminal article on objectivity, a reporter's values are necessarily injected into the story. Of the reporter, McDonald said "The value judgments he must make at every critical stage in his investigation and interpretation of the facts must reflect the values he already holds. Again, these values flow from his personal history. They are products of his education, his religious experience, his childhood, family life, social and economic background, friendships and associations, national ties and culture, as well as his emotional life and experiences, and his reason."[16]

What McDonald is saying so well is that it is impossible for the journalist to really be divorced from the story. Most readers would probably share McDonald's views. People instinctively understand that the thing is not the report and that the total complexity of the event "out there" is not treated adequately by the journalist's story of it. And they understand that a reporter's "personal history," as McDonald calls it, impinges on the way the reporter sees and shapes the story. In short, people are rather sophisticated—when they seriously consider it—in the area of epistemology. As the well-known Italian writer and journalist Luigi Barzini has written: "All people are resigned to the occasional differences between what they have seen and what the newspapers print the next day. Everything, they discover, has been touched up and simplified, often as unrecognisable as the picture taken from a plane of an intricate jungle, filled with wild beasts, colourful birds, and monstrous flowers, is to the traveller on foot."[17]

Some commentators on objectivity in journalism consider the concept simply a term that can give the journalist an upbeat feeling that goes a long way toward crowding out any sense of inadequacy he or she might feel. As Thomas Winship, former editor of the Boston *Globe,* said at the 1971 convention of the American Society of Newspaper Editors: "Objectivity is such a nice trip for an editor. Every morning he swallows his little objectivity pill. It shuts him off from all the long-haired kids in the city room

---

15   Friedrich Nietzsche, *The Twilight of the Idols,* trans. R. J. Hollingdale (Baltimore, 1968), 73.
16   Donald McDonald, "Is Objectivity Possible?" in John C. Merrill and Ralph Barney (eds.), *Ethics and the Press* (New York, 1975), 69–82.
17   Luigi Barzini, "The Anatomy of Expertise," *Encounter,* XXX (January, 1968), 33.

who whisper dirty talk over the water cooler. . . . Objectivity is a code word for playing it safe, covering up superficiality."[18]

Erich Fromm, on the other hand, grasps the essence of Dionysian objectivity. Objectivity, according to Fromm in *Man for Himself,* requires more than simply seeing an object dispassionately and neutrally; it requires the observer to become related in some way to the object being observed or reported. The nature of the object and the nature of the observer (or subject) must be merged and given equal attention if genuine objectivity is to be achieved. Fromm argues that "objectivity is not, as it is often implied in a false idea of 'scientific' objectivity, synonymous with detachment, with absence of interest and care. How can one penetrate the veiling surface of things to their causes and relationships if one does not have an interest that is vital and sufficiently impelling for so laborious a task?"[19]

But what about "facts"? Are they not undistorted and objective reflections of reality? In another book, *The Revolution of Hope,* Fromm deals with that issue and makes some interesting observations about so-called "facts." Not only can facts be meaningless, he says, but they can be untrue by their very selection, "taking attention away from what is relevant, or scattering and fragmenting one's thinking so much that one is less capable of making meaningful decisions the more 'information' one has received."[20] How can this be? It can happen, according to Fromm, because simply the selection of facts implies evaluation and choice. So even the *presentation* of facts (however *fact* is defined) is subjective.

Fromm makes a point not often heard in journalism schools: If a person, such as a journalist, is objectively reporting on the activities of a certain individual, the journalist must know that other person very well if those activities are to be evaluated properly. The journalist must know him "in his individuality and suchness, his character—including the elements he himself may not be aware of"—if the evaluation is to be meaningful.[21] But one might ask, why not just *present* the actions and not evaluate them? Because, Fromm would say, the evaluation of each act—its morality, the motive for doing it, etc.—is the important part of the story of the act and is necessary for meaningful objectivity.

18 Quoted in Robert Stein, *Media Power* (Boston, 1972), 207.
19 Erich Fromm, *Man for Himself: An Enquiry into the Psychology of Ethics* (New York, 1966), 111.
20 Erich Fromm, *The Revolution of Hope* (New York, 1971), 54–55.
21 *Ibid.,* 55.

Facts in themselves have little correspondence to objective reality. Often they distort and mislead. A fact, says Fromm, presented "merely descriptively" may make the audience member more or less informed, and "it is well known that there is no more effective way of distortion than to offer nothing but a series of 'facts.' " Pictures—which are in a sense "visual facts"—can also distort, whether they are still shots in the print media or filmed or live shots on television. Philip Wylie has expressed this point well, in spite of his cynical tone, in his book *The Magic Animal:* "It is claimed that TV has made a greater number of Americans better acquainted with more truth than they were in pre-TV days. Nothing could be less correct. More people doubtless have a slanted half-glimpse of more events, ideas, so-called scientific marvels, the faces and voices of prominent people and so on, than they had before. But fewer than ever have any background for appraising these unrelated, unevaluated, and random bits."[22]

Roger Poole, in his book *Towards Deep Subjectivity,* provides an excellent discussion of this subjective or Dionysian view of objectivity. In the chapter entitled "Objectivity" he offers many insights that can easily be adapted to journalism. Poole's view emphasizes process. Even if some story or set of facts could be objective at any one moment, he maintains, the facts behind the words would have changed greatly by the time the words were published or broadcast. So by then the story would have only a kind of "historical" objectivity, and for the purpose of real objectivity, journalists would be obligated to let their audience know the exact *date and time* at which their reports had been objective. This, of course, reporters never do. The unspoken, facile assumption is that, at the time the reader or viewer come to the story, it still exists as it was.

Why is Apollonian (or "real") objectivity impossible? Poole gives six reasons: 1) What one reporter takes to be true, evident, and obvious depends on the angle of vision, or perspective, of the reporter and the quantity of the phenomena (parts of reality) that are selected for the story. 2) There are also varying degrees of "subjective appropriation"—of how "open" or "closed" the reporter is to new perspectives. 3) Facts are "morally charged." Reporters and their audiences get interested in facts when they see the possibility of placing them in a congenial ideological context so as to add weight to an argument or position in which they are already

22 *Ibid.,* 56; Philip Wylie, *The Magic Animal* (New York, 1969), 205.

involved. 4) Reporters also select and arrange pieces of reality in accordance to their deepest fears and ambitions; often they are concerned not with finding what is true, but with finding what will best support existing positions. 5) Everything selected for a story is filtered through the affective constitution of the reporter. This affective constitution is already in existence, and by selection and exclusion of data, the journalist will construct a satisfying world view. The stories the journalist writes will fit this world view. 6) The journalist has a private "perspectival history" that determines the person he or she is, and when journalists frame a story, they manipulate the "facts" to fit this perspectival history.[23]

Facts are not facts, according to Poole. Or, said another way, there are different kinds of facts. Subjectivity impinges on facts, and it impinges on some facts more than on others. Poole, who has written much about subjectivity and morality, notes that a fact may be morally indifferent or morally charged. Too often journalists assume that morally charged facts are facts in the same unambiguous sense as morally indifferent ones. One can say, for example, that the Eiffel Tower is in Paris. That is a fact. One can also say that there is apartheid in South Africa. That is also a fact. But they are quite different kinds of facts. The first is morally indifferent, and the second, morally charged. Poole continues: "The modality of these two facts means that, while we shall all discuss the Eiffel Tower amicably enough, the second fact is going to involve the perspectival question. We are immediately plunged into the world of subjectivity, and it is a false or a cheap objectivity which claims that it is going to discuss the second proposition ('fact') with complete objective detachment. If the 'fact' is morally charged, it therefore follows that no one who feels it to be morally charged is going to be able to discuss it with full objectivity."[24]

The Apollonysian Synthesis

These two main perspectives on, or antinomies of, objectivity can be merged in the dialectic. Many of the comments I have quoted concerning the search for either Apollonian or Dionysian objectivity strongly suggest that their authors are proponents of some sort of merger or synthesis of the two. The scientific and artistic approaches are both important—if neither

23 Roger Poole, *Toward Deep Subjectivity* (New York, 1972), 120–21.
24 *Ibid.*, 118–19.

is taken too far and if the journalist does not get so wedged into a corner of one of these extremes that his or her journalism suffers from lack of intellectual oxygen. What is needed is a synthesis of the Apollonian and Dionysian orientations by the journalist: a stance that is Apollonysian. The Apollonysian journalist thinks *and* feels, is both rational *and* sensitive, is both concerned with facts *and* with interpretation, is dedicated to the world "out there" *and* to the subjective world "in here." Such a journalist is essentially a rational synthesizer—able to develop a journalistic philosophy that combines the epistemological stances of the realist and the idealist, of the Aristotelian and the Platonist, of the scientist and the poet.

As has been pointed out, institutionalized or "establishment" journalism in the United States is still tied rather closely to the more realistic, scientific, or Apollonian epistemology. Certainly journalism schools and departments give it significantly more emphasis than to the more subjective, artistic, or Dionysian journalism. The underground journalistic movement of the 1960s, coupled with the resurrection of subjective journalism (or "New Journalism") by such writers as Truman Capote, Tom Wolfe, Gay Talese, and Norman Mailer made a dent in the Apollonian orientation, but there is no doubt but that Apollo is still on the journalistic throne.

Those who are in favor of an "integrated" journalism, the dialectical synthesizers of Apollo and Dionysus, are still very much in the minority and are often felt to be the eccentrics of modern American journalism. But the Apollonian perspective is being challenged by an increasing array of voices, some of which have already been quoted in this chapter. Growing numbers of journalists and faculty members are beginning to recognize that there is no real demarcation between the stances of scientific objectivity and artistic objectivity. Apollo is merging with Dionysus, albeit slowly.

One such synthesizer has been William Stephenson, formerly a distinguished professor of journalism and psychology at the University of Missouri. He has insisted for years that the "separation of news and views" is unnatural and that what is needed is a synthesis that will make possible a fuller and deeper journalistic account. Fact, Stephenson says, is not enough; what is needed is what he calls "factuality"—something that goes beyond the surface and verifiable splinters of information and statements, something that brings the intelligence and insights and sensitivities of the reporter to bear on the story, something that fills in the gaps, something that puts flesh on the dry bones of fact and makes the story live in greater and more realistic dimensions. Facts are all right, but they need to be supplemented by interpretation and analysis, by background and by historical and psychological context. Then one gets close to the proper merger or synthesis—or "factuality."[25]

Stephenson, like C. P. Snow and Erich Fromm, believes that the scientist and the artist must not merely coexist; each should go further and develop characteristics and tendencies normally found in the other. Moreover, there is no valid reason why the scientifically oriented journalist cannot produce better journalism by injecting it with doses of subjective insight. The artistically oriented journalist, on the other hand, might do a much better job by employing the more systematic and dispassionate methods of the scientist. Such a synthesized orientation might well bring a new vigor to journalism; certainly it would bring more factuality. There would be a kind of artistic scientism. Journalism, like everything else, must change, and it is unrealistic to think that old ways of looking at it can prevail effectively in every age.

Apollonian objectivity is still the rule. A one-dimensional journalism dominates. Just give the plain facts in order of their importance, we are told. The journalist, at least in the United States, has been someone who, either because of an ability or desire to write or a penchant for prying open doors of secrecy, gravitated to a journalistic position. Or else the journalist has been a political agitator who landed in journalism instead of politics. Generally, the journalist has been an uninvolved, reportorial type who has been nurtured in an atmosphere of the Apollonian school of neutralism. When a journalist has been in the role of the opinionated and outspoken subjectivist, it was off in some segregated corner of journalism—in a syndicated column or in an editorial.

A journalist today must have deep respect for rational processes—the surface activities of institutions and persons—yet be sensitive to the psychological and poetic impulses that motivate these institutions and stir the depths of these persons. And these two aspects of journalism must be

25 Much of this chapter's final section is based on many conversations between the author and William Stephenson at the University of Missouri during the years 1964–1978.

93

integrated or synthesized, not segregated. The modern journalist must submit to a program of reading, conversing, thinking, and meditating to keep intellectually alive and emotionally atuned to the times, community, and nation. Apollo must join with Dionysus within each journalist, so that the person who emerges will manifest the transcending synthesis of the scientist's mind and the artist's soul.

Part II

FREEDOM AND ETHICS

Five

JOURNALISTIC FREEDOM

Press systems around the world have repeatedly been consigned to various pigeonholes based on the degree of freedom they possess. Then each nation is left either to luxuriate in complacent passivity or to fret and fume that the image of its press is being determined by some far-off theoretician or categorizer. Several scholars and press organizations (*e.g.*, the International Press Institute and the Inter American Press Association) have ranked national press systems according to some hierarchy of freedom, such as very free, free, moderately free, controlled, or very controlled. These classification schemes are of many kinds. Perhaps the simplest is my A-L Model, which divides press systems into authoritarian-leaning and freedom-leaning systems. There are also more complex and discriminatory models, such as the well-known "Four Theories" model of the early 1960s.[1]

In 1956 three professors of communication—Fred Siebert, Theodore Peterson, and Wilbur Schramm—brought out *Four Theories of the Press,* a book that went a long way toward establishing such a typology in the minds of journalism educators and students. In it the authors discuss press systems in the context of what they call the authoritarian theory, the libertarian theory, the communist theory, and the social responsibility theory. The little volume, in paperback since 1963, has become standard reading in journalism and communications departments and schools. Al-

---

1 Merrill, *The Imperative of Freedom,* 25–33; Siebert, Peterson, and Schramm, *Four Theories of the Press.*

most every article and book dealing with philosophical bases for journalism alludes to this book, comments on it, or quotes from it. Many have taken issue with it. It has had great impact internationally, in spite of its Western bias.

Since the 1960s there have been many other classification schemes that have attempted to label national press systems largely in respect to degrees of freedom and authority. One interesting model was provided by Ralph Lowenstein in 1971. He retains the authoritarian and libertarian theories of the "Four Theories" but abandons the communist theory, replacing it with what he calls the "social-centralist theory." This new theory admits a broad enough spectrum to include all the communist nations of Eastern Europe, yet removes the term *communist,* with its negative connotations, so that the new theory might also describe centrally guided systems in many developing nations. Lowenstein also discarded the social responsibility theory because the expression *social responsibility* is ambiguous. He substituted the term *social-libertarian* to indicate the new theory's close relationship to the libertarian theory. Under the social libertarian theory, self-regulation of the press is preferred, but some government regulation is unavoidable to keep factors such as monopoly and shrinkage of pluralism under control.[2]

More than ten years after Lowenstein revised the "Four Theories" model Robert Picard described his new model, which was an extension of my old A-L Model that classified systems as authoritarian-tending or libertarian-tending systems. Picard, however, added two intermediary classes between "authoritarian/communist at one end of his spectrum and "libertarian" at the other. These two types of systems he called "revolutionary" and "developmental." The first describes a press system that mainly concerns itself with overthrowing the existing political system, and the second describes a system seeking to promote national integration and socioeconomic development.

At the libertarian end of his model, he identified what he termed the "Western" type of media system, in which he placed the older libertarian and social responsibility models of the "Four Theories" typology plus a new one of his own creation—the "democratic socialist" press system, which he sees as the ideal. According to Picard, with the democratic

2 For a brief discussion of Lowenstein's model, see Merrill, *The Imperative of Freedom,* 37–40.

socialist approach, the press's purposes are "to provide an avenue for expression of the public's views and to fuel the political and social debates necessary for the continued development of democratic governance. Under such an approach, the state acts both to ensure the ability of citizens to use the press and to preserve and promote media plurality. Ultimately, ownership under such a system would be public and not-for-profit, through foundations, nonprofit corporations, journalist-operated cooperatives, and other collective organizations."[3]

Picard, interestingly, places his democratic socialist system to the left of the libertarian and social responsibility systems (toward authoritarianism), under the heading of "balanced or indeterminate tendencies." In other words, Picard sees his democratic socialist system as "balancing" some aspects of the libertarian press with some aspects of the collectivist or socialist press scheme identified with his "revolutionary" and "communist" systems. He mentions, for example, that the ownership of media in a democratic socialist system would be private—"at this time"—implying that such a system would evolve into a public or state-owned operation later on.[4]

The Media-Government Relationship

There is a natural symbiosis between the media and government. A media system reflects the political philosophy in which it functions. This is basic. The journalism of a nation cannot lag far behind the general development and values of the society, nor can it exceed the limits permitted by the society. Journalism is largely determined by its sociopolitical context, and when it functions essentially in accord with its society's natural ideology, it can be considered—perhaps should be considered—socially responsible in a political sense. Many persons, such as Siebert, Peterson and Schramm, would disagree, and they have postulated a separate theory of "social responsibility."

Certainly there are many ways to think about media or journalistic relationships to government. There are harmonic and disharmonic theories, functional and conflict theories, adversary and supportive theories, monistic and pluralistic theories, self-deterministic and governmental (or

---

3 Picard, *The Press and the Decline of Democracy*, 67.
4 *Ibid.*, 69.

"other-directed") theories, laissez-faire and control theories. When one begins to consider these, and there are many other ways to label them, it becomes obvious that they are really parts of broader or more inclusive theories.

Journalism's relationship to government can also be seen in another, rather simple way, as either 1) an equal contender, 2) a cooperating servant, or 3) a forced slave. In the first case, the press units are independent of government and of one another; there is competition among them; each is a self-developed and self-managed entity. In the second case the press units in a sense form a partnership with government, cooperating and aiding in overall objectives; government and "the social interest" would be considered synonymous and would motivate the press system into this partnership or cooperative relationship. In the third case, the press system would be wholly subservient to government, cooperating involuntarily with government as a result of coercion by the power elite.

Out of all the symbiotic relationships of government and media systems, a basic dichotomy always seems to emerge, and in spite of its dualistic oversimplifications and generalized structuring of reality, this dichotomy is probably still the best way to consider either press theories or political theories. This is the basic A-L (Authoritarian-Libertarian) Model, which really places the A-stance and the L-stance on a continuum instead of in two distinct categories. Media systems, like nations and people, tend to authoritarianism or to libertarianism—toward autonomy or toward social structure and control. Media or press systems in their relationship to the state are conveniently labeled authoritarian or libertarian, though of course they are all authoritarian to some degree and libertarian to some degree. Freedom always resides, in every system, with some person or social unit; the same can be said of authority. In this system the freedom is located in one of three places—with the state, with the press, or with the individual. The A-L Model actually loses its usefulness and validity when one considers these different modes of freedom. And it forces a crucial question: What *kind* of freedom are we talking about?

As for the first two modes, the freedom of the authority—the state—to protect and use the press as a social instrument, and the freedom of the press institution from state control, they illustrate two very different concepts of freedom. The first stresses positive freedom, and the second stresses negative freedom. These modes of freedom combine what Siebert, Peterson, and Schramm call the authoritarian and libertarian theories with various Marxist theories. I will call them the modes of state freedom and institutional freedom. Aside from these two government-related press theories or modes, there is also the more individualistic mode of journalistic freedom—the existentialist mode.

Analyses of press freedom normally deal with the cooperative or antagonistic relationship between the press system of a country and its government. This is one way to think about journalistic freedom, as Lowenstein did when he developed his PICA index to determine the press's independence (from government control) and its critical ability.[5] But freedom, as it concerns the press, has a wider context than just the government-press relationship, and I shall consider the two modes of freedom that concern this relationship in both so-called "open" and "closed" societies, and also the mode that relates to the individual journalist.

The Mode of State Freedom

Under the mode of state freedom, the state takes positive freedom (freedom to do, not freedom from) and projects it to the national context, provides it with a unified direction, and infuses it with a social consciousness that makes it a state-party instrumentality for national harmony, security, and progress. In this mode, the state has the positive freedom to harness journalism for the betterment of the total system. The press is simply seen as part of the government apparatus or the ruling party apparatus, and it is given the freedom by the state authorities *to do something helpful* for the country; in effect, the state utilizes the freedom through the press to bring about ends the state feels are necessary. This mode of freedom is a kind of monolithic—rather than pluralistic—freedom, and it is in the hands of the state rather than in the hands of the independent media managers and owners.

State freedom is what is called authoritarianism in *Four Theories of the Press;* it is also what is called "Marxism-communism" in the same book. The authority is centralized in either case, and it (the state or state-party) uses the freedom as it sees fit, uses it through the press. Usually, at least in

5 Ralph L. Lowenstein, *PICA: Measuring World Press Freedom,* University of Missouri Freedom of Information Center Publication 666 (Columbia, Mo., 1966). A more exhaustive explanation of PICA may be found in Lowenstein, "Measuring World Press Freedom as a Political Indicator" (Ph.D. dissertation, University of Missouri, 1967).

Western terms, this state freedom exists in what is called "closed societies"—authoritarian countries—whether they be fascist (on the capitalist right) or Marxist (on the socialist left). Such freedom is state dominated, and it is used in a systematic and determined manner for the benefit of "the people" rather than for the benefit of the independent media managers themselves.

Western scholars are likely to call such press systems "authoritarian," following Peterson, Siebert, and Schramm. Statist or collectivist scholars do not call them that. They see them as "people-oriented," democratic systems that attempt to provide a social service to the society rather than a profit for their owners. But it must be said that actually this state freedom mode is indeed authoritarian—in the sense that the state or state-party apparatus is the authority and, at the same time, the freedom user. However, calling the press system "authoritarian" is perhaps not very helpful, for the press system in the United States, for example, is also authoritarian—in the different sense of vesting the authority with the media owners and managers rather than with the state.

What one needs to recognize in considering these modes of journalistic freedom is that each is both an authoritarian mode *and* a freedom mode. The basic question is, Where are the authority and the freedom situated? In this first mode, the freedom is with the state, and, since the state is portrayed as a representative of "the people," the freedom of the press theoretically resides with the people.

Freedom of this type necessitates an authority to exercise the freedom, and the philosophical underpinnings of this symbiosis of freedom and authority are interesting. Authoritarianism—the mode of state freedom—has a beguiling quality, a neat and disciplined aura, a lure for orderly minds that desire structure, logical progression, and institutional harmony and stability. It is a giant invisible sociological magnet that pulls unceasingly at men and women and at nations themselves. It is extremely difficult and painful for the masses to be without an authority to direct and lead them. Even for journalists, to have autonomy is often an unpleasant, even traumatic option. It appears the more natural tendency is to embrace some person or group that offers guidance and protection. Commitment to personal freedom and willingness to accept responsibility for the consequences of exercising this freedom do not form a dominant philosophical stance today, even though existentialism has shown that there is a rather large group of devotees to personal autonomy. And in politics, libertarians and other anarchistically inclined persons are being heard from increasingly.

The philosophical base for what the West calls authoritarianism can be traced back to Plato, the first great proponent of "law and order" and of submission to an aristocracy of the best. According to Karl Popper, Plato recognized one ultimate standard—the interest of the state. Everything that furthers this interest, according to Plato, is "good and virtuous and just," and everything that threatens it is bad, wicked, and unjust. For Plato, actions that serve the state interest are moral, actions that endanger it are immoral. For Plato the moral code was strictly utilitarian—a kind of statist utilitarianism, under which the criterion of morality is the interest of the state.[6]

In recent times many national leaders have had this Platonic notion of morality stressing responsibility to the state, and they have applied it to journalistic ethics. In fact, Plato's statist utilitarianism may be the foundation of all political philosophy as it impinges on morality. In journalism, some manifestations of it can be seen in today's increased emphasis on press councils and other proscriptions and normative "help" given the press from outside the realms of the press itself. Increasingly, media autonomy is being made to appear irresponsible, and the old concepts espoused by Plato are returning to impress us with their elitist "wisdom"—concepts that do, admittedly, have a strong appeal to the multitudes who recognize the comfort of being "mass persons" and also to intellectuals who are titillated by the deterministic ideas of Freudians, Marxists, and Skinnerians.

Since Plato's day, many important thinkers have contributed to the development of this authoritarian or elitist political philosophy. A desire for strong government, a fear of the masses, a respect for power, a hatred for anarchy, a love for social stability and national objectives commonly sought—all of these are strong forces pulling men and women away from personal freedom.

Consistent with such a philosophy, the mass media are essential. Certain things, it is said, the citizens *must* know; other things—harmful things—they must *not* know. That is perfectly logical in a society that values social harmony and national progress. The goal is a political and social equilibrium brought about by a cooperative system, even if such

6 Popper, *The Open Society and Its Enemies*, I, Chapters 6–8.

cooperation results in some loss of personal liberty. This basic philosophy rings true, whether it is applied to an authoritarian country of the right or of the left.

Although there are some notable differences between a communist regime and a right-wing one in terms of organization and procedures, they are "basically alike," as Carl Friedrich and Zbigniew Brzezinski have contended in their superb book on totalitarian dictatorship.[7] Friedrich Hayek also demonstrates in *The Road to Serfdom* that there is no real difference in the basic philosophy of rightists and leftists. Both advocate statism and desire to direct the society in what is felt to be progressive directions. Both types of regimes constantly determine to use press freedom "correctly"—positively, helpfully, progressively, and "for the good of the people and the country"—in a sense.

Power, as Lord Acton stated, corrupts. Power is also active and insistent; it must intervene—it must direct, supervise, set standards, and define responsibility. This is true of both state power and the power of media owners. Solzhenitsyn, in his Nobel Prize lecture of 1972, was talking about literature, but he could just as well have been talking about journalism when he said: "Woe to that nation whose literature is disturbed by the intervention of power. Because that is not just a violation against 'freedom of print.' It is the closing down of the heart of the nation, a slashing to pieces of its memory."[8]

But this "freedom to print" that Solzhenitsyn said is at the "heart of the nation" is seen by many regimes as potentially harmful because it permits error to circulate in the society, damaging the social structure and impairing the achievement of social goals. Herbert Marcuse, one of the Marxist "gurus" of recent years and an example of the Platonic elitists who advocate the mode of state freedom, has been an influential guide for those who are escaping from personal freedom in the name of improving society. Alasdair MacIntyre has briefly described Marcuse's concept of free expression: "Freedom of speech is not an overriding good, for to allow freedom of speech in the present society is to assist in the propagation of error. . . . The truth is carried by the revolutionary minorities, such as

---

7 Carl J. Friedrich and Zbigniew K. Brzezinski, *Totalitarian Dictatorship and Autocracy* (New York, 1965), esp. Chapter 11.

8 Quoted in John Hohenberg, *Free Press, Free People: The Best Cause* (New York, 1973), 511.

Marcuse, and the majority have to be liberated by being reeducated into the truth by this minority, who are entitled to suppress rival and harmful opinions."[9]

The authoritarian maintains that people in general desire leadership; they like simple, straightforward, easy solutions and actions. They want decisions made for them. Eric Hoffer points out in many of his writings that authoritarianism tries to reduce greatly the variety of aims, motives, interests, human types, and, above all, "the categories and units of power." This being the case, Hoffer comments, the "defeated individual, no matter how outstanding, can find no redress."[10]

As the highest expression of institutionalized structure, the state supersedes the individual and makes it possible for the individual to acquire and develop a stable and harmonious life. This is the position of those who embrace the mode of state freedom. Mass communication supports the state and the government in power, so that the total society may advance and the state may be viable and attain its objectives. The state, or at least the elite that runs the state, directs the citizenry, which is not considered in a position to make critical decisions. One man or an elite group is placed in a leadership role; this person or group is the entity that exercises the freedom in the society—including through the press—in the name of progressive, enlightened, altruistic, and humanitarian ends. In journalism the mode of state freedom is thus a people-oriented pragmatism directed by a paternalistic state.

The individual citizens of the society submerge their own personal freedom in the collective will of the state. This is not considered a negative stance at all, goes the theory, for there exists in the human mind—as Herbert Read has said—"an itch for tidiness, for symmetry, and formality."[11] There does appear to be a desire on the part of millions to forsake a considerable amount of personal freedom for the "good" of the whole, for social harmony, for national security and progress, and for psychological hedonism. Read, however, does not think that life is really tidy and feels that it is rather "spontaneous in its manifestations, and

9 Alasdair MacIntyre, *Herbert Marcuse: An Exposition and a Polemic* (New York, 1970), 193.

10 Quoted in Nicholas Capaldi, *Clear and Present Danger* (New York, 1969), 269.

11 Herbert Read, *Anarchy and Order* (Boston, 1971), 21. For an excellent discussion of the tremendous attractions of a "closed" society see Jean-François Revel, *How Democracies Perish* (New York, 1984).

unpredictable in its blind drive to the light." He goes on: "Most Utopians forget or ignore this fact, and as a result their ideal commonwealth can never be, or ought never to become, real. I am convinced that Plato realized this—the Guardians upon whom the whole structure of his *Republic* rests are idealized super-human types, about as remote from realizable actuality as Nietzsche's supermen. The *Republic* is a fairy-tale full of beautiful fancies, and intended to teach a moral (that morality and beauty are identical)."[12]

One of the nineteenth century's leading opponents of this kind of statist freedom was P. J. Proudhon, a prominent anarchist. He provided a litany of characteristics of being governed by statist authorities—a summary of restrictive forces placed on individuals by government. Being governed, he said, is being spied upon, inspected, directed, numbered, regulated, indoctrinated, preached at, controlled, censured, censored, and commanded. And in Proudhon's opinion, this was all done by those who "have neither the right nor the wisdom nor the virtue to do so." He extended the list of verbs by taking into account the state's freedom to control. That meant being registered, taxed, counted, licensed, corrected, and punished. When there was resistance to all these actions, he said, that state would see to it that the governed were fined, repressed, abused, imprisoned, condemned, and shot. To "crown it all," he said, they were "mocked, ridiculed, derided, outraged, dishonored." Summing up, Proudhon pointed to his list of verbs and said of the state, "That is its justice; that is its morality."[13]

The advocate of the mode of state freedom, of course, would counter this anarchical barrage by maintaining that the individual needs to be restricted for the good of everyone. There must be social order, and persons must recognize that organization, discipline, respect for others, and correction of errors are all necessary in a just society. Freedom of a selfish media owner is in no way intrinsically good; in fact, undisciplined press (or personal) freedom is most likely to be bad—bad in the sense of restraining social progress, public morality, and manifestations of altruism and humanitarianism.

According to Karl Popper, there are really two types of society: one open, or libertarian, and the other closed, or authoritarian. He would call

12 Read, *Anarchy and Order*, 21–22.

13 P. J. Proudhon, *General Idea of the Revolution in the Nineteenth Century*, trans. J. B. Robinson (London, 1923), 293–94.

systems operating under the mode of state freedom closed systems. The classic analysis of this basic typology was made by Popper in *The Open Society and Its Enemies,* first published in two volumes in 1945 and revised in 1952. Popper traces the roots of the closed society back to Plato and even to Heraclitus, but he presents as its typical exponents Hegel and Marx. "If one believes, as these philosophers do," writes Herbert Read of Hegel and Marx, "that a law of history can be deduced from the incomplete records of past events, it is then merely 'logical' to wish to apply this law to the present and the future." But, believes Read, "a law must always be sanctioned by force, and so these prophets became authoritarians, ready to enforce their 'law' by the power of the State."[14]

What about Plato and laws? Plato believed that his "philosopher kings" would describe "good" laws—ideal laws, the best possible laws—for the governance of the state. Therefore, the citizens would automatically be led to do what is good. Not being philosophers, the ordinary citizens would be ignorant of the nature of virtue and why they should pursue it. But by simply abiding by the state's laws, they could attain to such virtue as lies within their capacity. So in a Platonic state the morality of the citizen would come, not from personal understanding of what is good, but simply from following public opinion and the laws—an obedience that, as a result of training and education, would become second nature.[15]

Plato in effect admitted that the ordinary citizen's morality is always conventional, and this admission formed his main argument against democracy. The ordinary citizen, according to Plato, is too busy—or too ignorant—to discover and solve moral problems. Yet it is necessary to believe something and have some code of conduct. So the person's sense of right and wrong is formed from without—by the social environment as it expresses itself in law or in public opinion. Plato is often seen as the father of the mode of state freedom, and Leonard Peikoff, like Popper, presents him in a negative light. He has said that for Plato the good life is "essentially one of renunciation and selflessness," with a person escaping this world's pleasures in the name of allegiance to the state, "just as he should negate his own individuality in the name of union with the collective."[16]

14 Read, *Anarchy and Order,* 18–19.
15 C. E. M. Joad, *Guide to Philosophy* (New York, 1957), 289.
16 *Ibid.;* Peikoff, *The Ominous Parallels,* 30.

Peikoff contrasts this view with that of Aristotle, a philosopher far more to his liking. The good life, according to Aristotle, is a life of self-fulfillment, and Peikoff sees Aristotelian man as one who enjoys life in this world, uses the mind to the fullest, and works hard to achieve personal happiness. Aristotle believed that pride—a rational and earned pride in oneself and in one's moral character—is "the crown of the virtues."[17]

Hegel followed in the philosophical footsteps of Plato and also reflected many of the ideas of Kant, who had great influence on him. Hegel saw the state as the creature of God and called for all citizens to obey and revere it. Hegel called the state "the Divine Idea as it exists on earth," and even went so far as to refer to the state as the individual's "true self." For Hegel, the state was not a means to some human end, but an absolute end in itself—an entity that had "supreme right against the individual." The person, to Hegel as to Plato, must be considered inferior to the society, the state, the collective. In ethics and political philosophy, Hegel's foundational ideas may be clearly seen in these two sentences from his *Philosophy of Right:* "A single person, I need hardly say, is something subordinate, and as such he must dedicate himself to the ethical whole. Hence if the state claims life, the individual must surrender it."[18]

The British philosopher Robert Tucker has called Hegel's political philosophy one that conceives the state as "the supreme form of human association" and the "highest form of objectification of *Geist.*" He goes on to inject Hegel's own dialectic into an explanation of the philosopher's political stance: "The state is the supreme social being, of which the family on the one hand and 'civil society' on the other are only incomplete expressions. In terms of the triadic formula, the family is the thesis, civil society is the antithesis, and the state is the higher synthesis in which both lower forms of association are transcended and perfected."[19]

Marx is said to have turned Hegel's political philosophy upside down. Hegel saw society as a manifestation of the state. Marx found this unsatisfactory and believed that the truth is exactly the opposite, that the state is an outgrowth or manifestation of civil society. Marx maintained: "Hegel proceeds from the state and turns man into a subjectified state. Democracy proceeds from man and turns the state into an objectified man.

17 Peikoff, *The Ominous Parallels*, 30.
18 G. W. F. Hegel, *Philosophy of Right*, trans. T. M. Knox (London, 1967), 156, 241.
19 Tucker, *Philosophy and Myth in Karl Marx*, 103.

Just as religion does not create man but man religion—so the political system does not create the people but rather the people create the political system."[20]

It is obvious that in any kind of society under the mode of state freedom, a press system would adhere to the basic theoretical underpinnings of the society, and this press system would see its duty as serving the common good and depreciating its own "selfish endeavors." The Germans have a slogan that well sums up the guiding principle of journalism in this mode: "Gemeinnutz geht vor Eigennutz" ("The common good comes before private good"). This principle would satisfy all advocates of the state freedom mode, a Hitler as well as a Stalin. Adolf Hitler, a firm believer in subjugating oneself to the state, was keen on reminding individual Germans: "Du bist nichts; dein Volk ist alle" ("You are nothing; your people is everything"). This saying would carry over nicely into the realm of journalism and would explain the particular locus of "freedom" in such a political system.

Mass Media and the Mode of State Freedom

In the mode of state freedom the mass media are seen as educators and propagandists through which the power elite exercises its proper positive freedom. Media may be privately owned (such as in Portugal or Paraguay) or publicly owned (such as in Cuba and the German Democratic Republic). But public or private, the leader or the elite group in power controls the exercise of press freedom. Mass communication supports the state for the good of the people. Mass media cooperate with the state— they are either part of the state or controlled by it—and are not seen as adversaries; rather they are considered as partners of the state or as cooperating instruments in the hands of the state, consistently working toward social harmony and national progress.

A basic assumption under this mode is that a person engaged in journalism is doing so as a special privilege granted by the state; therefore, the journalist owes an obligation to the leadership. This press concept has formed, and forms today, the basic rationale for journalistic work in many press systems of the world. Freedom is looked on as belonging to "the people," in the sense that it is an instrumental freedom, admittedly located

20 Quoted in *ibid.*, 104.

in the power of the state, to be used for the welfare of the collective citizenry rather than, as the theory goes, the selfish purposes of the journalists and media managers themselves.

The socialist type of the mode of state freedom is found in Marxist-Leninist countries. The communist theory was drawn from Marx and modified later by Lenin. The influence of Hegel was also important. The mass media in a communist society, said Marx, would function basically to perpetuate and expand the socialist system. Transmission of social policy would be the main rationale for its existence. Mass media, under this theory or in this mode of freedom, are owned and operated by the state and directed by the Communist party and its agencies. Some criticism, such as criticism for failure to achieve goals, is permitted in the media, but criticism of basic ideology is forbidden. The press is to be a "positive" force, not a destructive or negative force.

The mass media propagandize, agitate, and organize. In other words, they provide useful information, show how it is useful and meaningful to the people, and form public opinion and channel it in socially helpful ways. Mass media are to do what is best for the state and party, and what is best is determined by the party elite (the *Nomenklatura,* to use the Russian term) leadership of state and party. Whatever the media do to contribute to communism and the socialist state is moral; whatever is done to harm or hinder their growth is immoral. The influence of Plato is clear in this Marxist-communist press tenet, and stems from what William Shaw has called the "normative relativism" of Marx: "What is right is what the social formation in question deems right and, thus, that rightness frequently varies from place to place or time to time. The claim is not simply that what societies take to be right differs (since no one doubts this) nor that what is right in one circumstance may be wrong in another (since the same ethical principle may oblige different actions in different situations), but that what actually is right is solely a function of what the society in issue believes."[21]

The Marxist press system really began with the rise to power in 1917 of the Bolsheviks in Russia; to reach the scattered multitudes over vast distances, the Bolsheviks established a network of publications and radio

---

21 Quoted in William H. Shaw, "Marxism and Moral Objectivity," in Kai Nielsen and Steven C. Patten (eds.), *Marx and Morality* (Guelph, Ontario, 1981), 23. *Cf.* Eugene Kemenka, *Marxism and Ethics* (New York, 1969).

stations. The purpose was to educate the public about communism and to forge a unity of knowledge and purpose. Ever since, the Soviet media have been filled with "positive" news and views. Mass communication is up-beat, and the tone is optimistic, with Soviet society depicted as progressive and caring about "the people." The only negative notes found in the Soviet press are stories about the failure of capitalism and the weaknesses of other systems that exploit the workers and dehumanize the masses. The constitution grants its citizens press freedom; in theory it is a kind of class control of the press—in this case, control by the working class, which in fact means the Communist party and the state. The party leaders, the Nomenklatura, determine press policy, direct the media, and exercise press freedom in the name of the people.

Citizens in a communist country, especially in the Soviet Union, are serious readers of newspapers and, where possible, enthusiastic viewers of television. Part of the concept of press freedom in the Soviet Union is dialogue between the government or party and the audience; letters to the editors of newspapers, for example, are considered vital. They are an-swered by letters back to the writers or printed in the publication, or they are followed up by press representatives (and often by government offi-cials) in visits and conversations with the writers. Thus, the people partici-pate in the press—*their* press.[22]

There are capitalist press systems, as well as socialist ones, that are considered authoritarian under the "Four Theories" typology. They also belong under the mode of state freedom. They are usually called right-wing authoritarian regimes or fascist systems. The press in these countries is controlled by the authority, which may be a party, a military clique, a strong man, or a combination of these. The press is normally in private hands, but it is restricted and directed for the good of the country and for national progress and security. Freedom is being used, again, in the name of or for "the people." Many countries in Africa, South America, and Asia exemplify this type of press system. They are substantially capitalist coun-tries, but they have press systems that are directed by the leader or the elite in power at the time.

In contrast to the socialist systems under the mode of state freedom, in which journalists usually enthusiastically and voluntarily cooperate with the system and the party, the "closed" systems on the right often include

22 See Altschull, *Agents of Power,* esp. 85–109.

journalists who rebel against such direction and have to be coerced into cooperation. The national leader in such countries has the authority over the press, through police and military power as well as through a host of press laws. So this leader can use the press freedom at his disposal in whatever way is deemed necessary for the good of the country. The concepts of informational pluralism, ideological variety, and the press as a watchdog on government are not considered important in this kind of system; in fact, they are considered by the leader and the governing elite as counterproductive to the welfare of the nation.

The power elite in such "closed" capitalist countries see their audiences in basically three categories, and they might be defined as Hitler defined them. The first and largest group consists of the great masses who are "the simplest part" of the nation. These people are prone to believe everything that is put before them; they are the lazy segment of the population, and the most malleable. Therefore, the mass media can have enormous influence on them.

The second group in Hitler's typology of audiences is much smaller, composed of cynical dropouts from the first group. They no longer believe anything at all that comes to them in print. They hate newspapers and are annoyed by their contents, seeing their analyses and opinion pieces as only lies and half-truths. These people are very difficult to handle or influence through the media, since they will always face journalism—even if it is true—with great mistrust.

The third group is by far the smallest of the three. It is composed of the truly fine minds. These people, through natural gifts and good education, have the capacity to think independently. They try to form a judgment of their own about everything, and they submit everything they read to careful analysis. Journalists like such readers only with reserve, for such readers are prone to see every journalist as a scoundrel who plays fast and loose with the truth.[23]

Hitler and other proponents of state-directed societies have claimed that their exercise of authority and freedom is for the good and advancement of the people. They argue that such societies, in a very real way, give the people what the people want—a psychological security and sense of well-being. Carl Jung, speaking from a psychological perspective, tended to agree that people generally want direction and even paternalistic con-

23   Adolf Hitler, *Mein Kampf*, trans. Alvin Johnson (New York, 1941), 328–29.

trol. He pointed out that, contrary to popular Western notions, such directed societies do not result from the imposition of ideological and political pressure from the top, but are actually formed by social and psychological desires and expectations stemming from the masses.[24]

At any rate, regardless of the causes of statism, the world is filled with statist societies in which collectivism, cooperation, and the ideals of social progress are considered indispensable and in which freedom is centered— along with authority—in the state or its instrumentalities. When people voluntarily or under coercion give up their power to the state, they also give up their individual freedom—or much of it. In exchange they then get a kind of "collective freedom"—a freedom from interpersonal exploitation and a freedom to expand their talents and potential within a safe, harmonious society.

The Mode of Institutional Freedom

The mode of institutional freedom is the one most popular in the United States. When Americans talk of press freedom, they generally really mean freedom of the press (the institution) vis-à-vis the government. The mode of institutional freedom is what *Four Theories of the Press* called the "libertarian theory." And though I, too, have used this term *libertarian* as a kind of generic term for American-style press freedom, actually in political philosophy the term has a more individualistic, even anarchistic, meaning than it does in the "Four Theories" typology. Perhaps the term *liberal* —in the nineteenth-century sense—would be more precise, or perhaps *press libertarianism* would be better than just *libertarianism*.

At any rate, in this mode the press, as an institution, has the freedom. This translates into freedom of the press units vis-à-vis government— freedom from outside interference or control. Actually, however, it is the owners and media managers who have the freedom, with some (but not much) filtering down to the lower ranks of journalists. There appears to be little or no concern for the freedom of the individual journalist, for it is assumed, as part of the theory of capitalism, that the journalist is simply another employee and will conform to the corporate structure, taking orders and relinquishing his or her autonomy in journalistic matters to the institutional freedom of the press.

24 Odajnyk, *Jung and Politics*, 51.

Institutional freedom is the freedom enjoyed by the media of the press system—either individually or collectively—from outside interference, especially from the government. It is this press freedom that is protected by the First Amendment to the United States Constitution. This mode deals with the press's relationship to government, in particular with the limits in that relationship so far as governmental control mechanisms are concerned; in essence, institutional freedom concerns the degree of separation of press and state. The institution—the press—has the freedom in this mode. Or more accurately, the authorities—owners, editors, *et al.*—of the media have the freedom.

This philosophical or political stance, which Siebert, Peterson, and Schramm called "libertarian," developed in the seventeenth and eighteenth centuries and quickly had a significant impact on the press and public expression. John Milton, with his "self-righting process," and John Locke, with his concept of popular sovereignty, were pioneers in England, and they were followed by such spokesmen as Thomas Jefferson and his revolutionary colleagues in eighteenth-century America. It was Jefferson who clearly expressed the necessary relationship between a free (even if irresponsible) press and good, sound democratic government. And John Stuart Mill in nineteenth-century England further increased the philosophical status of press libertarianism.

These men and numerous others propounded a philosophy that was new. Unlike disciples of Plato and later Hegel, they basically trusted the common man and believed that all kinds of information and ideas should be made public. They despised secrecy; they rebelled against prior censorship and felt that open criticism is essential to personal, as well as national, happiness and growth. Of course, there are certain flaws in this generalization, for all of these men would draw the line on freedom at some point. But they were determined to keep expression of opinions in society tied to press autonomy just as tightly as possible. They saw press freedom as residing in the hands of the press owners, and they saw government's main role as keeping hands off.

In this stance there is a trust in the citizens, a belief that the majority—even if not always right—should be taken seriously and generally comes closest to the truth and makes sound decisions. This trust in the people is related to the mass media in that it is the media that can best inform the people in a way that the people know enough to intelligently govern themselves. But this stance also has a basic trust in the few people who own and control the mass media, which may seem rather strange for a democratic society. The assumption is that they will, in their diversity, do a good job of informing the citizens. In any event, these owners have the freedom to inform well or to inform poorly.

There is a theoretical assumption in libertarian press theory that a free and unhampered press will serve the idealistic function of adequately informing a democratic people. But there is no *obligation* that the press do so, for this would contradict the principle of press freedom. In a society under press libertarianism there is a basic emphasis on divorcing government from journalism, and so-called libertarian journalists have always shuddered at the thought of government meddling in the affairs of the press.

There is, however, in libertarian press theory a kind of built-in paradox, and it is this paradox that really is at the root of so much of the controversy going on today about press freedom and responsibility. The paradox arises from, first, the basic philosophical assumption that a democratic people need information upon which to base their decisions, and, second, the basic principle of a free press, which is protected by the First Amendment to the United States Constitution (and by the constitutions of many other nations). Quite naturally there are many citizens who look at the mass media, or certain of them, and see weaknesses in the way they are informing the public. So their natural inclination is to develop and affirm the principle that if the press, or any unit of the press, fails to provide the kind of service the citizenry is entitled to have in a democracy, it must forfeit its freedom. However worthy or unworthy such an argument is, it clearly points out the paradox. For quite simply, under the libertarian theory the press is free *not* to be responsible to the very principle undergirding its freedom—that of providing the citizenry with reliable information.

Often the paradox is expressed in other terms: for example, some press libertarians refer to two strains of freedom—positive and negative. Negative freedom implies the freedom to act autonomously—even if one does not really act. Proponents of positive freedom emphasize doing a good or at least doing something. Basically those supporting positive freedom are really utilitarians and have restricted their concept to freedom to doing something "good." This is a limited view of freedom held by the elitist descendants of Plato. The libertarian who favors negative freedom is the real supporter of the mode of institutional freedom, since the libertarian believes that the autonomous journalistic medium does not have to *do* anything to be free, that it is only necessary that it be unrestrained.

Defenders of this mode make this main argument: A free press functions to present the truth, however splintered it may be in a pluralism of voices. It is impossible to do that if it is controlled by an authority outside itself. Libertarian advocates have a strong faith that a free press, working in a laissez-faire, unfettered situation, will naturally result in the abundance of information and pluralism of viewpoints necessary in a democratic society.

From Thomas Hobbes in the seventeenth century, who has been called the father of modern democratic theory, to the contemporary philosopher Robert Nozick, who sees government's role as no more than a "night watchman," there have been many political philosophers who recognize the absolute need for government but would limit it greatly.[25] Although Hobbes manifests many signs of being an authoritarian, he champions a politics of choice, competition, and the market—what Karl Marx would surely see as the politics of bourgeois acquisitiveness. In many ways, Hobbes's thought was very close to the "possessive individualism" of John Locke.[26]

Hobbes said that natural man thinks first of himself and that in a state of nature everyone is primarily egoistic. He knew that the nature of man required government. That is why he called for a sovereign with absolute powers to use in case the citizens got completely out of hand. This sovereign was Leviathan, who would be dedicated to keeping the peace but would otherwise leave men alone. Personal autonomy must, according to Hobbes, give way to government. If individuals want peace, protection, and reasonable harmony, they must settle for government. So Hobbes came up with a plan for such a government, and according to Walter Berns, today the society envisioned by Hobbes is known as the "liberal state."[27]

Locke went somewhat further than Hobbes. He asserted that each

25 There is considerable debate over whether Hobbes was really libertarian and democratic or authoritarian. In spite of the fact that he would have the people voluntarily give up many rights to the sovereign, they would still have external control of their lives. Nonetheless it appears that Hobbes would definitely be an opponent of radical libertarians and of anarchism.

26 See Michael R. Dillon, "Defending Democratic Government: The Failure of Contemporary Theorists," *Intercollegiate Review*, XV (Fall, 1979), 36–38.

27 Walter Berns, "The Need for Public Authority," in George W. Carey (ed.), *Freedom and Virtue* (Lanham, Md., 1984), 29.

mature person should be regarded as free and independent of the authority of others and subject to legal authority only with his or her own consent. Government is needed only to protect all individual freedom that does not harm another person. Nozick also expresses the Lockean view that individual rights should be emphasized and that the state should serve only as a protector or "night watchman."[28]

Most of the writers who defend the mode of institutional freedom, or what might be called the nineteenth-century liberal position, do not, however, believe in *absolute* freedom. Some, like the contemporary anarchists or radical libertarians, sometimes come close to advocating absolute freedom, but there are always some limits. Robert Nisbet, a social critic and contemporary neoconservative, declares that though freedom is important, it is but one of several necessary values in the good or just society. In pointing out differences between libertarians and conservatives, Nisbet comments on their perspectives on freedom. He says that, for libertarians, individual freedom "is the highest of all social values." But for conservatives, freedom "is but one of several necessary values in the good and just society." Freedom not only may, but must, according to Nisbet, "be restricted when such freedom shows signs of weakening or endangering national security, of doing violence to the moral order and the social fabric."[29]

Just what is the basic position of libertarians? Philosopher John Hospers says that their motto is: "Leave the individual alone." (The press libertarian's motto, therefore, would be "Leave the press alone.") The libertarians, according to Hospers, favor "laissez faire in economy, laissez faire in religious belief, laissez faire in achieving one's individual goals as long as these do not interfere with the freedom of others to achieve theirs." He adds, "Libertarians believe in the minimal (night-watchman) state, so under limited government, most of their decisions, unless they violate the rights of others, can be exactly what they would have been without government."[30]

Most lovers of institutional (and personal) freedom are not opposed to

28 Nozick, *Anarchy, State, and Utopia.*
29 Quoted in Berns, "The Need for Public Authority," in Carey (ed.), *Freedom and Virtue,* 4; *Ibid.,* 35. Cf. David L. Norton, *Personal Destinies: A Philosophy of Ethical Individualism* (Princeton, 1976), for another good discussion of what I call the mode of personal freedom.
30 John Hospers, "Differences of Theory and Strategy," in Carey (ed.), *Freedom and Virtue,* 65.

voluntary associations; they are simply against having associations forced upon people. Frank Meyer, in his influential book *In Defense of Freedom*, expresses it in these words: "To assert the freedom and independence of the individual person implies no denial of the value of mutuality, of association and common action between persons. It only denies the value of coerced association. When men are free, they will of course form among themselves a multitude of associations to fulfill common purposes when common purposes exist."[31]

Some libertarians—those of the radical or anarchistic type—would, perhaps, be suspicious even of voluntary organizations and associations, feeling them a danger to personal liberty. For example, many contemporary journalists of a libertarian persuasion are opposed to journalistic professionalization for this very reason. Hierarchical and powerful organizations certainly do have the potential to strip the individual of much freedom.

Philosophers have long warned of such a danger, and modern-day libertarians, such as Murray Rothbard, Friedrich A. Hayek, Ayn Rand, Albert Nock, John Hospers, Jerome Tuccille, Tibor Machan, and Robert Nozick—would caution the individual to approach institutionalization and any kind of "groupism" very cautiously and to be ready to fight constantly against the invidious extensions of institutional power into the lives of individual members of the organization. This suspicion of, and warning against, institutions and their power to depersonalize leads naturally to a consideration of freedom on the individual or personal—the existentialist—level.

The Mode of Personal Freedom

The third level of journalistic freedom is the one at which the individual journalist works. He or she always has *some* control. It is at this level, or in this mode, that the journalist confronts freedom directly. It is true that the state's freedom, as well as the press institution's freedom, constrains or regulates the personal freedom of the journalist, but the fact remains that a considerable degree of freedom can be used by journalists who want to use it.

Notwithstanding political and institutional control and pressures, the

31   Frank S. Meyer, *In Defense of Freedom* (Chicago, 1962), 146–47.

journalist who is existentially oriented can, and will, find ways to give vent to personal desires and to push back the confining limits of social control. The existential or personal mode of freedom pits the individual journalist against the system; at least it calls on the journalist to maximize personal decision making and to expand the dimensions of self-determination in the institutional situation.[32] Existentialism is basically a philosophy of personal pride in independent thought and action; it is a stance against the massification process, against the forces that cause one to lose authentic selfhood in modern group-oriented society.

For the existentialist in journalism, the self and its enhancement rank very high on the list of priorities. Existentialists such as Kierkegaard, Nietzsche, Jaspers, Marcel, Buber, Camus, Sartre, Heidegger, Nikolai Berdyaev, and José Ortega y Gasset have all expressed their deep concern about the disappearance of the authentic self, about the tendency of mass society to swallow up the person in a kind of dehumanizing spirit of collectivism. By this process of sacrificing self to a collective, one enters an inauthentic mode of existence. To escape this inauthentic existence, a person must fight constantly for authenticity, for a person, says Ortega in his *Historia como sistema,* is "not like a stone which is given its existence." The Spanish philosopher continues: "Man . . . has to make his own existence at every single moment. He is given the abstract possibility of existing, but not the reality. . . . Man must earn his life, not only economically but metaphysically."[33]

How does an existentialist journalist make or create self and maximize personal freedom? By "engaging himself," as Kierkegaard explains in *Either/Or*—by making a "leap" beyond the immediate situation. Routine ways of doing things, to the existentialist journalist, are anathema, since they are not on a truly human level; there is no engagement, no commitment, and no real choosing. On such an inauthentic or subhuman level, a journalist would be acting merely as an automaton and not as a real, existing person. It is through choosing, pushing back the limits of group pressure, and making a commitment to self-enhancement that a person retains personal freedom and individuality.

In any society, the journalist who wants to live in the mode of existen-

---

32 See Merrill, *Existential Journalism.*
33 Quoted in José Ortega y Gasset, "Man Has No Nature," in Walter Kaufmann (ed.), *Existentialism from Dostoevsky to Sartre* (New York, 1975), 153–54.

tialist freedom, and who determines to affect the journalistic situation, will take one of two paths: 1) an external rebellion concerned with directly changing the outer conditions of existence (this was Sartre's approach); or 2) an effort to alter society indirectly through changing one's own values and outlook (this approach was exemplified by Camus). Germaine Brée has called the first of these two paths the "Promethean," and the second "Orphic."[34]

The Promethean journalist defies the established order frontally, directly; the Orphic journalist, on the other hand, stresses a transformation from within—an internal development concerned with the self more than with direct social reform. Prometheanism, in effect, seeks to change the outer conditions of people's lives; Orphism seeks to alter society indirectly through changing the person first, which then leads to a change in society. Journalists in all kinds of societies and press systems can be Orphic existentialists; Promethean journalists would have to be very courageous—or foolhardy—to operate with vigor in societies in which the system permits little or no independent overt activity or rebellion.

What is most important about both Sartre and Camus, in spite of their tactical differences, is that both thinkers stressed the importance of the individual, or, more precisely, "the priority" of the individual. Sartre, the atheistic rationalist, succumbed to the pull of the logic of Marxist communism and, at least for a while and to some extent, abandoned the individual. On the other hand, the more mystical and moralistic Camus withstood the temptation of communism and insisted on an unconditional separation between the individual and the state.[35]

The journalist who is concerned with freedom in the personal mode must, to some degree at least, have a sense of rebellion against the organization. Collectivities lead to uniformity, and, as Herbert Read said, "Uniformity is an unintelligent nightmare . . . that can only be created by the tyranny of a totalitarian regime."[36] But journalists should realize that uniformity can be created in *any* regime; conformity is not the result of the system of politics, but of the inclination of people to join groups and

34 Germaine Brée, *Camus and Sartre* (New York, 1972), 240–45.

35 For a more detailed discussion of the similarities and contrasts between Sartre and Camus as well as their relationship to Marxism, see V. W. Odajnyk, *Marxism and Existentialism* (New York, 1965).

36 Read, *Anarchy and Order* (Boston, 1971), 88.

submit to the dictates of the leadership of those groups. A journalist in the United States can be a conformist just as easily as one in the Soviet Union.

One of the main problems of modern American journalism is the journalist's temptation to lose all individuality in a highly centralized, all-powerful journalistic enterprise. According to Carl Jung, this can be partially avoided through a conscious development of individual awareness, moral self-reliance, and psychological self-knowledge.[37] The individual alone (and this is a basic existentialist tenet) is capable of recognizing the problem and altering the situation.

There is no doubt that the centralization and growth of bureaucracy makes it almost impossible, even for journalists who desire to do so, to be aware of, and feel responsible for, the developments and policies of the news medium for which they work. A sense of helplessness often leads to a compensatory identification with the power of the medium itself or with a power group in the so-called "profession" of journalism. "If you can't beat 'em, join 'em!" This saying represents a powerful urge in all journalists. To fight it, the journalist must first achieve an "inner autonomy," as Jung calls it; then there can often emerge a will to extend this inner freedom to the surrounding structures of society. This was also the view of Camus. But this sense of freedom and self-determination is primary, according to Jung; it is essential to the action of a person who is separate from "an anonymous mass."[38]

The personal, or existentialist, mode of freedom—in its emphasis on choosing and the development of the self—has often been viewed suspiciously by journalists who see in it a lack of concern with ethics. Many feel that this philosophy of self-enhancement naturally results in the ignoring of moral considerations. Such an attitude, of course, reinforces my fundamental contention that most journalists have an "either-or" mentality and shy away from the mutualistic thinking of the dialectic. At any rate, it must be said that an extreme version of existentialism might, as Burton F. Porter has pointed out, have little or no concern for morality. But as he goes on to say, most existentialist thought is not that extreme or anti-intellectual. He elaborates: "Camus' existentialism has a strong humanistic component. Rilke has been compared to St. Francis, and Sartre

37 Odajnyk, *Jung and Politics,* 67.
38 *Ibid.,* 186.

maintained that we should share our freedom with other people. The existentialists do assert the primacy of emotion over reason but relatively few would be in favor of total spontaneity, particularly in situations where destructiveness would result."[39]

Paul Johnson, in his influential book *Modern Times* (1983), states that the moral foundation of existentialism is largely derived from Kant's "categorical imperative." In essence, the existentialist would want to universalize—or to project onto everyone—the values that he or she has developed.[40] So the existentialist journalist is no more amoral or immoral than anyone else; the existentialist can choose good acts or bad acts, can have helpful motivations or harmful motivations, just as anyone else can. But to assume that a journalist who respects the self will be immoral, or will not be concerned with ethics, is to say egoism excludes choosing virtuous or moral actions, which is clearly not true.

The existentialist orientation defines the mode of personal freedom in journalism. Much of this mode concerns enhancing the self, choosing and acting in ways to retain maximum individualism. It is through these personal inclinations that other existentialist characteristics—such as integrity, authenticity, forthrightness, and honesty—develop.

The Journalist and the Mode of Personal Freedom

The great majority of journalists are devoid of a sense of self—a sense of personal worth and unique potency. They generally go through their days content without rocking the boat, without saying the "wrong things," without antagonizing those who might cause them harm or anxiety. In short, most journalists are timid souls. They have rationalized their inauthentic existence by flying the insipid banners of group loyalty and institutional cooperation. "Harmony" is their theme song, "cooperation" their life's strategy. A fear of putting themselves in personal danger has led them down the road to stagnation of the self. Journalism today has, by and large, become a world of purring machines, operated by machinelike functionaries passively packaging standardized news and mass-approved opinion.

---

39 Burton F. Porter, *The Good Life: Alternatives in Ethics* (New York, 1980), 219.
40 Paul Johnson, *Modern Times: The World from the Twenties to the Eighties* (New York, 1983), 576–77.

The average news operation disdains individualism. The person with integrity, a sense of self-respect, and a love for individuality is seen as a threat to the organization. This type of journalist is looked upon increasingly as a "poor team player," one who does not fit nicely into the system of corporate journalism. In short, the mode of personal freedom is not a very popular or profitable one.

This state of affairs has several causes. One, of course, is the natural inclination of human beings to "escape from freedom" and from the traumatic experiences that often come from exercising one's own choices and accepting responsibility for them.[41] Another cause is today's system of education, which tends to package journalists in conventional ways, so that they will be more marketable in the conservative world of American journalism.

Finally and perhaps most important are the great rewards for "creative conformity." The person who functions well at any assigned task is looked upon as efficient and productive even if the person's actions are not conducive to self-enhancement. The temptation is great for the journalist to "conform creatively" in this sense, working away passively in a little corner and never breaking out into the sunlight of personal (as opposed to institutional) creativity.

The existentialist journalist who values personal freedom rebels against this dismal spectacle and is determined that, in the midst of this depersonalizing situation, he or she will retain a substantial degree of individualism. Kierkegaard, in *The Present Age,* criticized his society and proved to be quite prophetic. This work has been a source for much existentialist criticism of modern society. For example, David Riesman, in *The Lonely Crowd,* and William Whyte, in *The Organization Man,* popularized some of Kierkegaard's insights. The individual is dying and the self is being dethroned, Kierkegaard pointed out. There is a drift toward mass society. Increasingly the social thinking is being determined by what William Barrett has called the Law of Large Numbers. Karl Jaspers related this idea to journalism, noting that when journalists perform their work day after day in a routine way, they sink "into the fathomless abysses of oblivion." And, of course, it is easy to sink into such

---

41 Erich Fromm, *Escape from Freedom* (New York, 1965), provides a strong rationale for a person's reluctance to remain in the "captivity" of freedom and discusses a range of enticements for escaping.

oblivion in the typical corporate journalistic medium, which, John W. Gardner has noted, loves and promotes stability, not efficiency or experimentation. With the media's natural tendency toward stability, a kind of mediocrity develops, and functionaries become ever more alike or equal. Mediocrity breeds mediocrity; Gardner has pointed out that organizations protect their "least able members." In fact, oftentimes it is quite obvious that organizations take a kind of pride in, and give various kinds of rewards to, their mediocre members rather than their superior ones, who pose some kind of threat (at least a psychological one) to all others concerned.[42]

An observant person, looking at the world of journalism, must be struck by the increasing conformity, the growing mechanization and regimentation, the submission of the individual to an ever-growing number of authorities. Journalism is, in short, increasingly subsuming the individual, depreciating the self. "He is drowned in the mass," says Jacques Ellul, "and becomes convinced that he is only a cipher and that he really cannot be considered otherwise in such a large number of individuals."[43] Looking into the average newsroom, one sees unsmiling faces and the overly serious demeanor of men and women unenthusiastically going through activities devoid of a spirit of vitality and creativity. The scene is dominated by piped-in music, wall-to-wall carpets, and robotized functionaries staring with glazed eyes into the hollow reaches of video display terminals.

"The individual feels himself diminished," says Ellul. "For one thing, he gets the feeling that he is under constant supervision and can never exercise his independent initiative; for another, he thinks he is always being pushed down to a lower level." There is a way out, of course. The temptation is strong for the journalist to follow a "spirit of consensus," to give in to numbers. But the existentialist journalist strives constantly to follow Gabriel Marcel's admonition to reject "the fascination of numbers" and "remain at the spiritual level, that is, at the level of truth."[44]

Nietzsche certainly recognized the accelerating trend toward the loss of the individual's importance. Individualism was dying, he believed, and he felt that he should present the world with the heroic figure of his *Übermensch*, his spiritual Superman. Like Nietzsche, Kierkegaard was

42 Barrett, *Irrational Man*, 173; Jaspers, *Man in the Modern Age*, 204; John W. Gardner, *Excellence* (New York, 1971), 17–33 *passim*.
43 Jacques Ellul, *Propaganda* (New York, 1969), 221.
44 *Ibid.*; Gabriel Marcel, *Man Against Mass Society* (Chicago, 1969), 221.

troubled by the spread of the "herd mentality." The two philosophers agreed that the individual is being emptied of all value and engulfed in some organization. Kierkegaard called the typical person a "cipher-man" or "fractional man," having purpose and importance not in self but only in the social whole.[45] Kierkegaard would see myriads of "cipher persons" filling our mass media today.

A journalist, operating in the mode of personal freedom, unlike these cipher or fractional persons, will daily seek to enhance the self, striving for individual fulfillment in the face of organizational pressures. However, self-enhancement or large-scale individual fulfillment is extremely difficult in a social system such as is known at present. As Gardner has said, "Individual fulfillment on a wide scale can occur only in a society which is designed to cherish the individual, which has the strength to protect him, and richness and diversity to stimulate and develop him, and the system of values within which he can find himself—and lose himself!—as a person."[46]

The journalist may never find such a society in pristine form. But it is up to the journalist to help make an effort to create such a society by personal pushing, striving, and choosing. The journalist must venture beyond the safe confines of expectations and determine to retain—and expand—the self. When journalists stop making this effort of willing and acting (or never start), their individuality slips away, and they become inauthentic. The mode of personal freedom has ceased to exist for them.

Press Freedom in the United States

The American concept of press freedom, as noted, stems from Enlightenment ideas in Britain and France. Milton, Locke, Mill, and others articulated the rationale for what has been called a libertarian press. At the core of this concept are these four tenets: 1) that the press is free from government control, 2) that the press operates in a laissez-faire system, 3) that the press is in private hands, and 4) that the press is at least a quasi-public service. Onto this basic core of beliefs about press freedom in America have been grafted some additional characteristics, though unlike the first four, they are all still subject to debate: 5) that the press is a check on

45 James Collins, *The Mind of Kierkegaard* (Chicago, 1967), 184.
46 Gardner, *Excellence*, 173.

government excesses and corruption, 6) that the press is diversified and presents a wide range of information and pluralism of viewpoints, 7) that the press is accessible to the public, and 8) that the press has a responsibility to use its freedom for the good of society. This last one is still in its developmental stage, for there are many journalists who refuse to accept it, because of its incipient danger to media freedom and pure journalistic autonomy.[47]

One of the problems with press freedom is that, though it is "protected" (from legal restrictions) by the First Amendment, the precise definition of freedom of the press is nowhere given. In addition, there is no consensus about other governmental restrictions that might be placed on press freedom. So the formulation and extent of press freedom is highly debatable. Immediately there arises the question of what limitations exist, if any, on such a freedom. Such a question presumes that what press freedom means is pretty well known, and, of course, it is not. When ethics rears its head, one thinks of limits to freedom immediately or, perhaps more precisely, of *how* the freedom will be used. Individual sensitivities and social consequences must be considered. National security and progress must be considered. So-called professional objectives must be considered, and also the problem of keeping the journalistic medium economically viable. A list of considerations related to press freedom and its use could go on for several pages. Most thinkers concerned with the issue of freedom have recognized that, to be worthy of its name, freedom must be limited. But how, to what extent, when, and by whom? These are questions, of course, that have persistently troubled those who are seriously concerned about freedom and related issues.

There have been and will be continuing controversies and endless discussions among journalists and others who ramble around in the thorny thickets of this question of press freedom. There are those who say that the United States does not have a free press, and such voices are heard not only from socialist and Marxist critics of capitalism. They are often heard from mainstream journalists and journalism educators. Perhaps the main reason for such arguments is that we are simply confused about what press freedom is; semantic "noise" tends to drown out rational discourse. Ideological biases, politics, and other factors play their role in determining how one conceives of press freedom.

---

47 For a good recent discussion of the development of the American concept of the free press, see Leonard W. Levy, *Emergence of a Free Press* (New York, 1985).

Everette Dennis, director of the Gannett Center for Media Studies at Columbia University, has summed up well the basic conundrum in discussions of press freedom:

Freedom of the press is usually defined as the right to communicate ideas, opinions, and information through the printed word without governmental restraint. A deeply held value in America, press freedom is also legally guaranteed in the free press clause of the First Amendment to the Constitution of the United States. A central purpose of freedom of the press is to encourage the existence of an educated and informed electorate that can make decisions about public affairs. To some early commentators, freedom of the press simply meant the absence of government licensing of printing and publishing. Later it came to mean "no prior restraint" of publication. This is the idea that pre-publication censorship is out of bounds. Freedom of the press is said to assure satisfaction of society's need for a maximum flow of information and opinion and the individual's right for self-fulfillment. Freedom of the press is also a promoter and protector of other rights. In America, a free press is regarded as central to the functioning of democratic government and a free citizenry. There is much continuing debate about the essential nature of this concept of freedom, what it actually means, to whom it extends, whether it is an individual or institutional right.[48]

Dennis' one-paragraph exposition throws considerable light on the complexity of the problem of press freedom in the United States. One thing is certain. Nobody is really sure just what press freedom is, but whatever it is, there is rather general opinion that at least the *idea* of such freedom is a good thing and should be valued and protected. In addition to the general lack of agreement about the concept's meaning, there is the recognition—at least among most people—that press freedom must coexist with other rights found in the Constitution. Throughout the years of debate and discussion of press freedom, two main views have emerged. The first is the narrow or "strict constructionist" view, and the second is the broad or

48 Everette Dennis and John C. Merrill, *Basic Issues in Mass Communication: A Debate* (New York, 1984), 1. This book also presents pro-and-con analyses of such related issues as the media-government relationship, the people's right to know, public access to the media, media pluralism, journalism as a profession, and press councils and ethical codes.

"populist" view. It is out of the clash of these two views of press freedom that most of the controversy has arisen.

The strict constructionist might also be called the press-centered view. According to its proponents, the First Amendment gives freedom (both negative and positive) *to* the press. The press alone has press freedom, and the possessive nature of such freedom is emphasized. The press, in this view, is free from government interference and, at the same time, free to do what it wishes to do editorially. It is free even to do nothing; it is free to publish or not publish. This is the view of those who advocate journalistic autonomy or what is more frequently called "editorial self-determination."

This press-centered view is the one held by most journalists, and it is probably the commonly accepted belief about press freedom in the country at large. The concept of the press being free means just that: the press is free. Naturally, there are problems with such a view, especially when ethics comes into the picture and the issue of responsibility is raised. The press is free, but always with some restrictions. There are in fact innumerable restrictions and countless moral imperatives that various citizens would place on press performance.

And as responsibilities are prescribed for the press, the strict constructionist or press-centered view recedes ever further into the shadows of institutionalism or into the light of populism. Responsibility implies obligation, and obligation implies accountability. Accountability implies some kind of agent to police this accountability, and such an agent implies an authority from outside the press. And such an authority implies "authoritarianism," anathema to the press-centered or libertarian freedom fighter.

The second view is the broad or populist view. Its supporters consider freedom of the press to be the people's freedom. Responsibilities of the press in a humane society require that the people have the freedom that is usually assigned to the press. It is quite common to hear press freedom referred to as really "belonging to the people, not to the press." Journalists themselves often say such things. They are expressing the spirit of the second view—the populist conception of press freedom.

The populist view leads to a consideration of the people's rights in the area of the press. The people are said to have rights "to know," to access to the press, to a pluralism of information treatment. This is a people-centered view of press freedom in contrast to a press-centered view. Its theoretical underpinnings seem similar to those of popular sovereignty in the political sphere. The government belongs to the people, and, it is argued, so does the press.

Although the people are enthroned in the broad or populist view of press freedom, the press is cautioned in many overt and subtle ways to be responsible—to use its freedom positively, for example, in order to educate the people, uplift them, better their social institutions and private lives, and generally help them to progress. The press also is admonished to refrain from causing harm to the body politic. Thus, under the populist view, if the press has any freedom at all, it is the positive freedom to serve the public interest. In a sense, then, the public interest becomes the total justification for press freedom, and the line of demarcation between the press and the public becomes blurred.

The Hutchins Commission, in its report of 1947, gave great attention to such responsibilities and thereby did much to shift thinking from press-centered to people-centered freedom. Since that time, a proliferation of advocates of people-centered freedom have continued to urge, almost to the point of insistence, that the press be responsible, ethical, positive, and utilitarian. In spite of the incipient governmental authoritarianism lurking in such a view, its proponents (from the Marxist Herbert Marcuse to the liberal Walter Lippmann to the conservative Walter Berns) insist that, in the long run, virtue is preferable to freedom for the press. And the debate goes on.

The old dialectical problem again presents itself, in the antinomies of press-oriented freedom and people-oriented freedom. The clash occurs, and there emerges a synthesis or middle way superior to either the thesis or antithesis. Such a clash is taking place today in American journalism. The dialectic is at work, and the reasonable journalist is one who recognizes this dialectical movement and merges into it with a consciousness that evidences aspects of *both* views of press freedom. Such a journalist will recognize the importance of institutional freedom vis-à-vis a powerful government but at the same time will acknowledge his or her responsibility as part of the press to serve the public good and use freedom ethically in the service of society.

Such a "middle way" of freedom implies respect on the part of the journalist for self and others, commitment to self and others, authenticity and honesty, involvement and choosing, and a firm dedication to both personal and social progress. These are largely existentialist traits, and such a middle way will be largely existentialist, though it will reflect a moderate and socially concerned type of existentialism that creates self as it creates a better society. The authentic journalist, ultimately, must give precedence to the self as an essential "cell" of society.

This middle way of freedom might be called responsible freedom, virtuous freedom, positive freedom, or enlightened freedom. At any rate, it is an ethically based freedom that also respects authenticity, self-enhancement, and truth. It insists that the freedom user seek not only self-esteem and self-fulfillment but also social concern and social enrichment.

Six

FREEDOM'S MIDDLE WAY

The dialectic works within the context of freedom, as well as in the broader area of freedom and ethics. It leads to a rational and socially relevant middle way of freedom that connects with an emphasis on ethics. At one end of the spectrum of freedom is self-indulgent or nihilistic freedom, often called license, and at the other end is ultracautious or self-sacrificial freedom. What is needed in journalism is a synthesis of these antinomies, a synthesis that might be called "social existentialism," since it balances the personal *and* the social aspects of freedom. Social existentialism is freedom's "middle way."

This middle way of freedom is really a bridge from freedom to ethics, from a concern solely for autonomy to a synthesis of both freedom and ethics, both the individual and society. In short, the middle way of freedom is ethically based freedom. It is personal, and it is also social. In terms of the dialectic, it is a merger of egocentric existentialism and collectivistic altruism. It is also a kind of freedom that is found between passive (negative) freedom and active (positive) freedom—a synthesis, an ethical freedom. Also, this middle way of freedom is a synthesis of irrational freedom, which is thoughtless and self-contained, and rational freedom, which is thoughtful and projective.

If this seems somewhat fuzzy, it is not surprising. We are so accustomed to antinomic thinking (thinking in opposites and in discrete terms) that when we try to think dialectically, we find it somewhat imprecise and feel uncomfortable. But freedom's middle way is a construct of interconnections composed of autonomy, social concern, self-respect, and cooperation. When these four ingredients are mixed or synthesized, there emerges a fusionist concept that is really a moderate kind of existentialism, a rational and ethically based existentialism that can be the foundation of a free and responsible journalism.

In order to describe this middle way of freedom, it is necessary to consider existentialism as it relates to journalism. Existentialism stresses personal freedom, of course, but the middle way emphasizes that this personal freedom is to be used rationally and ethically. In short, the individual must think of society as well as the self. The stereotypical view of existentialism almost obliterates concern for others, stressing self-development and personal decision making; this is unfortunate, for existentialism is really a synthesis of private and public use of freedom and personal and social sensitivity. The existentialist is no island. Choosing for self is choosing for others, and valuing freedom for self is valuing it for others. Thus, freedom and self are fused with ethics and others; Nietzsche is fused with Locke, Sartre with Kant, and Jaspers with Mill.

Existential Dimensions

Existentialism has many dimensions. In fact, it is a very eclectic philosophy that embraces ideas from many schools of thought. It is a philosophy of both egoism and altruism, espousing personal development along with the development of society. It is a philosophy of subjectivism, but with overtones of searching for essences of people and things. It is a quest for authentic existence and is concerned with freedom and its responsible use. It is undergirded by a search for self-reliance and at the same time for interpersonal relations. It is dedicated to a sense of commitment and personal integrity. It extols taking chances, living dangerously, experimenting, and making choices.

Themes such as freedom, choice, and responsibility are found in the thought of all existentialist philosophers. Another group of themes includes alienation, despair, death, and finitude—the negative themes that need to be overcome. In some existentialists' writings the tone of pessimism is strong; in others there is optimism or at least hope. All seem to be conscious of a tragic cloud hovering over human existence. For the existentialist, the cards are stacked against freedom and the development of authentic being. But even so, a person must combat the odds and try to shed traits that tend to diminish or eliminate his or her true being.

Because of their basic love of freedom and their spirit of rebellion against being pigeonholed or subsumed by a group, most existentialists are reluctant even to be called existentialists. In addition, they are a diverse lot. There are Christian existentialists (such as Kierkegaard, Heidegger, Jaspers, and Marcel), Jewish existentialists (such as Martin Buber), and mystical and aesthetic existentialists (such as Jaspers and Heidegger). There are other existentialists such as the great Russian novelist Dostoevsky, the Russian Orthodox thinker Berdyaev, and the quixotic Spaniard Unamuno. Finally, there is the atheistic existentialism of Sartre and Camus, probably the purest of the genre since it rejects any religious claim and asserts the complete autonomy and responsibility of the individual.

Existentialism provides the foundation of the middle way of freedom and it has several basic dimensions. It is necessary, first, to stress the Kantian (ethical) dimensions of the orientation so that freedom's middle way can be seen as a synthesis of negative and positive freedom—of freedom *from* and freedom *to*. Sartre, perhaps the leading contemporary existentialist, agreed with Kant that acts are self-determined. Certainly Sartre was a champion of personal freedom and, in his imposing book *Being and Nothingness,* argued that we are, always, absolutely free. To Sartre (and to Kant) this meant that insofar as we *act,* our decisions and actions are not determined by outside forces. We need to make decisions; we need to act. We can, of course, refuse to make decisions and refuse to act, but even then we are still making decisions—"choosing not to choose," in the classic Sartrian phrase.

So, first of all, existentialism stresses freedom—freedom to act. This is not what Isaiah Berlin meant by his concept of negative freedom.[1] Positive freedom is much more than simply being free from restrictions. Freedom is choosing, say the existentialists; choosing is acting, and one must act as one would want others to act. So here is the connection between freedom and ethics. Both concepts are built into the existentialist position. The existentialist extols freedom but endows it with responsibility and with the willingness to live with the consequences of the action; in this sense the rational existentialist is quite different from Kant, who eschewed consequences.

---

1 See Berlin, *Two Concepts of Liberty.* His dichotomy between positive and negative freedom is, in many ways, unfortunate, since it only helps perpetuate nondialectical thinking in this area.

Thus, existentialists advocate action, and action implies freedom. Therefore, existentialist journalists would have freedom near the heart of their philosophy. As a basic postulate for action, freedom is present as a condition for human existence. It is, of course, dangerous; it even tends to contain in itself the seed of its own demise. Nikolai Berdyaev, a Russian existentialist who has written much on freedom, puts it this way: "The tragedy of the world process is that of freedom; it is born of the inner dynamic of freedom, of its capacity for changing into its opposite."[2] In taking this view, Berdyaev is consistent with many of his fellow existentialists. Centuries earlier, Plato, in his classic "paradox of freedom," anticipated the existentialists in pointing out this danger when he noted that free people could freely decide to become enslaved. What if it is the will of the people, asks Plato in criticizing democracy, not to rule but to have a tyrant?[3]

Freedom is also dangerous because it may be used harmfully. In other words, it may not be used positively at all. Harmful freedom may be tolerated by a society, as it sometimes is in the United States, but it again has in it the seeds for its own destruction. Society will permit such license only so long; by some mechanism, harmful freedom will be brought under control or even eliminated. Irresponsible journalism in the name of freedom is a dangerous enterprise—not only for the society but for the practitioners of such freedom. The journalistic freedom that is viable, that is healthy for a society, is the freedom used by socially concerned journalists who think of the public good, not solely of a personal right or right of the press.

Hegel, though no existentialist, caught the essence of existential freedom. For Hegel, freedom was not license. He insisted that a more moderate stance was needed—a rational or responsible freedom. Philosopher Henry Aiken has described Hegel's concept of freedom: "Initially one thinks of freedom as doing just as one pleases. Such a notion of freedom, Hegel thinks, is the barest of abstractions, completely devoid of ethical significance. Freedom, for him, is the power to realize one's self. The self is not a pure ego; it is concretely a personality invested with determinate

2 Quoted in John Macquarrie, *Existentialism* (New York, 1973), 140.
3 "Plato as Enemy of the Open Society," Karl Popper, in Thomas L. Thorson (ed.), *Plato: Totalitarian or Democrat?* (Englewood Cliffs, N.J., 1963), 68–69.

tendencies and capacities. . . . The first step toward self-knowledge and self-culture . . . is the recognition of one's membership within an historically-evolving community."[4]

The middle way of freedom—the existentialist perspective—is not an extreme or totally individualistic path. It does not accept the premise that a person has no moral claim on others or that there should be no loyalties outside one's self. It does not claim, with the extreme individualists, that there should always be uncoerced personal choice. Extreme individualism, which lives on in the writings of Ayn Rand and her followers, seems to be slowly dying out in today's world. The existentialist, of course, preserves remnants of such freedom, but it is modified considerably by a sense of responsibility for the consequences of decisions. Make no mistake: the existentialist is an individualist, but a socially concerned one. The existentialist journalist will strive for individualism and try to be authentic, but he or she will also be related to others through a moral sensitivity. Integrity is a dominant aspiration for the individualist, and the journalist seeking the middle way of freedom holds tightly to integrity. Emerson's words sound familiar to this journalist: "Nothing is at last sacred but the integrity of your own mind."[5]

The existentialist has great faith in freedom—of *all* types. Negative and positive freedom are both to be respected; one must be free from many restrictions before being able to use such freedom positively, for good purposes, both personal and social. The dialectic is at work again as negative and positive freedom merge and the synthesis has traits of both. As Mortimer Adler has said, "A man lacks freedom to whatever extent he is passively affected, or subject to an alien power, the power of another rather than his own." In stressing the value of all types of freedom, Adler continues, "In every conception of freedom, the self is the principle of freedom through possessing the power to be actively the source of whatever kind of activity is thought to manifest human freedom."[6]

4 Henry D. Aiken (ed.), *The Age of Ideology: The Nineteenth Century Philosophers* (New York, 1962), 79.

5 Ralph Waldo Emerson, "Self Reliance," quoted in Raymond Van Over, *The Psychology of Freedom* (Greenwich, Conn., 1974), 112.

6 Quoted in Robert E. Dewey and James A. Gould, *Freedom: Its History, Nature, and Varieties* (Toronto, 1970), 75.

Existentialists and Freedom

Perhaps the best example of a person who took this middle road of free-dom and qualified as an existentialist journalist is Albert Camus (1913–1960). He joined the underground group called Combat in 1943 and struggled against the Nazi occupation of France. A sensitive, intelligent individual, Camus edited the group's newspaper which was also called *Combat,* and wrote hundred of articles that record his reactions to events during the occupation. These articles add up to an extended profile of an existentialist in journalism, evidencing vigor but restraint, anguish yet hope, historical perspective yet concern for the future, individualism yet social awareness, and a love for facts coupled with a subjective orienta-tion. He was the classic dialectical journalist. What is probably more important, Camus in his articles exhibited a deep love for positive freedom but at the same time an appreciation of logical argument and reason-ableness. He was, in effect, the quintessential existentialist—part free-wheeling, mystical artist and part socially conscious social scientist. Dur-ing the bleak days of World War II, *Combat* was, for millions of Frenchmen, both a source of information (hard facts) and a source of hope, inspiration, and pride. Later Camus continued in journalism by writing for the serious weekly of Paris, *L'Express.* At the time of his death in an automobile accident in 1960, he was a contributor to many French newspapers.

What is a good journalist? Camus answered that a good journalist is one who has a deep concern and respect for oneself, for others, and for the truth, one who has ideas and a sensitivity to social progress, who desires to act responsibly and is not unwilling to become involved in the social issues of the day.[7] He treasured the rebel, to be sure, but he realized that re-bellion—like freedom—implies responsibility. Maturity demands realism and moderation, and for Camus, these are the twin necessities of good journalism. He was, in a profound sense, a dialectical journalist, believing that every journalist must seek the harmony and the order that ensure his or her own freedom and integrity and—equally important—the freedom and integrity of all others. In Nietzschean terms, Camus would say yea, not only to life, but to freedom and responsibility. He chose the middle way of freedom. His general impression of journalism was rather gloomy,

---

7 Jean Daniel, "Camus as Journalist," *New Republic,* June 13, 1964, p. 19.

for he felt that the field was filled with dull, passive, inauthentic persons devoid of much real commitment.

Another person who, like Camus, saw journalism generally as a rather dismal field of endeavor, was the noted Spanish philosopher José Ortega y Gasset. Ortega referred to journalism as being on a "very low spiritual plane," and called the typical journalist "one of the least cultured types in contemporary society," who "reduces the present to the momentary, and the momentary to the sensational." He, like Camus, urged journalists to relish their freedom but also emphasized their responsibility. Karl Jaspers, too, was less than happy with journalism. He wrote that it is very difficult to find a "terse and highly polished insight . . . amid the multifarious rubbish of what is printed from day to day."[8]

Jaspers expressed his views on journalism mainly in his book *Man in the Modern Age*. The journalist's position, he said, is extremely important, and the person who occupies it should have a keen sense of honor. He accords the press much power. He warns, however, that a potentially disastrous feature of the press's position is that its responsibility and creativity might well be endangered by the fact that journalists must depend on the needs and expectations of the masses and upon political and economic centers of power.[9]

Jaspers referred to the press as "a caste with an ethic of its own," one that exercises a mental dominance over everything. In fact, he claimed that without a press the modern world could not exist. The big question is, according to Jaspers, whether "mass-qualities will hopelessly ruin everything which, through the exercise of these possibilities, human beings might become." And in a passage of soaring rhetoric Jaspers provided perhaps the best description of the existentialist journalist that has ever been given: "The journalist can realise the ideal of the modern universalised man. He can merge himself in the tension and the reality of the day, adopting a reflective attitude toward these. He can seek out that innermost region where the soul of the age takes a step forward. He deliberately interweaves his destiny with that of the epoch. He takes alarm, he suffers, and he balks when he encounters Nothingness. He becomes insincere when he is content with that which brings satisfaction to the majority. He

8 José Ortega y Gasset, *Mission of the University* (New York, 1944), 90; Jaspers, *Man in the Modern Age,* 134.
9 Jaspers, *Man in the Modern Age,* 136.

THE DIALECTIC IN JOURNALISM

soars towards the heights when he sincerely fulfils his being in the present."[10]

Jaspers also had something to say about the inauthentic journalist—a person he referred to as "the sophist." This sophist, or passive journalist, according to Jaspers, often poses as an intellectual but is really a kind of coward who "endeavors to avoid any fundamental conflict." He is a social person to a rather ludicrous degree, entering into relations everywhere. According to Jaspers, this inauthentic journalist is "pliable when vigorously resisted, brutal and disloyal when he has the upper hand; pathetic when it costs him nothing; sentimental when his will is crossed."[11] Such a sophistic journalist, Jaspers thought, is a pitiful person, standing for nothing except egoistic expediency. In fact, he is actually without character and without sincerity. Such a sophist is guilty of deceptions and frauds, though most of these may be minor. So this type of journalist is usually not really bad, but is never really good either.

Jaspers' ideal journalist would be straightforward, honest, well informed, rational, sincere, authentic, and willing to accept responsibility for his or her actions. Such a journalist would relate to others, care for others, and be sensitive to the needs of others, all without surrendering basic personal integrity. Interconnections in society—between the journalist and others—were very important to Jaspers. He expressed this dialectic between self and others in these words, which capture the essence of existential journalism: "What frees us from solitude is not the world, but the selfhood which enters into ties with others. Interlinkage of self-existent persons constitutes the invisible reality of the essential. . . . The best gift the contemporary world can give us is this proximity of self-existent human beings."[12]

Two main orientations, as previously noted, seem to dominate among existentialist journalists: 1) the Promethean, which is concerned with changing directly the outer conditions of people's lives in the kind of external rebellion exemplified by Sartre; and 2) the Orphic, which seeks to alter society indirectly through the individual journalist's efforts to change himself or herself, as exemplified by Camus.[13] Camus, following the tradi-

10 *Ibid.*, 136–37.
11 *Ibid.*, 182–83.
12 *Ibid.*, 209.
13 Brée, *Camus and Sartre*, 240–53 *passim*.

tion of Orpheus, sought to achieve the transformation from within, and Sartre, in the tradition of Prometheus, sought to change the outer condition of people's lives. The Promethean would defy the established order, trying to liberate men and women and make them the equal to the gods. Such a journalist stresses open defiance of the established powers. This Sartrean type of journalist, who wants to change others immediately, becomes a social rebel and ideological revolutionary. Change society first, and then the individual will change—that is the Promethean plan.

In contrast, the Orphic existentialist desires to develop personal possibilities and to change and renew the self. But by so doing, the Orphic journalist wants to have an impact on society. Change oneself first, and then society will change—that is the plan of the Orphic journalist. In short, Camus wanted to create an aesthetic order, whereas Sartre wanted to change the physical order. Sartre set two main goals for the journalist or writer. First, the journalist or writer should unveil to readers the developing social world and judge social weaknesses, and second, he or she should personally engage in actions to close the gap between what is and what can be. In Camus' view the journalist should be concerned mainly with "the present, with the practical needs of the moment," since the journalist pays attention mainly to the self; struggle against others may be necessary, but the major problem is self-development and persuasion of others. This is in contrast with Sartre, who would take a more forceful role—to make people see needed changes and assist in bringing about these changes.[14]

Many journalists are outward rebels, even revolutionaries. They are Promethean existentialists. Others are more introspective, more self-concerned, anxious to change themselves, touching others only tenuously and indirectly. They are more evolutionary than the revolutionary Prometheans. Aesthetic development, personal growth, and individual moral progress dominate the lives of Orphic existentialists. Both types are true existentialists, valuing freedom, authenticity, self-development, social impact, honesty, openness, and choosing. The difference is one of degree. But there is no reason why the journalist cannot synthesize the Orphic and Promethean traits, developing self simultaneously with engaging in overt activities designed to change the social situation. Personal growth and morality do not preclude social action and altruistic morality. The dialectically oriented journalist will merge these two tendencies almost uncon-

14 Ibid., 253, 240–41.

sciously, bringing a synthesized and superior ethical stance to bear on journalism and society.

One important characteristic of existentialist journalism is self-respect, which is closely related to ethically oriented freedom, positive freedom, and responsible freedom. Journalists desiring and cherishing freedom must also respect themselves and the capacity they have to contribute to the total range of information and pluralism of viewpoints that have a positive impact on society. Actually journalists who are not ethically motivated in their use of freedom will find it difficult to have much self-esteem. They may be negatively free, but they cannot be responsible. Therefore, they have no reason to respect themselves. Freedom by itself and in itself is nothing for a person to be proud of. Self-respect comes with using freedom responsibly.

What Kant referred to as "the dignity of ends" is possible through freedom of will, and it is this freedom that is the ground of personal value and self-respect. Dignity or worthiness comes from self-respect and has no substitute.[15] A person, of course, often has freedom to act in such a manner as to lose self-respect; one who habitually acts in such a way is a vacuous person who has freedom but no ethical purpose for such freedom. The individual journalist is harmed in such a case, and what harms the journalist harms others and, when projected widely, can harm the whole society.

Self-respect causes a journalist to believe that he or she can do something with freedom—something useful and socially significant—and even when this freedom leads to trouble and causes the journalist pain, his or her self-respect is still intact through the realization that an action has been taken and that there is personal acceptance of responsibility for that action. Self-respect grows with freedom—positive, responsible freedom—and freedom grows with self-respect. And freedom is necessary for both personal and social development. A member of the Hutchins Commission, William Ernest Hocking, has stressed that freedom is essential to a press system for it not to become stagnant. In his book *Freedom of the Press* he insisted that freedom is as necessary to one's being as is breathing; a person suffocates when freedom is taken away. He continued: "To the individual the value of his freedom lies simply in the enjoyment of his capacity for

15   H. J. Paton, *The Categorical Imperative: A Study of Kant's Philosophy* (New York, 1967), 188–89.

self-direction. It is not separable from the value of being alive; for to live is to act, and action *means* free action—the adjective adds nothing to the natural fact. It is only as spontaneous action is interfered with that the notion of freedom comes to consciousness or receives a name."[16]

The journalist with self-respect is proud of the freedom that gives him or her the chance for self-expression, regardless of its hazards, and is eager to take a stand, become committed, and to take the consequences for this exercise of freedom. This is nothing less than freedom's middle way, the social or rational existentialist view of freedom. Such a journalist is committed to freedom and responsibility, to moderation and authenticity, and to self-respect and respect for others.

To have respect is to have more than negative freedom. One must use this freedom, activate it, and put it to use for good. There is no self-respect in simply being free of outside control; a dignified slave can have more self-respect. The journalist who is permitted freedom of expression and fails to use it has no reason for self-respect. In other words, freedom in itself is valueless; it is what is done with it that matters. And what is done with freedom is dependent on one's value system, moral motivation, and ethical direction. This is why the journalist who has nothing but freedom, has nothing. Freedom takes on significance when it links up with morally determined personal action. This is ethical freedom—freedom that is neither passive nor extreme. It cannot easily become license. In short, it is compromising freedom, a middle way of freedom, that the morally concerned journalist lives in.

Although the existentialists' emphasis on the authentic free person frustrates their proposing a precise code of ethics, their humanitarian concern leads them to suggest a principle for guiding moral decisions. According to this principle, when a person makes a choice, it is accompanied by great responsibility, for the choice is made for all humanity. The basic moral maxim for the existentialist, one that restrains existential freedom, is that one should choose what one would wish all people to choose under the same circumstances. By and large, this Kantian strain in existentialism provides an altruistic dimension. However, such a universalizing concept does not necessarily imply altruism, for the existentialist may, of course, like Nietzsche, take the extreme position that altruism is a fraud perpetrated by religiously inspired slave mentalities. It should also

16 William Ernest Hocking, *Freedom of the Press* (Chicago, 1947), 56–57.

be remembered that Heidegger did not let his existentialism deter him from becoming a Nazi. He said at one point that all that "is great is in the midst of the storm," and maintained that it was through having such a realization deep within that Germans could have an understanding of "the glory and the greatness of the Hitler revolution."[17]

The Importance of Individualism

If one had to give a prime characteristic of existentialism (with the possible exception of its stress on freedom), one would probably point to individualism. The existentialist's emphasis on subjectivity, free choosing, and authenticity results naturally in an individualistic stance. Collectivism and determinism are concepts contrary to existentialism. Nevertheless, existentialists and others have recognized that individualism and authority are not necessarily mutually exclusive and that there need not be a conflict between the two. Kant, for example, though a champion of maximum autonomy, insisted that the only individualism worth defending was the ability of the person to participate in universal morality. This dialectical consideration has been found also in Socrates, Plato, and Aristotle. In more recent times this argument has found a large following among thinkers who have seen disastrous results of overly individualistic thinking. Hegel, for instance, in the nineteenth century, noted that it is very important that there be "the preservation of a people, a state, of the well-ordered spheres of life. This is the activity of individuals participating in the common effort and helping to bring about its particular manifestations."[18]

Hegel argued that each of us is insignificant in our tiny place in history; he said that no other view of ourselves is realistic. He went on to contend that even the greatest among us is no more than an expression of the "universal," of the grand forces of society as a whole. Individualists such as Kierkegaard would react sharply to this Hegelian idea. Such a de-emphasis of the self would cause Nietzsche to lapse into anti-Hegelian poetry and Ayn Rand to fly into self-esteeming rhetoric. But such spokesmen as Hegel—and even Marx—are not really denying the indi-

---

17 Benjamin Piunkel, *The Existential Adventure* (Marina del Rey, Calif., 1976), 142; Martin Heidegger, *German Existentialism*, trans. D. D. Runes (New York, 1965), 178.
18 G. W. F. Hegel, *Reason in History,* trans. R. S. Hartman (New York, 1953), 178.

vidual or individual rights. They are insisting that the individual deserves respect only insofar as he or she is a contributing member of a community. What Hegel and like spirits are denying is what has often been called "vulgar individualism"—the form of individualism that denies all social relevance and social obligation.

Certainly the existentialists are not guilty of vulgar individualism. Social consciousness or collective cooperation is much in evidence in their philosophy.[19] Individualism is, of course, of prime importance to existentialism, but social concern is attached. The individualist movement is not unique to existentialism, for it has been in the mainstream of Western thought from Socrates through Reformation Christianity to contemporary capitalism. The rebellion of Socrates was in fact largely an existentialist rebellion in the Orphic tradition; he stood up for personal values against the prevailing opinion of his society. And Martin Luther's Reformation reasserted the individual conscience against the authority of the Church.

Individualism, needless to say, has always had its scoffers and doubters, and these doubters have played an important part in the dialectic. It has been noted that when individualism becomes so powerful that egoism eclipses social interest and the community is endangered, then it may be time to point out the limits of individualism. And this is a valid perspective. Runaway individualism and unethical use of freedom cannot be sustained by rational and moral persons. Are there not limits to the degree to which one can challenge the values and customs of our society? Are there not social responsibilities that rise above individualism? It is often said that our individual selves are so bound up in our communities that we must sacrifice many of our personal proclivities to the values of our fellow citizens. Such a social emphasis must be balanced against individualism; it leads to a more moderate, rational, and moral concept of individualism. It is of the spirit of the dialectic and is consistent with the middle way, or the existentialist concept, of freedom.

In spite of the reasonableness of the middle way, individualism should not be deprecated. Individualism should be thought of as the American sociologist David Riesman has thought of it. He has maintained that though we are part of society, that is no reason to deny individuality. Although emphases on social integration may well be a useful corrective to

19 Mary Warnock, *Existentialist Ethics* (New York, 1967).

an earlier solipsism, he said, it should not hold that social conformity is a necessity and duty. If we go to that extreme, he said, it will destroy freedom, which gives life its savor and its potential for advancement. The Enlightenment's philosophical stress was on individualism and also on equality and democracy, with their tendencies toward egoism, selfishness, and anarchy. Then in the nineteenth century there was a new emphasis that brought a reversion to a collectivized society, which, however, was quite temporary, as a resurgence of individualism soon followed. Of course, in the late nineteenth century and into the twentieth century the dialectic was at work again with a new reaction, as collectivism reasserted itself against individualism.[20]

Against this collectivistic resurgence in the present age, the ideas of Carl Jung have been a major force. He was a passionate defender of the freedom and basic rights of the individual, which, in his opinion, should be protected not only by a just state but also by the maturity and wisdom of all the members of the community. "The individual matters more than the system," said Jung, reversing the idea of Plato, Hegel, Marx, and other statists. Jung was a kind of Orphic existentialist; he reflected the view of Camus in believing that change must begin with self-improvement and not with trying to improve other people. Jung believed that the relatedness of the individual to his or her inner self is coincident with social relatedness. "Nobody," said Jung, "can relate to others if he has not first a relationship with his own inner Self." He went on to say that to a large degree "all political dissension and conflicts are exteriorizations of inner conflicts that each human being should resolve within himself, thus taking the weight of his neurotic dissociation away from society."[21]

The dialectical antinomies are found in the contrasting views of individualism held by Nietzsche and Marx. These two men represent, respectively, the subjugation of the mass to the individual and the subordination of the individual to the class. Nietzsche was the prototypical individualist, and Marx was the prototypical collectivist. Nietzsche placed the individual above everything, thus illustrating individualism; Marx subordinated the individual to the group, the class, the society, and the nation, thus exemplifying collectivism. As E. L. Allen has said, "For Nietzsche the

---

20 David Riesman, *Individualism Reconsidered* (New York, 1954); Odajnyk, *Jung and Politics*, 35.
21 Odajnyk, *Jung and Politics*, x.

individual is the wheel; for Marx, the individual is a cog in the wheel." Nietzsche saw the individual as an autonomous, self-determining will—a typical existentialist position; Marx saw the individual as a cooperating, dominated, self-sacrificing functionary of society—a typical socialist or statist position. Allen suggested that the rational person must not opt for either extreme: "We can be content with neither [the position of Nietzsche or Marx]. For events have taught us that there is a secret alliance between them; the mass-movement and the tyrant call for each other. Our task is to create a society in which persons will come into their own, in which the man of outstanding ability will not provoke resentment and the common man will not be an object of contempt. Did not the Christian love that both Marx and Nietzsche despised aim at something of this order?"[22]

Yet it may be somewhat unfair to classify either Nietzsche or Marx as embracing extreme positions of individualism or collectivism. Certainly Marx, especially in his early, humanistic period, cared for the individual and individual rights. And Nietzsche's "true Superman" recognized the importance of the individual's concern for the group, at least to some degree. Herbert Read has characterized Nietzsche's thinking about individualism and the group: "When an individual has become conscious . . . of his own closed circuit of desires and potentialities (at which stage he is an egoist) but also of the laws which govern his reactions to the group of which he is a member, then he is on the way to become that new type of human being which Nietzsche called the Superman." But there is no doubt that Nietzsche did personify the individualist spirit. In fact he spoke of morality as "the herd-instinct in the individual." A similar emphasis was given individual rebellion even earlier by Kierkegaard, the religious philosopher who is often considered the father of existentialism. Like Nietzsche, he deplored what he sarcastically called "the public," and urged an end to collective identity and social roles in favor of a respect for the individual. Kierkegaard argued that a person who follows the crowd and does not choose his or her own identity as an individual cannot even be said to exist.[23]

In the twentieth century, borrowing heavily from Kierkegaard and

---

22 Allen, *From Plato to Nietzsche,* 185.

23 Read, *Anarchy and Order,* 40; Friedrich Nietzsche, *The Joyful Wisdom,* trans. Thomas Common (New York, 1964); Søren Kierkegaard, *Concluding Unscientific Postscript,* trans. David F. Swenson and Walter Lowrie (Princeton, 1941).

Nietzsche, the German existentialist Martin Heidegger argued against collective social identity in terms of what he (ironically) calls *das Man,* an extremely useful German expression that roughly translates as "they," as in everyday remarks such as *"They* say that you can't believe what you read in the newspapers." Who are "they"? No one at all, Heidegger said, just an anonymous no one. The contemporary American scholar Noam Chomsky also sees individualism as threatened by a number of growing power centers within the system, that he calls "State capitalism." To him this new situation is far from classical liberalism; in fact, he says that it is what is now called conservatism. At any rate, he sees the individual disappearing in this new system, which is "highly authoritarian." It is one that accepts a number of centers of authority and control—the state on one hand, clusters of private power on the other, all interacting, "while individuals are malleable cogs in this highly constrained machine." Chomsky adds that such a system "may be called democratic, but given the actual distribution of power, it's very far from being meaningfully democratic, and cannot be so."[24]

Chomsky's observations can be productively related to the journalistic context. The press in the United States is not conducive to journalistic individualism. It is, in Chomsky's terms, really quite authoritarian—in the sense of having a number of centers of authority and control. On one hand, there is the government, with considerable power. On the other hand, there are the big chains and conglomerates and other corporations of the press. They are definitely authorities (power centers) directing American journalism. Such a system may still be called democratic, or libertarian, or pluralistic, but it does not really have these characteristics. The individual is minimized in this scheme; as Chomsky says, the individual journalists are simply "malleable cogs in this highly constrained machine." So on the social level, the press centers of power combine with the government centers of power to keep journalism as a whole from being truly oriented toward the individual. And on the microcosmic level (the level at which the journalist works within the institution), individual journalists are not free, since they find themselves controlled and directed constantly by authorities within the press system itself.

---

24 Martin Heidegger, *Being and Time,* trans. John Macquarrie and Edward Robison (New York, 1962); Magee (ed.), *Men of Ideas,* 193.

Journalism and Existentialism

As Erich Fromm and others have contended, people are inclined to try to escape from freedom because of the pain attached to making decisions. Existentialists maintain that persons who attempt to shed freedom are living inauthentic lives—living "in bad faith." In spite of the personal pain it may cause, freedom—especially positive freedom—is necessary in an open society, one in which democracy and a pluralistic journalism are important. There can be no real human dignity, say the existentialists, without freedom, and as John Macquarrie has insisted, "The risk of increasing freedom must constantly be taken." Without freedom, there is no creativity, no pushing toward progress in journalism. Even if the masses do not fully appreciate the value of freedom, journalists should constantly defend it and project it. The journalist must be a kind of rebel against tyrannizing and conforming influences of the masses; the journalist must protest against attempts to diminish freedom, for, as Camus said, "Freedom preserves the power to protest and guarantees human communication."[25]

The modern journalist will recognize the potential danger of manipulating and enslaving others and will prize freedom. Journalistic freedom will mean freedom for all; journalistic authenticity will mean authenticity for all. In other words, existentialist journalists will try to expand freedom (both negative and positive) for others as well as for themselves.

Existentialist journalism is largely a subjective journalism, in the sense that much stress is placed on the *person* who creates the journalism. But it does not ignore the world "out there"—the objective world of reality. It is just that the *perception* of this objective world is emphasized, with substantial attention given to the journalist as the creator of the verbal or symbolic world that reflects the real world. This existential subjectivism is not extreme subjectivism; rather it is modified or temperate. It endows journalism with a personal perspective while it retains a demeanor of reasonableness and a concern for verifiable potential, which are necessary for good reportorial journalism. The aspect of reasonableness impinges on both freedom and subjectivity, limiting both by a rational dialectical pro-

---

25 Macquarrie, *Existentialism,* 141; Albert Camus, *The Rebel,* trans. Anthony Brower (New York, 1956), 291.

cess. Existentialist journalism in such a sense is a moderate journalistic stance.

Although the will to be objective is important, subjectivity in journalism should not be repressed. The journalist is a subjective creature unable to escape from self. Trying too hard to become a detached reflector of the environment will cause the journalist to assume a false nature, as the existentialists say, becoming an inauthentic person. Freud has pointed out that a person's unconscious motivates and influences his or her conscious choice of words and messages and that the idea of detachment or aloofness is a myth. Existentialists in journalism would agree. Fromm has insisted that objectivity does not mean detachment, but that it means no more than respect—that is, "the ability not to distort and to falsify things, persons, and oneself." Very often journalists will assume a stance of detachment, of disinterest, of aloofness; they are trying, they say, to be true to objectivity. Fromm discredited such a stance, saying that the idea that "lack of interest is a condition for recognizing the truth is fallacious."[26]

The dialectic is at work again. Existentialism is not a philosophy of the object alone; it emphasizes relationships, especially between the objective world and the subjective person. The existentialist journalist is not obsessed with the thing or person being written about. The existentialist journalist stresses the writer's perception of what is being reported. This does not mean that the event, thing, or person is ignored; it simply means that straining this reality "out there" through the subjective reportorial process is not thought of as detrimental or dangerous to the emergence of the truth. The existentialist journalist knows, in the first place, that "truth" in an objective sense will never really emerge and that only subjective reflections of bits and pieces of the truth will filter through. The existentialist journalist knows that when he or she writes about an event or person, to a very large extent the journalist is writing about himself or herself. There is no way to separate self from story, and as the story becomes more complex and controversial, this basic principle of journalism becomes even more valid.

Existentialist journalists are users and expanders of freedom. They see their freedom as everyone's; when they choose freedom, they are philo-

---

26 Erich Fromm, *Man for Himself: An Enquiry into the Psychology of Ethics* (New York, 1966), 111. See also Karl Mannheim, *Ideology and Utopia* (New York, 1935), for another good discussion of detachment and truth.

sophically universalizing themselves. In so doing, they introduce a Kantian dimension into their existentialist demeanor. Therefore, self-indulging, strictly autonomous journalists who do not think of others are not really existentialists. They may be nihilists, or anarchists, or radical libertarians, but they are not choosing the middle way of freedom.

The journalists of freedom's middle way are vital, dynamic, passionate, and committed; they are repelled by stagnant, conformist, routine, passive, and uncommitted journalism. Existentialist journalists thrust themselves into the social maelstrom, seeking to harmonize their own self-interest with the wider public interest of society. The journalist who is passive and who lives in a little private world is not an existentialist journalist, even though such a life may be freely chosen. The existentialist is not passive, isolated from social concerns, or uninvolved in the ebb and flow of practical affairs, but is anxious to push forward, to experiment, to explore, to take chances, and to seek social progress. In addition, such a journalist is one who values personal independence and wants to avoid being simply a cog in the wheel of journalism. The existentialist journalist also brings into sharp relief the uniqueness of individual personalities and develops a distinctive character, projecting it into society through journalism. And such a journalist rebels against being anonymous and lost in journalism, prizes freedom and responsibility, and enthrones personal decision making. He or she also considers the situations of self and of others, wants freedom for self and others, and wants freedom to be used and not just possessed. Finally, the existentialist journalist desires self-respect and authenticity.

Anxiety, Alienation, and Authenticity

Three of existentialism's most pervasive themes are anxiety, alienation, and authenticity. The first two are negative and form psychological hurdles for the existentialist; the third is positive and will help the existentialist conquer the first two. Dread, concern, fear, and pessimism are all tied closely to anxiety; the feelings of loss of self, isolation, personal insignificance, and impotence in the face of mass society, are related to alienation. The existentialist journalist must fight anxiety and alienation constantly in order to maintain a balanced life and mental sanity. Helping the journalist to achieve such balance is the quest for authenticity. Only when the journalist respects himself or herself, acts honestly and forthrightly, and chooses positive and self-satisfying action can anxiety and alienation be held in check. Only then can the journalist function creatively, pushing forward into areas of social concern with vigor, imagination, and responsibility.

First comes anxiety. The journalist is anxious, assailed by a certain sense of dread, of anguish, or *Angst,* as the Germans call it. Such anxiety largely stems from the traumatic nature of freedom, a freedom that at once is prized and feared, a freedom that forces the conscientious journalist to make choices and accept responsibility for them. It is an anxiety born of uncertainty. It is an anxiety resulting from a recognition of personal inadequacies and limitations—and, ultimately, of the temporariness of life. The journalist knows that his or her actions can have a very significant impact on others—and on society generally. Such actions can ruin lives, harm reputations, damage relationships, and even endanger national security and social stability. The sensitive, conscientious journalist is therefore anxious.

The fact that the existentialist journalist knows that personal journalistic decisions have important results, that personal choice must be universalized, and that responsibility must be accepted causes a sense of unease, dread, or anxiety. The existentialist journalist tries to use a universal standard when making decisions, but the decisions are still subjective. "What would happen if everyone chose to do as I am doing?" the journalist must ask. This is an existential question, as it is also a Kantian question. What would happen? The journalist really does not know. Subjectivity is utilized, and a decision is made. It may not be a good decision. Bad consequences may flow from it, and the ethically motivated journalist is understandably uneasy about this. Such choices and decisions must be made, however, and in journalism they must be made continually and without much time for deliberation. This increases the sense of *Angst.* As responsibilities of the journalist increase, the anxiety increases. One is often tempted to do nothing, but inaction is itself an action and may lead to worse consequences than doing almost anything else would.[27]

Journalists are anxious about their decisions, about their impact on others, about their relationships with their fellows and with their superiors. They are anxious about their work schedules, about their status, and

27 See Jean-Paul Sartre, "Existentialism is a Humanism," in George Novack (ed.), *Existentialism Versus Marxism* (New York, 1966), 75–78.

about their future. And always lurking in their subconscious is a deep concern about freedom—not only about restrictions and expansions of their own freedom, but about the freedom of the institutional press.[28] They sense that both types of freedom—personal and institutional—are being constricted, that freedom is being lost, and that they as individuals (and the media as institutions) are being depersonalized and subjected to increasing amounts of authority. This realization increases the anxiety of the sensitive and rational journalist.

Anxiety is more than being afraid of this or that thing, of making this or that specific decision. As Heidegger put it, anxiety is the "uncanny feeling of being afraid of nothing at all," and it is "this Nothingness that makes itself present and felt as the object of our dread."[29] This sense of *Angst* that hovers over the journalist portends something that "may not be good" for the journalist. But if he or she is asked what it is, there is no clear answer. It is a feeling, a sense, a presence, a premonition—a vague spirit of unease, of dread, of forlornness, of anxiety. It can incapacitate the journalist, it can make his or her work tentative, cautious, timid, and indecisive. The existentialist recognizes this anxiety, accepts it, but tries to transcend it.

Beyond anxiety, there is alienation to cause problems for the existentialist journalist. Perhaps it is not so much alienation as a sense of alienation. What causes this sense of alienation? For one thing, the journalist feels a certain isolation from society in the role of its reporter and interpreter, and at the same time, he or she is knowledgeable about social happenings. Journalists also sometimes feel as if they are pieces of the machinery of journalism, living in small, isolated corners of the mammoth institution, restricted to routinized functions. Such journalists find it difficult to retain their own selfhood, their own identity, their own authenticity as they routinely collect, package, and transmit "the world out there" to others. Jacques Ellul has pointed out that alienation actually means being someone other than oneself; he also said that it can mean to belong to someone else, to be deprived of oneself, or to be subject to the authority of, or even identified with, someone else.[30]

Journalists often feel that their identity is only that of their newspaper or their television station. As they fit in ever more comfortably with their

---

28 Merrill, *Existential Journalism*, esp. 71–74.
29 Barrett, *Irrational Man*, 226.
30 Jacques Ellul, *Propaganda* (New York, 1965).

medium, they increasingly become someone other than themselves. They feel detached from society and deprived of their true selves, and they live a robotlike existence in their own little corporate worlds of journalism. By the very nature of their mainly neutralist, dispassionate work, journalists have become largely detached from society. Even though they have connections with representatives of society, they are considered merely sources or spokesmen—in short, part of their work and little more. Camus and other existentialists have emphasized this growing isolation or alienation of persons and groups from society. Perhaps *The Stranger,* a novel by Camus, illustrates this estrangement as well as any other literary work; it combines the themes of alienation, self-estrangement, the mechanization of the person, and the general loss of selfhood.

Without a doubt the growing corporate nature of the press, coupled with technocracy and journalistic specialization, contributes to this sense of alienation. Press institutions get larger and larger and more and more impersonal, and individual journalists become estranged from one another and from the overall product. Together with a retreat from humanistic concerns and a general loss of religious faith, this growing mechanization of journalistic action pushes the individual journalist deeper into a feeling of loneliness and isolation. Such a situation combines with the natural sense of anxiety to create a kind of psychic despair or unease in the journalist. According to psychologists such as Erich Fromm, the modern person is forced into a kind of technical, mechanistic straitjacket in which material values tend to erase the capacity for deep emotional experiences and self-satisfaction. Fromm, for example, believes that the mechanistic, impersonal modern world that we have created has become so powerful that it has led to dehumanization.[31]

Carl Jung largely blames the mass state for this alienation, which he calls "psychic isolation." Jung sees a governmental duplicity in this, believing that the state desires individual isolation, for "the more unrelated individuals are, the more consolidated the State becomes." Gabriel Marcel, the French Christian existentialist, also believes that giant institutions, large groups, and technocracy contribute significantly to this personal alienation. Such alienation gives a general pessimistic tone to many lives.[32]

31 Erich Fromm, *The Revolution of Hope* (New York, 1968), 2.

32 C. G. Jung, *The Undiscovered Self* (New York, 1958), 115; Gabriel Marcel, *Man Against Mass Society,* trans. G. S. Fraser (Chicago, 1969), 204.

Not everyone thinks existentialism is a philosophy of pessimism. Mary Warnock, for example, believes it is basically optimistic. She points out that Sartre, for instance, encouraged people to action by teaching them that their destiny is in their own hands, that they themselves have a say in what they will become. This is an optimistic note, and it pervades existentialist philosophy. Sartre saw no despair in a theory that says that we must decide for ourselves how to live, that we become whatever we are by making decisions. And besides being optimistic in that sense, it is also a philosophy of morality. According to existentialism, when we choose for ourselves, we choose a particular course of action because we think it is good. It also teaches that one should not choose a course of action unless it is good for everyone. What a person chooses, that person chooses for all. And of course, such choosing for all injects a Kantian deontology into existentialism and gives it its moral base. Some optimism is always present in a philosophy that has a moral base.[33]

It may well be, as many critics of existentialism contend, that this alienation is being exaggerated and that people today are far from being the isolated, despondent creatures so often depicted. But there is little doubt, as suicide rates increase and people more often take refuge in drugs, that such "psychic isolation" is rampant among us. The robotlike atmosphere pervading the modern offices of the mass media indicate a substantial degree of personal alienation. Existentialists say that such a situation is to be expected, that it must be faced and conquered, and that it can in fact serve as a catalyst for intensive life. Fortunately, the existentialists emphasize the third theme, authenticity, which provides a person with an escape from alienation as well as from anxiety. And this authenticity, so much valued by the existentialist, plays its part in the dialectic of journalism. As Kierkegaard stressed, a person must function as an individual but use this individuality to connect self with other individuals in meaningful relationships. Such relationships, he believes, can conquer the corroding effects of alienation.[34] The authentic person can be a true self and at the

---

33 Warnock, *Existentialist Ethics,* 39–40.

34 N. A. Horvath, *Philosophy* (Woodbury, N. Y., 1974), 106. See Carl B. Kaufmann, *Man Incorporate* (Garden City, N.Y., 1969), 164–203, for a good discussion of the danger of alienation and loss of individuality among people working in corporations and other large organizations and for suggestions for the preservation of a sense of identity in a world of growing institutionalization.

THE DIALECTIC IN JOURNALISM

same time merge into a group, becoming simultaneously an individualist and a collectivist.

Authenticity, the third major theme, is the positive one. It is the factor that can overcome the two negative ones and lead the person to harmony, progress, hope, and optimism. Authenticity, probably the most old-fashioned of all the existentialist values, is also the supreme virtue of existentialism. When journalists are truly themselves, when they are authentic and not playing roles, they can overcome such debilitating factors as alienation and anxiety. Existentialism is basically a revolt against loss of self; therefore, when authenticity comes to the fore, the journalist is able to find satisfaction unknown in the pseudo lives that so many modern persons live. And with authenticity comes integrity.

Every notable existentialist—Kierkegaard, Nietzsche, Jaspers, Marcel, Berdyaev, Buber, Ortega, and others—has expressed concern about the lack of authenticity that pervades human existence. Too many people, say the existentialists, have no authentic existence simply because they refuse to recognize that they are what they make themselves. They are not like stones, Ortega said, which are given their existence and remain basically what they were. People are what they are and what they are making of themselves. As Ortega wrote, "Man has to be himself in spite of unfavorable circumstances; that means he has to make his own existence at every single moment . . . to earn his life, not only economically but metaphysically."[35]

Nietzsche said that the main causes of inauthenticity are laziness and fear. What people fear most, according to Nietzsche, are the problems with which "any unconditioned honesty . . . would burden them." In order to be authentic, Nietzsche added, a person "must merely cease being comfortable with himself [and] follow his conscience which shouts at him: 'Be yourself!'" A person must, Nietzsche wrote in *Thus Spake Zarathustra*, "go into the open air and away from all dusty rooms." He or she must shed temerity, open self to the world, and cease being a spectator "sitting in cool shade."[36]

Authenticity will keep the journalist from the twin dangers of alienation and anxiety. When one is anxious, the self is sacrificed for the ap-

35 José Ortega y Gasset, "Man Has No Nature," in Walter Kaufmann (ed.), *Existentialism from Dostoevsky to Sartre* (New York, 1975), 153–54.
36 *Ibid.*, 123; B. V. Hill, *Education and the Endangered Individual: A Critique of Ten Modern Thinkers* (New York, 1973), 56.

proval of others. When one is alienated, the person is obsessed with guilt and a desire to conform. Courting the approval of others and the desire to conform in order to "belong" simply further erodes one's authenticity. The various key tenets of existentialism, such as integrity, honesty, commitment, and individualism, are related to authenticity. And authenticity is directly related to journalistic responsibility. It is the inauthentic journalist who will compromise ethics and seek to escape responsibility.

Journalists in the newsroom are too often subsumed in the corporate machine, finding themselves in well-defined little niches where freedom, creativity, and individuality are highly regulated and limited. Journalists may think they have considerable freedom, but really they are being ever more institutionalized and branded with the corporate mentality. They find themselves putting on their false selves in order to cope, to adapt, to prosper, to progress; they find that inauthenticity often pays and that authenticity often causes them social pain. So they often sacrifice authenticity for short-term results. They push their real selves back into the shadows, and they do it so often that ultimately they do not know who they are. Authenticity may, indeed, bring certain disapproval from colleagues, but it brings a wealth of satisfaction and self-knowledge, as well as long-term rewards, to the journalists who determine to be themselves.

The authentic journalist is the honest journalist, the committed journalist, the acting journalist, the caring journalist. The authentic journalist, in short, is the responsible journalist. And responsibility is freedom's anchor. Freedom thrusts the journalist into the storms of daily life, and existential responsibility restrains the underlying surge of freedom, channeling it into the moderate "middle way," where it merges with the less turbulent waters of ethics.

Seven

MERGING ETHICAL PATHS

As the journalist follows the transitional "middle way of freedom," with its emphasis on moderate existentialism, he or she is soon in the territory of ethics, where many paths wind through a tangle of practical, expedient, and egoistic journalistic concerns. Existential freedom—if treated rationally—is really an eclectic *ethical* orientation that merges personalism and Kantian duty ethics. This synthesis of freedom with ethics evidences the dialectical nature of a sound journalism—one that respects duty to principle as well as free choosing in an atmosphere of change and self-respect. There are several wide-ranging ethical stances, orientations, and concerns facing the journalist today.

Finding the best paths to ethical action is difficult, for they all tend to be rather rough and narrow paths, winding through metaphysical and problematic thickets and underbrush. Scientific proof concerning ethics has not been forthcoming, and if the journalist chooses a path at all, he or she is forced to take it for no sound reason. In fact, one's general journalistic demeanor may be determined by whim, not by any deep concern for rational ethical determination. There are some journalists who take a purely pragmatic approach to their journalism, in each case doing what seems expedient or profitable at the time.

Even though many journalists seem to push through the dense wilderness of journalistic activity without following any path, most of them, at least on most occasions, seek some clear byway that will facilitate (and rationalize) their travels. Ethical paths seem to go off in many directions, crisscrossing here and there, and some even disappear in the thickets.

Philosophers have contemplated the various paths through the years and have come up with a large number of "theories" or "schools" of ethics. Paths not only crisscross here and there, run parallel, and disappear, but they also often merge and run along together. This capacity of ethical theories to merge is consistent with my dialectical emphasis.

Will Durant has said that there are only three paths (or systems) of ethics—what he calls "three conceptions of the ideal character and the moral life." The first is the ethics of Jesus and the Buddha, which stresses feminine virtues, considers everyone equally valuable, resists evil with good, enthrones love, and inclines in politics to unlimited democracy. Second, the ethics of Machiavelli and Nietzsche stresses masculine virtues, accepts the inequality of people, sees virtue in power, and exalts hereditary aristocracy and meritocracy. The third path is the ethics of ancient Greeks such as Socrates, Plato, and Aristotle, which maintains that only the informed and mature mind can judge—according to the circumstances—when love should rule and when power should dominate, an approach that suggests a merger of the feminine and masculine virtues. This ethical system also identifies virtue with intelligence and advocates a synthesis of aristocracy and democracy in government.[1]

Spinoza the Synthesizer

Durant goes on to point out that Baruch Spinoza (1632–1677), who basically took the Greek path, was able in his ethics to reconcile these seemingly distinct ethical positions—to weave them "into a harmonious unity, and give us a system of morals which is the supreme achievement of modern thought."[2] Spinoza said that the goal of conduct is happiness, which is the presence of pleasure and the absence of pain. For Spinoza, however, pleasure and pain are relative, not absolute, and not static states, but transitions. He believed that we should act to seek what is useful, and this seeking the useful is virtue.

Spinoza was in large part an Aristotelian. He did not believe that one should sacrifice oneself to another's good, and he thought that egoism is needed for the supreme instinct of self-preservation. A person, for Spinoza as for Ayn Rand, must love self and seek what is useful. Personal striving is

1 Durant, *The Story of Philosophy,* 179–80.
2 *Ibid.,* 180.

good; attempts to block it are bad. Spinoza built his ethics not on altruism and the natural goodness of men and women, as do utopian reformers, and not on selfishness and the natural wickedness of human being, as do cynical conservatives, but on what he considered to be an inevitable and justifiable egoism. Spinoza's ethics taught that for a person to be weak is to be worthless.[3]

Like Nietzsche, Spinoza had little use for humility, for it implied absence of power, and Spinoza saw all virtues as forms of ability and power. He also saw remorse as a defect rather than a virtue. In many ways Spinoza's ideas resonate with a kind of Spartan coldness. But he struck a softer tone in his ethics. With this egoism he merges an ethics of altruism. He suggested that, in order to eliminate social ills, humankind must eliminate envy, recrimination, mutual belittlement, and hatred. He went on to say that hatred can be overcome by love much better than by reciprocated hate; in this he turned to the feminine virtues and away from his hard-line Nietzschean ethics. He even believed that love begets love. But according to Spinoza, hatred is a weakness revealing inferiority and timidity. So even in advocating such "feminine" virtues as love, Spinoza was really taking a hard line.

In essence Spinoza's ethics is rather more Greek than Christian; that is, he stressed reason over passion. But since humanity needs both reason and passion, he did not really oppose one against the other. He saw a need for passion to achieve freedom and a need for reason to achieve freedom's proper use. Neither passion nor reason should become passive, he thought. He believed that they should be used constantly, and in this he struck an existentialist note. According to Spinoza (and this is important for the journalist), persons are free only when they know, and they are free only when they passionately use this knowledge in responsible ways.

Spinoza's ethical journalist would use reason to keep passion under control. Spinoza would say of journalistic freedom that no journalist should be free from the restrictions of social justice. Acting from blind instincts should not be justified by freedom, for freedom is guided by reason only. If the journalist uses freedom for the good of society, guided by reason, then he or she becomes complete, has integrity, and, Spinoza adds, is wise. Such a person represents the dialectic. Absent is the aristo-

3 *Ibid.*, 181. See also S. E. Frost, Jr., *Basic Teachings of the Great Philosophers* (Garden City, N.Y., 1962), 92.

cratic self-complacency of Aristotle's hero, and absent also is the super-cilious superiority of Nietzsche's Overman. The synthesis is a person with "a more comradely poise and peace of mind."[4]

Finally, Spinoza believed that people who are good through reason, who are guided by rationality, desire and seek what is useful to them and have a Kantian imperative to desire nothing for themselves that they do not also desire for the rest of mankind. So Spinoza's ethics is essentially an altruistic or rational egoism that fits well with the middle way of freedom, which leads to ethical concern.

Four Perspectives on Ethics

One way to apply reason to ethics and to consider ethical problems is to differentiate among ethical perspectives, or ways of looking at ethics. Four significant perspectives are those of 1) the social scientists, 2) the casuists, or applied ethicists, 3) the moralists, and 4) the ethical theorists. It should be noted that these perspectives are not mutually exclusive and that often a person can deal with ethics from more than one of them.[5]

The social scientists attempt to describe how various people or groups behave, what their systems of values are, and the like. They are the empiricists of ethical study. Their dialogue is mainly descriptive, but they may or may not draw conclusions from their study. Their examination of moral behavior yields definitions, classifications, and generalizations. They observe and compare customs, morals, and laws in different societies and formulate theories about the role of ethics in a society. They are mainly concerned with what is called "descriptive ethics."

The casuists who are also known as special-case ethicists, try to decide specific cases involving moral issues by drawing on moral principles, laws, religious tenets, and related bodies of thought. They deal with individual moral problems, serving as moral guides or advisors to individuals or groups in their choice of action. They might also be called "applied ethicists"; they bring to bear ethical principles that are felt to be relevant to particular cases and judge the rightness or wrongness of an action in view

---

4 Durant, *Story of Philosophy*, 185. See also Baruch Spinoza, *The Ethics: The Road to Inner Freedom*, trans. R. H. M. Elwes (New York, 1957).

5 Ethel Albert, T. C. Denise, and S. P. Peterfreund, *Great Traditions in Ethics* (Belmont, Calif., 1984), 3–4.

of the circumstances of the case. Their main purpose is to resolve particular ethical quandaries.

The moralists are ethically concerned persons who prescribe the right way for humanity and attempt to persuade people to follow it. Quite often they are opinion leaders in society, such as literary figures and religious leaders. Basically they are propagandists, and in some cases even ideologues, who want to promote their esteemed values for the improvement of their groups or communities. They want to convince others to follow their ethical positions. Thus, they are mainly persuaders and rhetoricians, and they deal with what is often called "prescriptive ethics."

Although perhaps similar in some ways to the casuists, the moralists deal with ethics or morality generally—in a broad sense—providing people with general guidelines for action rather than dealing with specific cases. In addition, they seek converts, unlike casuists, and are not satisfied with merely giving guidance on an *ad hoc* basis.

Finally, there are the ethical theorists. These persons deal with metaethics. They might also be called "macro-ethicists," since they are concerned with the most basic or foundational principles of morality. They attempt to answer questions about concepts of justice, mercy, right, wrong, duty, obligation, fairness, absolute versus relative ethics, and the like. Rather than treating normative or regulative aspects of ethics, the ethical theorists' main function is to deliberate about underlying assumptions in ethics and to critically analyze moral principles. However, they usually do deal to some degree with normative ethical concerns.

So there are different approaches to ethics. But the four that have been presented could easily be reduced to two: normative ethics and metaethics. All the theories of ethics from Aristotle to the modern pragmatists and existentialists attempt to show what is good and bad, right and wrong. These theories, in other words, are normative theories of ethics. They are the ethical paths, providing principles, guidelines, norms, or standards to follow; they tell us, concretely or abstractly, what we should and should not do.

Beyond normative ethics, each of the great moral philosophers also deals with metaethics. For example, they engage in semantic analysis of ethical concepts. The various philosophers also formulate and discuss ethical principles. Aristotle, for example, justified his ethical statements by reference to the goal (*telos*) of being fully human. Kant appealed to reason and duty; Mill, to the principle of utility and personal well-being;

Nietzsche to the strength of the individual will. Such analyses of ethical terms and principles, as opposed to the advocacy of a prescriptive ethics, belong to the field of metaethics.

The Nature of Ethics

What is good and what is evil? This is perhaps the most persistent question in the history of humankind. In spite of the great attention given it, however, there still is no completely satisfactory answer. Some have argued that there is an absolute, ultimate, unquestioned standard for good and evil, one that goes beyond special particular societies, eras, and circumstances. The Ten Commandments of the ancient Hebrews exemplify this absolutist, universalist moral approach. At the other extreme have been philosophers who thought that good and evil are relative to place, time, and other factors, and that thus one cannot expect all people in all situations to act in the same ways. And between these extremes are various other theories of ethical behavior.

There seem to be three main views of ethics from the perspective of appraisal of actions. There is the view that the morality lies mainly in the actor or person; this is often called the "intentional" (or will-oriented) theory. It is what the actor wills or intends that gives ethical meaning to the action. There is also the view that morality consists of following a maxim, a principle, from a sense of duty. That was Kant's position. Finally, there is the view that morality is defined by the consequences of an action. Good consequences mean good ethics. That was essentially the position of John Stuart Mill. These are the three main ways of looking at ethical theories, but there are many others. The journalist, seeking a road to follow, is faced with numerous ethical paths. The problem, perhaps, is not that there are inadequate guidelines, but that there are too many. Therefore, what the journalist does—as do we all—is to mix, merge, synthesize, and connect those paths that best seem to suit his or her basic philosophical, psychological, and religious inclinations.

The journalist thus typically comes up with a synthesized ethical position. Of course, there are some journalists who care little or nothing for ethics. Either they are nonethical (amoral) in their indifference, or else they are unethical (or immoral), purposefully disregarding the ethical path they have chosen for themselves.

The term *moral* is basically equivalent to the term *ethical*. The two words are actually etymologically synonymous. with the former coming from the Latin *mores* and the latter coming from the Greek *ethos*. Both *mores* and *ethos* refer to customary behavior. Usually the opposite of moral is immoral. A moral person is one who is good and who acts rightly, and an immoral person is one who is bad and acts wrongly. A person can also be amoral—meaning that moral issues do not enter into the situation. For instance, a journalist may type slowly or poorly, but ethics is not involved, since typing is an amoral activity. If he or she consciously distorts the facts of a story, then the journalist may be said to be immoral, though in such a case the term *unethical* would probably be used. It does not have quite the negative stigma of the word *immoral*. In addition, it should be noted that the antonym of *ethical* may be either *unethical*, which refers to wrong actions, or *nonethical*, which applies to actions (or to objects, such as trees) that are beyond, or immune to, ethical evaluation. In other words, *nonethical* is the rough equivalent of *amoral*.

What should a person do? What should a person avoid doing? What acts are good? What acts are bad? These are ethical questions. The core of ethics is morality, a set of fundamental rules that guide human actions. The moral standards that most persons follow are the ones adopted from parents, friends, and others of their own society. Whenever one defends or criticizes a moral belief, he or she is in the realm of ethics, where the various ethical paths are located. Some ethical theorists—the utilitarians—believe that any good moral rule should promote the greatest happiness for the greatest number. Other ethical theorists have seen it quite differently. For example, Aristotle and Kant argued that a good moral rule is one that helps people to act in the most rational way possible.

Four of the many different ways of thinking of ethics and justifying ethical beliefs are these: 1) Aristotelian ethics, based on Aristotle's concept of virtue and the idea that a person is a social and rational animal. Aristotle argued that being virtuous (disciplining one's feelings and acting rationally) helps a person to be fully human. 2) The ethics of David Hume and Jean Jacques Rousseau, according to which morality is essentially a matter of feeling. 3) Kantian ethics, which insists that morality is a matter of practical reason, divorced from personal desires and based entirely on universal principles. According to Kant, the ethical person acts solely out of a sense of duty to principle, refusing to consider consequences. 4) Utilitarian ethics, which, in contrast to Kant, states that moral rules are those that achieve the greatest good for the greatest number of people.

Utilitarians, who give a lot of weight to consequences, also try to reconcile the interests of the individual with the interests of society.

A Network of Ethical Paths

One set of paths that the various ethicists have laid out might be described in this way: 1) the Hedonist Path, exemplified by the Cyrenaics, Epicureans, and utilitarians; 2) the Path of Self-Realization, exemplified by Aristotle; 3) the Evolutionist Path, exemplified by Darwinian ethics and by Herbert Spencer's ethics of social evolution; 4) the Duty Path, exemplified by Kant's duty ethics; 5) the Naturalistic Path, exemplified by "natural ethics," transcendentalism, and Stoicism; 6) the Religious Path, exemplified by those who live by a holy book; and 7) the Existentialist Path, exemplified by the Kierkegaardian ethics of commitment, integrity, and authenticity.[6]

Indicating the complexity of ethical paths is the typology provided in 1984 by Ethel Albert, T. C. Denise, and S. P. Peterfreund, who discussed a total of twenty ethical systems. Here is the list, with a person or persons exemplifying each: knowledge and virtue (Plato), moral character (Aristotle), the pleasant life (Epicurus), self-discipline (Epictetus), the love of God (St. Augustine), morality and natural law (Thomas Aquinas), self-interest (Thomas Hobbes), nature and reason (Spinoza), conscience in morality (Joseph Butler), morality and sentiment (David Hume), duty and reason (Kant), the greatest happiness principle (J. S. Mill), the transvaluation of values (Nietzsche), scientific method in ethics (John Dewey), the indefinability of Good (G. E. Moore), prima facie duty (W. D. Ross), ethics as emotive expression (A. J. Ayer and C. L. Stevenson), ethics as radical freedom (Simone de Beauvoir), good reasons in ethics (Kurt Baier), and ethics and social justice (John Rawls).[7]

Clifford Christians has provided five basic paths for the ethicist. They are 1) Aristotle's Golden Mean, which locates virtue between two extremes; 2) Kant's categorical imperative, according to which a person should act on the maxim that he or she wills to become universal; 3) John Stuart Mill's principle of utility, which seeks the greatest happiness for the

---

6 See Porter, *The Good Life: Alternatives in Ethics*. The book is organized to fit this typology of ethical systems.

7 Albert, Denise, and Peterfreund, *Great Traditions in Ethics*.

greatest number; 4) Rawls's "veil of ignorance," which teaches that "justice emerges when negotiating without social differentiations"; and 5) the Judeo-Christian principle of treating persons as ends, which urges, "Love your neighbor as yourself."[8]

Many other typologies of ethical paths could be given, but generally they are variations on the ones already presented. There are absolutist and relativist paths, rationalist and instinctivist paths, formalistic and consequence-oriented paths, egoistic and altruistic paths, secular and religious paths, contextual and universal paths, optimistic and pessimistic paths, authoritarian and libertarian paths, socialist and capitalist paths, individualist and collectivist paths, paths of self-realization and paths of social service, conservative and liberal paths, and on and on.

Seldom does any one of these paths run discretely through the thickets of daily journalistic experience. A path will normally merge with, and exhibit many of the characteristics of, other paths. Seldom does a journalist take only a single path—unless it is a dialectical path. It is quite common for egoistic paths to exhibit signs of altruism and for rationalist paths to have an admixture of emotion and instinct. Paths are constantly changing, merging, narrowing, and widening. And often the substantive nature of a path is quite different from the label it carries, because, unfortunately, language is unable to keep up with the ever new reality produced by the changes and connections of the dialectic.

Justifying Journalistic Conduct

Most journalists are not satisfied with simply practicing their craft in a mechanistic manner from day to day. They feel compelled to evaluate their performance, not merely in terms of technique, but also in terms of their purposes, motivations, and values. They normally wish to know if their conduct toward others is right or wrong, just or unjust, fair or unfair. Not only do they want to justify themselves and their work to others, but they also want to justify it to themselves. In short, they are concerned with ethics.

They are constantly measuring their conduct against some ideal that they have as a standard. To some journalists this standard is conscience, to

8 Clifford G. Christians, K. B. Rotzoll, and Mark Fackler, *Media Ethics: Cases and Moral Reasoning* (New York, 1983), 9–17 *passim*.

others it is God, and to others it is a desire to reach a higher stage in self-development. Whatever the motivation, it usually comes into play during times of introspection and deliberation. The great majority of journalists want to have good reasons to support their actions and commitments. In other words, they raise ethical questions and try to develop strong grounds for doing what they do and for not doing what they do not do.

How can the journalist justify his or her values and ethical actions? It cannot be done scientifically. There are no empirical tests that can be used, though the utilitarians came close with their "greatest happiness" principle. When a journalist says that sources should be quoted accurately and fully the statement may be seen as merely a personal opinion or private desire on the part of the journalist, revealing something about his or her belief system or psychology. It is, indeed, difficult to justify values, to prove anything in ethics. But this does not mean that one should despair and not try. Although scientific empiricism is inadequate in ethics, this does not mean that there are no criteria at all to use in separating the good from the bad, the better from the best.

One standard that is important is reasonableness. A person often chooses an ethical action most in accord with reason. Or if reason demands it, the person can combine several theories or use parts of more than one to form a better theory. Application of a standard of reasonableness to an ethical stance concerning a situation means that the ethical stance must 1) be consistent with itself, 2) consider all the relevant facts, and 3) provide the most probable interpretation of human experience.

A theory that one should always tell the truth, for example, is consistent within itself, and it can be carried out conscientiously. But it fails, in a moral sense, to take into consideration certain consequences of actions based on it. Many journalists would consider consequences an integral part of an ethical decision. Simply giving all of the truth (*e.g.,* the name of a rape victim) might not be as ethical as not giving all of the truth.

All relevant facts must also be considered. It is not good enough to consider only some of the facts or principles in an ethical situation. For example, there is the principle that, for the development of truth, it is good or necessary for a pluralism of facts and ideas to be made known. But one must not forget that audiences can extract erroneous facts and distorted perspectives from such a pluralism of information. In short, falsehood as well as truth may flow from the principle of pluralism.

When a journalist assumes that he or she was not promoted or did not

THE DIALECTIC IN JOURNALISM

get a certain desired assignment because of failure to please the editor or do a good job on a prior assignment, such an interpretation may not be the most probable. A little thought and investigation might show that the situation resulted from a number of impersonal factors—such as a cut in the budget, the hiring of new reporters and editors, or a renovation project that siphoned away salary money. Journalists—whether thinking about themselves or others—must take care to provide the most probable interpretations of events. All three factors must be considered when one tries to apply a standard of reasonableness to ethical matters.

The Journalist and Ethical Concern

Seeking and following an ethical path is an exciting activity for the journalist. It forces the journalist to consider basic principles, values, and obligations to self and to others. It forces the journalist to decide how he or she will live, conduct journalistic affairs, think of self and others, and act and react to people and issues. Ethics has to do with duty—duty to self and duty to others. It is individual and social, for the quality of human life has to do with both solitude and sociability. We do right or wrong by ourselves in that part of our lives lived inwardly and also in that part of our lives in which we are reacting and responding to other persons. This duality or synthesis of individual and social morality is implicit in the very concept of ethics. The journalist, for example, is not simply writing for the consumption of others, but as *self*-expression. What the journalist communicates is in a very real way what he or she is. Journalists please or displease themselves—not just those in their audiences. What they do to live up to some standard within themselves not only affects the activities and beliefs of others but the very essence of their own lives.

A concern for ethics is important. Journalists who have this concern obviously care about good or right actions; such a concern indicates an attitude that embraces both freedom and personal responsibility. It indicates also that the journalists desire to discover norms for action that will serve as guiding principles or specific directives in achieving the kind of lives that they think most meaningful and satisfying. Ethical concern is also important because it forces the journalist to commitment, to thoughtful choosing among alternatives. It leads the journalist to seek the *summum bonum,* the highest good.

What characterizes most journalists today is a lack of commitment and consistency, even a lack of a coherent life plan. Before journalists choose any ethical path, they must decide whether or not to be ethical: this is the first and most important choice. However, it may well be, as Sartre and other existentialists have believed, that "not to choose is already to have chosen" and that the "refusal to choose the ethical is inevitably a choice for the nonethical." There is a tendency today to identify as ethical any personal decision to act. Any action one wants to perform can be justified in some way. Many persons therefore think it is an ethical act. Hazel Barnes has pointed out that this is exactly what has happened to religion: "An age which is willing to apply the term 'religion' to communism, aesthetic awe, devotion to one's fellow man, and allegiance to impartial demands of pure science has no difficulty in labeling any guiding motif or choice a personal ethics." If this position is accepted, it means that no one is really nonreligious or nonethical, and if that is true, then all meaning will have been drained from the words *religion* and *ethics*.[9]

Ethics is the branch of philosophy that helps journalists determine what is right to do in their journalism; it is a normative science of conduct, with conduct considered primarily as self-determined, voluntary conduct. Ethics has to do with "self-legislation" and "self-enforcement"; though it is related to law, it is of a different nature. Law often stems from the ethical values of a society at a certain time (*i.e.,* law is often reflective of ethics), and law is something that is socially determined and socially enforced. Ethics, on the other hand, is personally determined and personally enforced—or should be. Ethics should provide journalists certain basic principles or standards by which they can judge actions to be right or wrong, good or bad, responsible or irresponsible.

It is well to establish that ethics deals with *voluntary* actions. If a journalist has no control over decisions or actions, then there is no need to talk of ethics. What are voluntary actions? Those that a journalist could have done differently. Sometimes journalists, like other persons, try to excuse their wrong actions by saying that these actions were not personally chosen but assigned to them—or otherwise forced on them—by editors or other supervisors. Such coercion may indeed occur in some situations in which the consequences to the journalist for failing to follow orders may be dire. But an American journalist is able to "will" most

9 Barnes, *An Existentialist Ethics,* 7, 5.

journalistic actions—at least to a considerable degree—and in doing so can exhibit ethical strength and authenticity.

The journalist's culture, of course, largely determines his or her basic ethical stances or suggests which moral paths are appropriate in the practice of journalism. Cultures instill habits, values, desires, and prohibitions, all of which are reinforced, or in some instances modified, by individual ideals and goals. Some ethicists see individualizing ethics as detrimental to cultural sanctions, and permissiveness as an outgrowth of privatizing morality. Others, however, see a greater need for a kind of private or personal ethics, a rational breaking away from majoritarian or socially sanctioned ethics. Regardless of the "paths" of ethics one chooses, there is a fundamental unease among journalists over the moral condition of the press, which can be considered healthy. At least it shows a concern, "an itch to be moral," and evidences a recognition that all is not right.

Journalists need an ethics that admits change, that looks at morality as an ongoing process. As Walter Lippmann stressed in a number of his works, the person who fails to recognize the importance of change is doomed to failure. An extreme version of this emphasis on change is seen in pragmatic moral philosophers such as John Dewey and William James. And a kind of relativism also can be found in the thought of Joseph Fletcher and other so-called "situation ethicists," who stress the primacy of the individual over general moral principles. This stance, of course, opens the door to "exceptions" (flexibility) in ethical action. Many journalists, however, find this situationism too frustrating and demanding; they seek moral principles, maxims, and laws to guide them and tell them when they are ethical and not ethical. Such a Kantian ethical legalism seems to lie deep within all journalists.

The Journalist and Virtue

Journalists who are concerned with ethics—with the quality of their actions—are, of course, desiring to be virtuous. Just what a virtuous journalist is, however, is somewhat circular and leads back to the question, What is a moral or ethical person? However, the nature of virtue is not really so relative or vague if one has any respect for the great thinkers of history; there has been a large measure of agreement among philosophers generally, even though "virtue" has been conceptualized in terms that contain considerable semantic noise.

The virtuous journalist is one who has respect for, and tries to live by, the cardinal virtues that Plato discusses in *The Republic*.[10] First is wisdom, which gives direction to the moral life and is the rational, intellectual base for any system of ethics. Wisdom is part natural and part acquired, combining knowledge and native abilities; it largely comes from maturing, from life experiences, and from contemplation, reading, conversing, and study. Second, there is courage, which keeps one constantly pursuing his or her goal, the goal that wisdom has helped set. Courage is needed to aid journalists in resisting the many temptations that would lead them away from the path that wisdom shows.

The third virtue is temperance, the virtue that demands reasonable moderation or a blending of the domination of reason with other tendencies of human nature. It is this virtue, giving harmony and proportion to moral life, that helps one avoid fanaticism in pursuit of any goal. Finally, there is justice, which is different from the other cardinal virtues in that it refers more specifically to social relations. Justice involves considering a person's "deservedness." Each person must be dealt with, but this does not mean that each person has to be treated like every other. For example, justice would not require that every person elected to a city, state, or national office receive equal attention on television or the same amount of space in a newspaper. Equal treatment simply does not satisfy deservedness and does not imply just coverage.

One sign of virtue in a journalist may well be a deep loyalty to truth. At least the pursuit of truth by the journalist surely takes wisdom, courage, temperance, and justice. John Whale, a former editorial writer for London's *Sunday Times* and now a staff member of the British Broadcasting Corporation, contends that at the base of journalistic ethics is an allegiance to truth. It is the authenticity of the information contained in the story that is the journalist's chief ethical concern, according to Whale. What methods should a journalist use in trying to get at this "truth"? Whale believes the journalist should use only those methods that he or she would be willing to publish as part of the story. This is one reason why Whale and many others are opposed to the passage of "shield laws." What is far more important than keeping a source's name secret, Whale maintains, is whether what the source says is true. It is hard to verify truth if the source's name is hidden from the public. This allegiance to truth and not to

10 See Josef Pieper, *The Four Cardinal Virtues* (Notre Dame, 1966).

some person (source) who reveals information is what is important. Too often those who reveal information and elicit the journalist's promise not to identify them have motives other than a desire to let the truth come out. Virtue in journalism, believes Whale, has to do with getting as much truth as possible into the story, and of course, the source of the information is part of the "truth" of the story.[11]

Most journalists think of truth as they do of objectivity—as temporary, splintered, and incomplete. Accuracy, fairness, balance, and comprehensiveness are generally related to objectivity by the journalist and, therefore, also are related to truth. Naturally, the main problem with such truth is that it must be considered in context with editorial authority. What truth—or what parts of what truth—will a journalistic medium choose to present? The New York *Times* replies, "All the News That's Fit to Print," thus proclaiming to all that certain matters (even if truthful or contributing to the truth) that are not considered "fit" will not be printed. Therefore, the *Times* is explicitly saying what journalists generally believe and practice: truth is what journalists consider fit to call truth, just as news is what they decide is news—nothing more and nothing less.

Consequences and Duties

Moral philosophers have at least given us a wide variety of alternative standards for determining virtuous actions. In general, these ethical standards boil down to two main ones: *teleological* theories and *deontological* theories. Teleological theories consider the moral rightness or wrongness of an action as the good that is produced. Deontological theories hold that something other than (or sometimes in addition to) consequences determine which actions are morally right or good.

Teleologists look at the consequences of an act; they consider consequences as the sole determinant of the moral rightness or wrongness of actions. Teleologists differ among themselves only over whose good it is that one ought to try to promote. Egoists, for example, hold that one should always do what will promote his or her own greatest good; this view was held by Epicurus, Hobbes, and Nietzsche, among others. Utilitarians—or ethical socialists—take the position that an act or rule of

11 John Whale, lecture at the School of Journalism, University of Missouri, Columbia, July 10, 1973.

action is right or good if and only if it is conducive to the greatest possible balance of good over evil everywhere. Some utilitarians, such as Jeremy Bentham and John Stuart Mill, have been hedonists, in that they believe that the good is the greatest happiness or greatest pleasure for the greatest number.

Ethical egoism, one of the teleological theories, holds that it is the duty of the individual to seek his or her own good. There is a lot to say in favor of this stance. For if one regards the goal of morality as perfection, it is likely that under this theory very little can be done to achieve the perfection of anyone other than oneself. A person may influence to some degree the activities of others, but one can control only his or her own activities. This is an Aristotelian ethical perspective; under it, self-perfection is the goal of a moral life.

The ethics of utilitarianism, on the other hand, holds that every person should seek the good of his or her group, community, nation, or world—as a whole. It claims, in a way, to combine the true elements of egoism and altruism, since the good of the group or community will include, of course, the agent's own good. Its appeal is that it sets no narrow limits on the range of moral obligations. One form of utilitarianism, the extreme altruistic stance, emphasizes the seeking of the good of other individuals with no regard for the agent's own good. That is the stance of self-sacrifice, with the emphasis being entirely on others.

Utilitarian ethical theory enthrones others—the group, collective, or society generally—and sees the good as that which benefits the life of the group or the society. This is usually called the ethics of collective altruism, and it has been expressed generally in terms of the utilitarian principle that good conduct is that which results in the greatest good to the greatest number. There are two practical problems with this theory: the problem of determining what is really good for most people and the problem posed by equating the good with majority opinion or action. The journalist, for instance, in deciding whether or not to present a story, has no sound way of knowing which of two or more actions will result in the greatest good to the greatest number, and can only guess and hope. The second problem leads the journalist to a kind of "give them what they want" ethical stance, abdicating personal commitment in favor of serving the majority.

Deontological theories are quite different from teleological ones, for they hold that something other than consequences determines which actions are morally right. Deontologists, who are often called "legalists," say that the important thing is the motive of the agent; an action is justified if the intentions of the doer are good, regardless of the consequences. A deontologist believes that producing the greatest possible happiness in the greatest possible number has nothing to do with morality and that personal satisfaction or gain is irrelevant to ethical action.

Kant is probably the best example of a deontologist. His basic principle, or supermaxim—the categorical imperative—lies at the base of his ethical system: "Act only on that maxim that you can at the same time will to be a universal law." Kant offered this maxim as the necessary principle for determining what more specific and concrete ethical rules persons should adopt to guide their behavior. He said in effect that a person is ethical only if he or she is—or would be—willing to have everyone act on this maxim. In other words, a person is acting ethically only if he or she would be willing to see everyone act the same way in a similar situation.

If one asks which actions are right, one is really asking for some method to identify right actions. Utilitarians say that right actions are those that maximize utility or that do the greatest good for the greatest number. Kant and other deontologists claim that right actions are those that pass the test of some personal and rationally accepted imperative. For Kant, for example, virtue had absolutely nothing to do with pleasure or with any other consequence.

Kant's formalistic ethics has been much criticized. By and large, the remarks in the following passage from Ayn Rand typify the spirit of much of this criticism: "As to Kant's version of morality, it was appropriate to the kind of zombies that would inhabit that kind of universe; it consisted of total, abject *selflessness*. An action is moral, said Kant, only if one has no desire to perform it, but performs it out of a sense of *duty* and derives no benefit from it of any sort, neither material nor spiritual; a benefit destroys the moral value of an action. . . . Those who accept any part of Kant's philosophy—metaphysical, epistemological or moral—deserve it."[12]

If consequences and states such as happiness are not important in determining ethical actions, then what is relevant must be something to do with basic maxims or principles. For the deontologists, what is important is the principle from which the action has been performed; in addition, the test applied to the maxim must be something independent of consequences. As Rand said, Kant saw duty to principle as absolutely necessary

12   Ayn Rand, *For the New Intellectual* (New York, 1961), 32.

for ethical action. The categorical imperative is not really a specific maxim from which one acts—rather it is a supermaxim, or grand principle, that serves to guide thinking about specific rules to be applied in specific cases. If a journalist accepts the categorical imperative, then it is unnecessary for him or her to carry around a printed code or creed with specific guidelines to follow. The guidelines are formulated on the basis of this supermaxim as the various occasions arise. If the guidelines followed for each case pass the test of the categorical imperative, then the action based on that supermaxim is ethically sound and the journalist may be considered virtuous.

Although Kant's philosophy has profoundly influenced Western thought, it is obvious that at least among modern intellectuals his strict and absolutist "duty ethics" has lost considerable appeal and force. Journalists, like many others, do not want to act solely out of duty; they feel that considering consequences is important to morality. A relativism or situationism is in ascendancy, an ethics that has a great appeal to those who like to think of themselves as rational and flexible. This new situationism is a kind of synthesis emerging from the clash of ethical legalism, on one hand, and ethical flexibility on the other.

Ethical Relativism: Seeking a Synthesis

The ethics of law, of duty and absolute obligation, is a little strong for most thinkers. So this legalistic stance in ethical thinking has been confronted by its opposite: antinomianism. The rebel against Kantianism and other legalistic ethics has accepted what might actually be considered a "non-ethics"—a completely different kind of morality that is against any rules. The antinomian has, in effect, tossed out all basic principles, precepts, codes, standards, and laws that might guide human conduct. Just as the legalist tends toward absolutist or universalist ethics, the antinomian tends toward anarchy or nihilism in ethics. Opposed to standards, the antinomian needs no a priori guidelines, directions, or moral rules, being satisfied to "play it by ear," making ethical judgments and decisions intuitively, spontaneously, emotionally, and often irrationally.

In journalism the antinomian is usually found in the free-wheeling ranks of rebellious journalists, among whom an antiestablishment stance is considered healthy. The antinomian journalist confronts mainstream journalism, making ethical decisions almost subconsciously. This ethical (or nonethical) system might be called "whim ethics," and its confrontation with mainstream journalism is not very potent or successful, because it is weakened considerably by a lack of rational force.

From the clash of these two ethical antinomies—legalism and antinomianism—a synthesis has developed that has had a significant impact on ethical thinking. It is usually known as "situation ethics." Although it is related to legalistic ethics more closely than it is to antinomian ethics in most of its characteristics, it does synthesize certain strains of both orientations. Like legalistic ethics, it is basically rational, and like antinomian ethics, it is relativistic and not tied securely to absolute principles. Situation ethics begins with traditional legalistic ethics but is willing to deviate from these basic principles when rationality and the situation call for it.

Another type of situationist is one who subscribes to what may be called "Machiavellian ethics." Maurice Cranston has pointed out that Machiavelli believed that persons, or at least statesmen, should not allow their relationships with other states always to be governed by the same ethical scruples that govern their dealings with private persons. Machiavelli's ethics, according to Cranston, were basically absolutist; he accepted one true morality, but believed the ruler should sometimes disregard it. As Machiavelli said in *The Prince,* the ruler "should not depart from what is morally right if he can observe it, but should know how to adopt what is bad when he is obliged to."[13] Machiavelli did not contend that the bad is anything other than bad; he contended only that bad things are to be done sparingly and then, if possible, only in a concealed manner.

Journalists like to point to Machiavellianism in others, especially government officials, but they themselves often operate under this variant of situation ethics. They usually contend that they believe in absolutes (such as giving their audiences the truth), yet they depart from such principles when they think they need to for some reason. The press would rather see Machiavellianism in government. This is natural and socially helpful, for certainly government is filled with myriad Machiavellian functionaries busy justifying to themselves (and sometimes to others) their departure from basic moral principles. The Machiavellian ethics of expediency is common in government, but journalists must not forget that it is also quite often found in the press.

Relativist or situationist ethical positions can be considered a part of

13   Maurice Cranston, "Ethics and Politics," *Encounter,* XXXVIII (June, 1972), 16–26.

"subjective ethics," for what one does in a certain situation is determined *subjectively* by the journalist at the time when an ethical decision is demanded. The temper of the times has thrust the subjectivist into a dominant moral position, or at least to the point of being in the majority. And for many persons today, if the majority believes something is ethical, then it is ethical. These are the days of the subjectivist, the relativist and the situationist. If there is to be a sense of duty, it is a kind of duty to situationism. These are the days when situationism and relativism have clashed with absolutism, and aspects of each are merging. But what the journalist must realize is that ethics contains both absolute principles and relative considerations. It is not a matter of either-or; it is a case of meaningful connections, of merger, of synthesis. What is demanded of the rational journalist is a respect for the dialectic.

Ethical Connections and Mergers

All of the various ethical paths and conceptual antinomies—teleology and deontology, relativism and absolutism, Kantianism and consequentialism, empiricism and existentialism, Platonism and Aristotelianism, feeling and reason, and on and on—might lead one to believe that they are so different that mergers are impossible. How can a teleologist, for example, follow the path of deontology, where respect for moral laws and principles in a kind of duty-bound or absolutist way is required?

This question can illustrate the merger of ethical paths. One can maintain that the journalist who respects ethical principles and feels a duty to abide by them sometimes simply needs to rethink the principles. Perhaps they are too narrow and too inflexible. What the deontologically inclined journalist might need to do is to synthesize his or her respect for definite principles with a more flexible, consequence-oriented stance that still retains a concern for principle. The fact is that, though it may be difficult, such a synthesis is possible, and the journalist needs only to think dialectically to achieve it.

There is no reason why an existentialist cannot be rational, why a mystical Platonist cannot also have a scientific, Aristotelian demeanor, why a relativist cannot have an absolutist ethical magnet pulling him or her back to basic moral principles, why the journalist who is Christian cannot use reason, and why the scientific ethicist cannot have intuitions and mystical experiences.

There is no reason why the ethical egoist cannot have sensitivity for the feelings and welfare of others, why the journalist who enshrines truth cannot—out of ethical principle—deviate at times from truth, why the journalist who looks to consequences for ethical value cannot also recognize ethical value in the intent or the will of a person, and why the ethical subjectivist cannot use this subjectivity to enhance or help reach ethical objectivity. Undoubtedly all of these "merged" ethical paths complicate the journalist's trip through the experiential territory of daily activity. Which path is the best one? This is a basic question.

Some paths are better marked and smoother than others; indeed, some paths seem to fade out in the underbrush of irrationality. Other paths are so narrow that it is difficult to squeeze along them at times. However, other paths are found to be quite effective in getting the journalist through the tangles of daily moral problems. Perhaps "paths" are the best analogy for ethical theories, for paths are not mutually exclusive avenues, each of which leads directly to its end or destination. But in morality, there is no reason why these paths cannot be considered as rational, though often overlapping, ways to reach a higher ethical level of experience. The important thing is that they are helpful in the moral progress of the journalist. The progressive nature of the paths, their mergers, and their connections indicate the spirit of the dialectic at work. And the journalist, immersed in this spirit, should be able to find the best paths—or mergers of paths—and proceed on the ethical journey with confidence and self-respect.

Eight

DEFINERS OF JOURNALISTIC ETHICS

Journalistic ethics, in the eyes of most journalists and other persons, is a vague area of concern with no agreed-upon authority. Books and articles, as well as pronouncements and speeches of all kinds, provide recipes for ethical behavior in the field of journalism. Persons and groups observe society and the press. They record data and proceed to dispense prescriptions and proscriptions on how to make the press more ethical and responsive to society.

The Hutchins Commission in the 1940s was an early and rather typical arbiter of press responsibility and ethical behavior among journalists in the United States.[1] Other persons and groups have followed, giving advice to American journalists for making their activities more responsible. These definers of responsibility, sitting on the baseline of media morality, judge journalistic actions against their own self-developed standards. This is, of course, exactly what the Hutchins Commission did, and myriad theorists of social responsibility have followed in the commission's footsteps.

The literature of journalism and communication is full of rhetoric about press ethics and responsibility—admonitions, directions, guidelines, and ethical codes. Today one can hardly hear a speech, attend a conference, or read a book or article on journalism without being plunged into a wilderness of pleonasm surrounding the subject of journalistic ethics.

Generally the overriding points of such rhetoric are that the press is

[1] Commission on Freedom of the Press, *A Free and Responsible Press.*

unethical and irresponsible, that it is getting worse all the time, and that something must be done about it. This plethora of criticism of the press's actions comes not only from ideological liberals but also from conservatives. It comes in the form of isolated bombasts, often in institutionalized declarations, from sensitive politicians, cynical academics, and so-called "average citizens" who are fed up with press excesses. It comes from Republicans and Democrats, socialists and capitalists, rich and poor—and even, increasingly, from journalists themselves.

Responsibility and Ethics

In the field of journalism the term *responsibility* can be used synonymously with *ethics* and often is; by and large, when one thinks of a responsible press, one thinks of an ethical press. Ethical journalism is responsible journalism. Acting responsibly is acting ethically. Perhaps there are shades of difference in the connotations of the two terms, but most journalists and press critics use the terms interchangeably, and they are so used here.

It should be pointed out that a journalist can, indeed, be responsible (in the sense of being accountable) to the editor by performing in a way that may well be unethical. But that is using the word *responsible* in a pragmatic sense, not in a moral sense. An authority may require "responsible" journalism, meaning journalism that conforms to the newspaper's policy or to the wishes of the editor. In such a situation, when a journalist deviates from policy or the editor's instructions, then that journalist can be considered "irresponsible." But I use the term *responsible* in a moral context to mean ethical. Responsible journalism is ethical journalism; a responsible reporter is an ethical reporter. Theodore Peterson put it this way: "The moral duties which are implicit in libertarianist theory become explicit in social responsibility theory."[2] Most writers on the subject, like Peterson, think of moral duties as having a direct relationship to social responsibility.

Those who contend that the American press is unethical are seeing in it some real or imaginary threat to the national security, to the public interest, or to those aspects of society that appear to these critics as most important. And those who might question the ethics of the press of the

2 Peterson, Siebert, and Schramm, *Four Theories of the Press,* 101.

Soviet Union, Iran, or Zaire, for example, would do so if in their views the press in these countries were exhibiting mannerisms that endangered the stability and progress of their respective national societies. *Responsibility* and *irresponsibility* are relative terms, like *ethics,* and must be handled gingerly, taking the particular circumstances and national system into consideration. Even within a single national society the terms have a multitude of meanings, depending on the degree of pluralism present.

Ethical Gurus Aplenty

It seems that everyone wants to dictate press morality—if not practically, at least theoretically. Even stalwarts of libertarianism such as James and John Stuart Mill evidenced the schizophrenia prevalent in this whole area. James Mill, perhaps the originator of the concept of the "watchdog" function of the press, advocated press freedom because it "made known the conduct of the individuals who have been chosen to wield the powers of government."[3] Would he, then, have cancelled liberty of the press for those press units that failed to live up to his rationale for such freedom? One is left contemplating that question, since Mill does not answer it.

And his son John Stuart Mill wanted to hold the individual to a high standard of responsibility to his fellow men. But he was a lover of freedom to the extent that he preferred that "the conscience of the agent himself" should enforce the agent's responsibility and that a free society should put few restrictions on its members' behavior.[4] And if the agent's conscience did not enforce his or her own responsibility, then what? Again, one is left wondering. One could in fact go on and on citing persons who have duties and responsibilities in mind that they want the press to accept. It appears that such definers of responsibility like to standardize their definitions; they seem generally dissatisfied with the idea of permitting each journalist and each medium to frame an individual sense of responsibility. There is something both noble and arrogant about such definers of responsibility.[5]

Almost everyone today seems to know what is wrong with the press and how it should change in order to be ethical or socially responsible. Increasingly one hears that the press is irresponsible or that this or that

3 Zashin, *Civil Disobedience and Democracy,* 25.
4 *Ibid.,* 49.
5 I developed this theme extensively in *The Imperative of Freedom.*

journalistic decision was unethical or in some way socially irresponsible. Few, if any, of these critics would admit that they want to dictate to the American press, but they are not reluctant to try to influence the press to come around to their concept of press responsibility. This shows a praiseworthy attitude of concern for ethics, but it also indicates a self-righteous and closed concept of morality. How can this goal of press responsibility be attained? What are the means of achieving responsible journalism? And which of the means is the best one? How do we know when responsible journalism has been achieved? Such questions are difficult, but they must be asked.

Underlying such questions is a basic one: Who defines or approves press responsibility? There are at least four principal ways that journalistic ethics can be defined. Elsewhere I have referred to them as "approbative theories" of press responsibility.[6] Under this scheme, the problem is to locate the defining, approving, and enforcing agent: Ethics or responsibility can be 1) legally defined by government, 2) professionally defined by the press organization, 3) pluralistically defined by the individual journalists themselves, or 4) defined by market forces.

Government as Definer

Americans could choose to accept the first way, allowing press responsibility to be defined by law and guided by the government. But this would be a direct affront to the First Amendment. Few persons would deny that if such a definer were accepted, the press would, in a sense, be more "responsible"—at least to the governmental and legal system. The amount of sensational material could be controlled in the press or eliminated altogether. Some kind of "proper balance" in the press could be maintained by following strict governmental guidelines. The press undoubtedly could be made to manifest a more positive attitude.

Under this approach, the press could be more progressive and socially helpful in the sense that news about the positive achievements of the society—stories about art exhibits, educational concerns, road building, upbeat political speeches, and national progress in general—could be

6 John C. Merrill, "Three Theories of Press Responsibility and the Advantages of Pluralistic Individualism" (Paper presented at the Annual Conference of the International Communication Association, Honolulu, May 23–27, 1985).

emphasized. In short, the press would stress the affirmative and eliminate or minimize the negative. Then with one voice the press of the nation would be responsible to its society; the definition of "responsible journalism" would be functional in a monolithic way—defined by the courts and monitored by functionaries of the government.

This model, of course, presumes a nonpress authority, and that would not find favor with many people who see in government interference a danger to society. In a way, this attitude is strange, even in a country such as the United States, since theoretically the government is "of the people, by the people, and for the people." Why should it be that government interference in the affairs of the press, especially in the area of social ethics and responsibility, is bad for the people or dangerous for society? As most people know instinctively, there are limits to freedom, and in the area of the press there is no better authority to set these limits than government. At least, this argument is often made by critics of a statist hue. As representatives of the people, such critics maintain, government should have the public interest as a priority and see to it that the press acts in such a manner as to enhance this public interest.

Government and the law are already involved in the press in many ways—such as mail subsidies, antitrust matters, libel and slander litigation, document classification, executive orders and policies, and Federal Communications Commission regulation of broadcasting. Certainly the case could be made that governmental and legal factors already restrain freedom of the American press, such restraint being justified in the name of ethics and social responsibility. Of course, in many other countries of the world, governmental and legal sanctions are much more overt, constant, and sometimes even draconian. But whatever the degree of interference, control, or guidance, or whatever press system is involved, it is always supposedly done for the good of society.

For government to have the power to define press responsibility can be good or bad, depending on the intelligence and moral consciousness of the government officials involved. So one could say that the model is not necessarily faulty; rather any weakness in such a system might stem from immoral or defective administrators within the system. This is also true of the other three approbative models. After all, the professional elite of the press can define press morality erroneously or unintelligently. So can individual journalists acting out of their own moral autonomy. And so can the market mechanism, composed as it is of people with varying degrees of moral concern and sophistication. Therefore, in theory at least, there is no logical reason why the governmental and legal model could not work as well as the others.

The Profession as Definer

In spite of the neatness and basic appeal of the governmental and legal model, it is the professional model that currently seems to be carrying the day, at least in the United States. Without a doubt it is more appealing constitutionally, and it does not smack so obviously of incipient governmental authoritarianism. This second approach—having press responsibility defined and regulated by the journalistic profession itself—is gaining much support in the United States and is even being championed around the world by UNESCO. The government would not be involved, it is maintained, and yet there would be an enforcement mechanism—all the professional screening and control normally found in exclusive professions. Large numbers of press people are, or want to be, on the road to professionalization today. In spite of its basic appeal for journalists, however, professionalization has some obvious dangers, and many journalists are cautious about proceeding too rapidly in that direction.[7]

The professionalizers are calling for a kind of system by which the press would regulate itself, with trappings of ethical codes, licensing, minimal entrance requirements, and a mechanism for ridding the profession of unsuitable journalists. This would not endanger the provisions of the First Amendment, they say, but would give incentives for the press to act responsibly. This professional model would, in fact, provide a solution to the problem. Journalists could forget about governmental and legal power over their field, forget about a pluralistically defined system of individual morality among journalists, and forget about the whims and crass appetites of the journalistic market. A professionalized journalism would pro-

---

7 Much has been written in recent years about journalism as a profession. See, for example, John Hohenberg, *The Professional Journalist* (New York, 1973). For a partial bibliography of such writings, see Marianne Allison, "A Literature Review of Approaches to the Professionalism of Journalists," *Journal of Mass Media Ethics*, I (Spring–Summer, 1986), 5–19. This entire issue was given over to articles about the professionalization of journalism. For a look at both sides of the question, see Dennis and Merrill, *Basic Issues in Mass Communication*, 149–60. Cf. Goldstein, *The News at Any Cost*, Chapter 8, for a view from a practicing journalist.

vide an institutional concept of responsibility—a kind of self-regulation—projected into the field of journalism. Therefore, advocates argue, the professional model would bring responsibility.

But would it? The field would, of course, be responsible in the eyes of the elite leaders in the profession who defined "responsibility." But would it be responsible journalism to every member of the profession, especially if, solely out of fear of being blacklisted, they conducted their activities according to this professional concept of responsibility? What is probably more important, would the professionally defined responsibility be accepted and supported by the citizenry, who would be the consumers of this "responsible" journalism? In a diversified and opinionated society such as the United States, there is no doubt that there would be considerable disagreement with much of this "socially responsible journalism" defined and practiced by the profession of journalists.

Pluralistic Individualism as Definer

Both the governmental and legal model and the professional model have as their main problem the restriction of individual journalistic freedom. The third approach, the pluralistic model, gives more emphasis to the personal ethical beliefs of the individual journalist. It seems to be philosophically more compatible with Anglo-American tradition than the first two. That tradition has stressed, at least since the time of John Stuart Mill, individual and independent editorial decisions and efforts to raise journalistic moral consciousness through sound education and competitive persuasion. But the emphasis is on individual journalists and on having a great pluralism or diversity of them.[8]

In this model of journalistic responsibility, the individual journalists set their own standards. In effect, each acts as the "court of last resort" for his or her ethical actions. This is self-determination of ethical practice in which the journalists themselves define, approve, and enforce their ethics without looking to some internal or external authority for guidance. It is obviously a theoretical concept, since in the practical world of journalism today, no journalist really has the ultimate power for such ethical definition. Always standing in the epicenter of power is some person such as the

8 An extensive case for pluralistic individualism and the market philosophy is provided in Merrill, *The Imperative of Freedom.*

editor or publisher, or some group or institution such as the government, the courts, or a professional organization, ready to define and enforce journalistic ethics.

Theoretical concept or not, the fact remains that such a model, expressing a pluralism of ethical concepts, is consistent with the individualistic philosophy that American journalism inherited from the Age of Reason. The acceptance of such a concept of journalistic responsibility would, in effect, represent a true journalistic freedom, something American journalism has never really had. It would shift freedom and responsibility to the individual journalist or to large portions of the working press population, and it would diminish the power of the corporation and the government. This is not a very likely prospect in our capitalistic system, which assumes rights of domination for employers and a willingness to submit to orders on the part of employees.

In spite of the unrealistic or idealistic nature of the pluralistic model, there is no doubt that journalists as individuals can—even under the employer-employee system—exercise far more autonomous ethical decision making than they usually do. There are many areas of responsible action and ethical definition that lie in the hands of individual journalists. Simple passivity, unconcern, and inaction are what keep most of them from creating their own ethical standards. This is the area in which the existentialist thrust should manifest itself, in which the journalist *wills* to choose his or her own ethics, to act accordingly, and to be ready to accept responsibility for these actions.

The Market as Definer

The fourth approach—the market model of press responsibility—is, like the pluralistic model, closely tied to American tradition. American society is diversified, having a large number of communications desires. The journalistic market caters to these desires, and in theory—and seemingly also in practice—provides a wealth of information and perspectives to satisfy the demands of these various consumers of messages. The objective of the market is to permit the maximum of individual and independent editorial decision making in what ideally will be a very pluralistic system. Media that people accept and support will survive and thrive; others will suffer and die. This may be thought of as the ultimate accountability under this model. And it is an accountability, market proponents believe, that is in harmony with the spirit of individualism, democracy, and freedom. However, critics contend that it may not be in harmony with the spirit of ethics or social responsibility. Many of them say that the market in fact cares little about morality and that it is an economic, not an ethical, barometer.

At any rate, at least five historical ideas have advanced and perpetuated the market model. Not necessarily in order of their importance, they are 1) the Age of Reason's emphasis on freedom and individualism; 2) the Protestant ethic's emphasis on hard work and competition, as explained by Max Weber in *The Protestant Ethic and the Spirit of Capitalism;* 3) social Darwinism, which applies the concepts of natural selection and survival of the fittest to business competition; 4) Adam Smith's theory of laissez-faire capitalism, according to which the law of supply and demand determines the flow of goods and services; and 5) Justice Oliver Wendell Holmes's concept of the marketplace of ideas, which updated Milton's seventeenth-century idea of the self-righting process, and according to which worthy ideas have the power to win out over unworthy ones in the open competition of the market.[9]

The media, in this model, become the market, or they serve on the informational and opinion level of society as the main foundation of the market. That the market be as free as possible is considered essential. For, according to this model, a free market provides the greatest chance to reach the truth, the best way to produce a full range of information, ideas, and opinion.

There are nine important tenets of the market approach to press responsibility: 1) The media should be as free from outside control as possible; 2) the media should be as diversified as possible; 3) the media should be competitive, seeking to gain and keep an audience in order to have a firm economic base; 4) the media providing needed services will survive and thrive, whereas those failing to do so will languish and possibly die; 5) the economic support of the media reflects the public satisfaction or dissatisfaction of the various audiences with these media; 6) the media are accountable to the people for their existence and growth; 7) changes in the media are needed when public support wanes; 8) when public support increases, it is a sign of public satisfaction with the medium; 9) the media

9   John C. Merrill, "The Marketplace: Court of First Resort" (Paper presented at conference on media freedom and responsibility at the Gannett Center for Media Studies, Columbia University, New York, April 3, 1986).

are directed—indirectly—by the people, who demand that their wishes be fulfilled.[10]

Several assumptions of the market model should also be noted. First, there is the assumption of an audience that is informed about, and concerned with, ethics. Another assumption is that the audience is expressive and largely monolithic. Seemingly built into such a model is also a kind of Platonic assumption that when people know the good, they will do the good. In fact, the market model goes further and assumes that people, if they know the good, will see to it that others (in this case, the media managers) know and do the good.

The market approach holds that media are accountable to the public in the sense that they are rewarded (they gain circulation or viewership and thereby profits) or are punished (they lose circulation or viewership and possibly go out of business) to the degree that they satisfy or fail to satisfy the desires and expectations of their audiences. The whole process is seen in terms of a simple interaction. As Herbert Altschull has said, "If the reader reacts negatively to the content of his newspaper, he will cease to buy it, and the newspaper will be forced to modify its behavior in order to survive in the marketplace."[11] But it is not quite that simple. Individual or isolated readers, by ceasing to buy the newspaper, cannot force a modification in its behavior. *Many* readers would have to be alienated or outraged by the newspaper's actions, and what is clear from readership surveys is that readers typically like some things and dislike others in a particular newspaper. They seldom cancel subscriptions because of a dislike for portions of a newspaper or for particular stories. Also, they must consider what they can get to replace the cancelled newspaper. It is a complex situation that shows one of the big weaknesses of the market approach to assuring press responsibility.

The Responsibility Question Pursued Further

American troops in 1984 invaded the Caribbean island of Grenada. The press was not permitted to land with the troops to cover the initial phases of the operation. The majority of journalists saw this as irresponsible on the part of the government, since the press did not have the freedom to go in. However, according to the majority of Americans, the press could not

10   *Ibid.*
11   Altschull, *Agents of Power*, 289.

have been responsible if it had gone in with the troops to provide coverage. Such coverage would have been responsible (according to journalists) *and* irresponsible (according to the public). So the question arises: Based on this particular case, who determines responsible press action—the government, which kept the press out? The journalists, who wanted in? Or the majority of citizens, who sided with the government?

Press responsibility, it would appear, is in the eye of the beholder or commentator. If one wants something of the press and it is not forthcoming, then that person calls the press irresponsible. If the person wants something and gets it, then he or she calls the press responsible. As Arthur Ochs Sulzberger, publisher of the New York *Times,* said in a speech at Yale in 1984, "There seems to be a growing feeling that our free press is not consistently enough a responsible press, and that both regulation and punishment are called for."[12] Sulzberger made it clear that he wanted responsibility defined by the individual news decision makers in the press—at least in *his* newspaper. He also made it clear that he did not want it defined by the government or by the courts. A decade earlier, he likewise made it clear that he did not want it defined by a presumably independent body such as a press council. Sulzberger did not cooperate with the now-defunct National News Council and in fact was an outspoken critic of it.[13]

Sulzberger's position seems to be the classic position of American journalism, in spite of the voices one hears in favor of press responsibility being defined from outside the press. More and more there are calls for a responsible press, even if it must be brought about by government and law. Here is the position of Walter Berns, a well-known conservative political scientist: "Whatever the tension that exists between them, a responsible press need not be the opposite of a free press; and a government that, through its law, acts to promote a responsible press is not by that fact the opposite of a free government. Not only are such laws not incompatible with free government, they may be a necessary condition of it."[14]

Journalists would probably all agree that a responsible press is prefera-

---

12   William R. Greer, "Publisher of the *Times* Cites Concern for Press in Second Reagan Term," New York *Times,* November 11, 1984, Sec. A, p. 3.

13   See Richard S. Salant, "The Late—or Too Soon—National News Council," *Journalist,* II (October, 1984), 6–11, for a good summary of the problems leading to the death of the NNC.

14   Walter Berns, "The Constitution and a Responsible Press," in Harry Clor, Jr. (ed.), *The Mass Media and Modern Democracy* (Chicago, 1974), 135. For a more thorough explication of Berns's ideas for making the press more responsible through outside intervention, see his *Freedom, Virtue, and the First Amendment.*

ble to an irresponsible press. Certainly the press should be responsible to *someone's* concept of responsibility. But many critics seem to want the press to be responsible to *everyone* at the same time. Of course, any reasonable person knows that this is not possible. Interests conflict, reportorial perspectives vary, editorial biases go in different directions, and perceptions of readers and audiences are not the same. One person's responsible journalism may well be another's irresponsible journalism.

Berns's plan would remedy, at least to some degree, this relativism in the responsibility concept. Laws can probably be written that would force all segments of journalism to accept certain ways of doing things. And this idea is popular with many people who sincerely want to see a better press and a more responsible journalism. But to carry out this remedy would be extremely difficult in view of the First Amendment. But the First Amendment can be changed, many say, and perhaps one day it will be.

Another remedy might be proposed—other than the normal array of pressures on the press (such as press councils, critical journalism reviews, and letters to the editor)—and this is to raise the consciousness of journalists to a higher moral level at which they will voluntarily act more in accord with their own ethical principles.[15] This, of course, would not require institutional or structural change. Journalists in the United States already have the option to act responsibly, or to try to, according to their own standards. So in a way, at least for the present, one is back to the beginning. The question of responsibility in journalism, as always in an open society, today must be settled by the personal definitions of the persons who use it and by the market forces in the society, in line with the pluralistic model and the market model. In addition, laws, government policy, and professional direction, in line with the governmental and legal model and the professional model, will continue to be used to some extent as supplemental definers and enforcers of press responsibility.

Professionalization is becoming ever more popular as a definer and enforcer, but it raises problems. Even if the profession of journalism develops to the point that it can mandate that its members, for example, always

15 The literature of journalism is filled with books, chapters of books, and articles dealing with individual ethical perspectives. Admonitions abound for journalists to raise their moral consciousness. Feedback mechanisms such as audience surveys, op-ed pages, letters to the editor, courses in ethics, and ethical conferences and workshops have been used. See the Hutchins Commission's report for a lengthy plan designed to enable journalists and media to perform more responsibly.

reveal their sources of information, the controversy about responsible journalism will not be over. Even if all journalists were to conform to certain "ethical" standards set by the profession, the question of whether what they were doing was responsible would still exist. In the future the general rules (and their exceptions), will have, as they have had in the past and have today, their proponents and opponents. There is no way in a free and open society to settle once and for all this question of press responsibility.

A free press will always be considered responsible by some and irresponsible by others. Some individual press units and parts of press units will be considered responsible by some and irresponsible by others. Some persons will consider them responsible in some situations, irresponsible in others. Some persons will consider them both responsible and irresponsible to some degree. There is no way around it, short of adopting an authoritarian system under which some totalitarian or monolithic concept of responsibility is forced upon the entire press. This would, of course, pretty well settle the question from the point of view of the press, but a deeper question would persist: Is the press fulfilling its responsibility toward the society if it is forced to act according to a single standard?

The pluralistic and market models, under which American society has been operating, have certainly not eliminated charges that the press is irresponsible. Thus, as theories designed to eliminate differences of opinion about responsibility, these two models are certainly no better than the other two; they may even be inferior to the others. But no theory will prove completely satisfactory in this respect. The pluralistic and market models have the advantages of both retaining a maximum degree of freedom for the press and assuring a greater diversity of messages and practitioners than would probably result under either or both of the other two models. In the area of journalistic ethics, however, individualistic approaches have often had serious shortcomings, mainly in their stress on egoistic concerns and their neglect of larger social considerations. These weaknesses should certainly be noted. In spite of these weaknesses and the facts that societies are getting more complex and that institutions are bigger and harder to control, it is perhaps too early to rush headlong into collectivistic "solutions" without reconsidering the strengths of individualistic approaches.

Friedrich Hayek has warned against tendencies that would organize and direct intellectual pursuits, and certainly journalism is one such pursuit. In his classic work *The Road to Serfdom,* he wrote:

It may indeed be said that it is the paradox of all collectivist doctrine and its demand for "conscious" control or "conscious" planning that they necessarily lead to the demand that the mind of some individual should rule supreme—while only the individualistic approach to social phenomena makes us recognize the super-individual forces which guide the growth of reason. Individualism is thus an attitude of humility before this social process and of tolerance of other opinions and is the exact opposite of that intellectual *hubris* which is at the root of the demand for comprehensive direction of the social process.[16]

Hayek touches on the centrality of individualism—tolerance of other opinions. This is at the root of the theory of the pluralistic model as it impinges on the concept of press responsibility. By tolerating other opinions (even concerning the nature of press ethics), neither journalistic eccentricity nor press pluralism is discouraged. The result is a theory congruent with the basic avowed values and traditions of the American press and American society. But it should be noted that such a theory may be compatible with these values and traditions and still not lead to ethical or social responsibility.

In addition to those represented by the four models, other definers of press responsibility might be suggested. Individual media managers or employers might do it. Another possibility is a "theological" model. But though it is true that a church or a holy book can greatly encourage responsibility, both seem marginally relevant in the area of *press* responsibility.

Of the four approaches I have discussed, the pluralistic model seems to have the greatest number of advantages for American society. One major disadvantage of it is that there is no assurance that press ethics or media responsibility will improve; in fact, there is at least an equal chance that the moral situation of both the press and society will get worse.

This last problem is important and raises a compelling objection to the pluralistic model as a definer and enforcer of press ethics. This objection is that pluralistic individualism simply ignores the matter of press ethics and

16 Friedrich Hayek, *The Road to Serfdom* (Chicago, 1944), 165–66. See also an excellent discussion of responsibility in the context of individualism and existentialism in Thomas Flynn, *Sartre and Marxist Existentialism* (Chicago, 1984), parts I and II.

evades the evidence of public dissatisfaction with the way segments of the press actually operate. And it is true that this approach does at least appear to ignore ethics. But actually it does not *necessarily* ignore ethics; it simply puts ethics in the hands of the individual rather than of a group or institution. It places the ethical burden on the individual journalist—where it always falls ultimately—and seeks to attain, through the journalist's education and voluntary exposure to moral thinking, the progress in the areas of press responsibility and media ethics that is healthy and desirable for free people.

The acceptance or retention of the pluralistic and market models, of course, will not eliminate criticism of the press or dissatisfaction with its news and editorial decisions. To assure some social consciousness on the part of the press, there is a need to combine or merge all four models, including the legal and governmental model and the professional model. Such a synthesis of the four models would preserve freedom while insisting on responsibility. If a nation tries too hard to achieve press responsibility—by systematic, instrumental means—it runs the risk of sacrificing freedom. And if it neglects responsibility because of a passion for freedom, it faces the great danger of being unethical and using press freedom irresponsibly, a situation that also might lead to the sacrifice of freedom. A merger leading to a middle way is what is needed from the four models. And such a merger is well under way. The dialectic is very much at work.

Pointing Toward a Synthesis

At a time when a wide variety of analysts are bemoaning the press's arrogant concern with its own rights and insisting that the public be considered more important in press affairs, a group known as the Critical Theorists are making great progress in getting beyond the basic libertarian paradigm and pushing into socially relevant frontiers in which wider participation in public communication is possible. These communications scholars are providing substantial critical foundations for the public's dissatisfaction with the press, which has been growing since World War II. The insights and proposals of the Hutchins Commission are being taken seriously in the essays and books of the Critical Theorists.

They are, in short, doing much to give a counterbalance to the press-centered journalistic paradigms of American tradition; they are proposing that a "people-centered" factor be taken into account. From the clash of these antinomic orientations should come a concept of journalism with greater stress on ethics or responsibility and reflective of the concerns and values expressed by the Hutchins Commission in the 1940s.

The Critical Theorists derive much of their intellectual vigor from the so-called "Frankfurt School" in Germany, which showed great concern about alienated audiences of the media and about the people's powerlessness in the face of the media. They also have a deep-rooted suspicion of the status quo. Today they are interjecting certain Marxist orientations into communications research and criticism, and it is no longer possible to assert the efficacy of classical liberalism or the advantages of press libertarianism without being challenged.

The emphasis in mainline academic circles has been shifting since World War II from the media to the people, from press rights to people's rights. This trend has gained momentum as students of the 1960s have found themselves increasingly the young researchers, teachers, and social critics of today. Institutions—especially capitalistic ones—have become suspect, and empirical researchers are being replaced by critical analysts who are not reluctant to use their ideologies, biases, and passions in efforts to change society. Describing social problems is no longer enough; the essential thing is to have an impact on them. Theory alone is inadequate, they say; it must be harnessed to practice and concepts for fostering social justice. This pragmatic emphasis at least partially explains why theory and research seem to be enthroning the audiences and dethroning the communicators and media institutions—at least in the capitalist countries.

Media-centered paradigms are being challenged by audience-centered paradigms. The dialectic is at work. Theoretical attention is being given to analyzing audience needs, frustrations, and alienation; less and less attention is given to the problems and functions of the media themselves. Increasing attention is placed on audience desires, fears, hopes, and freedoms, and concomitant emphasis is being given to the media's shortcomings, obligations, and duties. Among others, the Critical Theorists, abroad and in the United States, are leading in this new scholarly direction.

Proponents of Critical Theory see it as a diverse and innovative approach to media criticism. They see it as seeking alternative press models, focusing on the sources of media power, being concerned with media dominance over oppressed social groups, and subjecting the status quo to much-needed criticism that will lead to social transformation. Behind all the work of the Critical Theorists is one priority—to demonstrate how capitalistic forces, operating in mass communication, enhance the power of a few media owners while diminishing the public's power and oppressing the people generally.[17]

Opponents of Critical Theory see it as dull, negative, and obsessed with media ownership and communications empires. They find Critical Theory destructive of Western capitalistic journalism, too unrelentingly Marxist, ethically unclear and politically unrealistic, scornful of empirical research, seduced by big words and fashionable jargon, prone to overgeneralize, and inclined to assume what it cannot demonstrate.[18]

But the new emphasis supplied by the Critical Theorists appears to be soundly entrenched. Robert A. White of London's Centre for the Study of Communication and Culture has sought to put Critical Theory's new dialectical emphasis, search for new journalistic approaches, and growing popularity into perspective. Scholarship must, according to White, give more attention to "authoritarianism *in the media,* media linkage with powerful interests, the roles and rights of receivers, the unmasking of self-serving ideologies of the media, and the power and mechanisms of social control in the media."[19]

It is difficult to disagree with White's observation that there is an "increasing interest in participatory communication, demand for public access to media channels, insistence on balancing libertarian rights of the media with the public's right to know, media reform movements, and the spread of education for critical use of media, and the greater appreciation of the value of popular culture."[20] The state of concern summarized by White is far advanced in Europe and in many places in the Third World, and it is also, more slowly, making inroads in the United States. Such a concern is clashing with—and merging with—the older press-centered emphasis.

In view of these tendencies in scholarship and social concern, it is quite natural that theories of pluralistic individualism (with their emphasis on individual journalists) and of market journalism (with their emphasis on competition) are outside the main channels of the new contemporary

17　Michael Real, "The Debate on Critical Theory and the Study of Communications," *Journal of Communication,* XXXIV (Autumn, 1984), 72–78.

18　*Ibid.*

19　Robert A. White, "Mass Communication and Culture: Transition to a New Paradigm," *Journal of Communication,* (Summer, 1983), 283.

20　*Ibid.*

theorizing. Journalist-centered theories (the thesis), already weak in 1974, when I wrote *The Imperative of Freedom,* have further eroded; audience-centered theories (the antithesis) and the concomitant criticism of institutionalized journalism have crowded in on them. A synthesis is under way.

This trend to lessen the press's power, to limit its freedom, to restrict its options, and to stress its ethical responsibilities has as its goal the restoration of a kind of balance in journalism. Critical Theorists, with their strong ideological proclivities, populist concerns, and social agenda, have taken up the banners of the Hutchins Commission of the 1940s and are effectively criticizing the Western press and shaking the very foundations of liberal theory. Marx and Locke are, in a sense, waging a vigorous battle. There is always hope that the vaunted dialectical process will push journalism to a synthesis position at which press freedom is protected in its essentials while the audience's desires and expectations are realized.

Nine

DEONTELIC ETHICS: A SYNTHESIS

For a long time now the American press, snug in its favored position under the First Amendment and basking in the libertarian theory that came out of the Age of Reason, has rather complacently—and often arrogantly—gone its own way, pointing out the shortcomings of the government and of every other social institution in sight. But this nearly two-hundred-year honeymoon is over. Today the American press is getting large doses of its own medicine. From both outside and inside its ranks, critics are noting a variety of journalistic weaknesses, especially those shortcomings that seem to result from a lack of ethics or at least from a distorted or ill-formed moral philosophy.

Biased reporting, uneven news flow, oversimplified images and stereotypes, unreasonable fascination with sensation and negative news, unfairness to minority groups and opinions, careless or purposeful distortion of quotes—these and other criticisms are mounting. Such charges, evidencing a strong dissatisfaction with American journalistic ethics, are heard at every press seminar and convention inside and outside our borders.

Today, as the press still rolls out its big guns to shell pockets of unethical practice in government and defends its own vested interests regarding its freedom (as in the Grenada affair), critics of the press are returning the fire with intensity. The real meaning of the theory that the press and society have an "adversarial relationship" is finally being brought home to journalists. The press increasingly finds itself portrayed in an image it does not like—as a powerful and largely unethical institution that needs to clean up its own house before it condemns so insistently the faults and moral squalor in the houses of others.

A Growing Concern with Ethics

By and large, the press, like the government, is touchy and defensive about criticism. Members of the press cannot quite understand why the public sees in journalism a bid for power and bigness, an insensitivity in dealing with institutions and citizens, a selfish and often harmful use of its considerable freedom, a defensiveness and arrogance, and a consistent pandering to low taste and sensationalism. The fact that press ethics is increasingly being questioned and the "social responsibility theory" is growing in popularity would certainly indicate at least that there is a general sense of dissatisfaction with press performance.

This mounting criticism of the press has touched off a defensive reaction among journalists—a growing concern with the purposes, objectives, and responsibilities of journalism. And this concern thrusts press people—in spite of themselves—into the area of ethics.

Specific questions of an ethical nature are raised. For example: Should sources of information be revealed in news stories? Should newspersons ever hide their identity when they are getting data for their stories? Should news persons accept gifts? There is no shortage of discussion of questions and possible answers. Few hard-and-fast conclusions—perhaps none at all—are reached, and every case ends as an open question.

In spite of journalists' failure to reach definite conclusions in their talk about ethics, the mere fact that such talk is taking place indicates a concern and an awareness that all is not right and that journalism can be made better. Perhaps this awareness is cause for optimism, and certainly it is reason enough for further discussion of the subject.

What journalists seem to need is a sense of ethics, or a reasonable ethical ground upon which to stand; in other words, they need a meaningful *theory of ethics* that will help them answer specific questions as they arise. Of course, journalists cannot escape from all the little practical moral quandaries of a day's work, but if they had some kind of broad ethical orientation, they would be much better equipped to face such questions.

A Broad Ethical Orientation

The search for a broad ethical orientation for journalists leads into more theoretical and metaethical areas of morality. The journalist needs an "ethical grounding," which cannot be gained by belaboring an infinite number of specific problems that may arise to confound the journalist in his or her daily rounds. It is not that this "practical" ethical emphasis is unimportant—this consideration of how this case or that case has been or might be approached from an ethical standpoint. But there are many books, articles, and conferences giving full consideration to this approach. Two excellent examples of books that have approached journalistic situations from an ethical perspective are Clifford Christians, K. B. Rotzoll, and Mark Fackler's *Media Ethics* (1987) and Tom Goldstein's *The News at Any Cost* (1985).

But in addition to ethical issues that deal with specific questions, the journalist also needs to be familiar with broader moral considerations. In my view a sound ethical stance for journalists is the synthesis of deontology and teleology that I have called "deontelic ethics."[1] Along with this synthesis, I propose an orientation toward moral situationism as a sensible alternative to absolute and universal ethics. Deontelic ethics—which is closely related to the dialectical thrust of this book—and this sympathetic approach to situationism in ethics combine to form a foundational platform from which the journalist can plunge into the waters of multitudinous specific ethical problems.

Journalists would be wise, in trying to find a meaningful ethical ground upon which to stand, to consider combining deontology and teleology. They would begin with basic principles or maxims to which they could reasonably pay allegiance and to which they feel a duty to follow. Some such principles might be: 1) Never fail to give the source of quotations in a story. 2) Never tamper with direct quotes—always use the source's exact words. 3) Never purposely omit from a story any pertinent information in hand. 4) Never purposely quote out of context. The journalist, then,

---

1 My concept of "deontelic ethics" is explicated in John C. Merrill, "An Ethics for the Journalist: Sound Principle, Judicious Deviation," *Freedom at Issue,* No. 75 (November–December, 1983), 15–18. See also John C. Merrill, "Sound Principle and Wise Deviation: Deontelic Ethics for the Journalist," in Louis Hodges (ed.), *Social Responsibility: Business, Journalism, Law, Medicine* (Lexington, Va., 1985), 15–22.

would start with deontology with a dedication to principle and a deep sense of duty to follow ethical imperatives.

Such guiding principles should be a very important factor in the journalist's ethical thinking. But journalists should also be willing to deviate from such a principle or maxim when they feel they *should*—such as when reason dictates another course or when projected or anticipated consequences warrant the desertion of these rules.

The important point is that journalists should not abandon basic principles or maxims of conduct; they should feel a strong duty to follow them. They should retain a body of principles to which they are basically dedicated. They must feel a duty to uphold them and to respect them as normal guides for action. These principles give the journalist's ethics a sense of meaningfulness and considerable predictability. Having an allegiance to such rules gives the journalist some concept of loyalty to principle, which most people need in order to consider ethics seriously.

But it is important to stress that the journalist must not follow these basic ethical tenets blindly or unthinkingly. Duty for duty's sake—Kant's version of deontological ethics—may well mean, if taken too far, that a person should act blindly in accordance with a rigid rule. This is not a very sound ethical road for the journalist to take. And many philosophers, such as H. B. Acton and Bertrand Russell, have criticized Kant's strict, legalistic ethics, which would insist that a journalist follow a chosen rule out of duty or allegiance to the rule and for absolutely no other reason.[2]

Reasonable and concerned journalists must think about particular ethical situations. In short, they must consider some modification of their principles when their ethically conscious intellect deems such modification imperative. Journalists must be flexible, or willing to moderate a basic ethical tenet in order to reach a higher ethical objective dictated by a reasoned analysis of the situation. The significant point, and it should be emphasized, is that the journalist should never capriciously or un-thinkingly break an ethical rule or maxim. An exception to a principle because of a specific situation must be made only after serious thought, or as Kierkegaard would say, "only with much fear and trembling."

It is reasonable, therefore, to say that it is incumbent on thinking journalists to bring anticipated or likely consequences into their analysis. When they do this, they begin shifting to a teleological orientation. To think ethically is to be concerned with consequences of actions as well as with conforming to guiding principles or maxims. Teleological determination of ethical action seems essential to journalists concerned with morality in decision making.

Teleology in ethics means a concern for consequences and a belief, basically, that good consequences stem from good ethics. So what I am proposing is that a reasonable ethical ground for the journalist is a merger of this concern for consequences (teleology) with a basic sense of duty to certain principles (deontology)—in short, synthesis of the two stances.

Deontelic Ethics

I call this higher synthesis of deontology and teleology "deontelic ethics" in hopes that the symbiotic name will indicate the dialectical implications of the theory. This theory of deontelic ethics is really not so strange. In fact, even a strict duty ethicist, or deontologist—one who is dedicated to rules and oblivious to consequences—is one who originally, at least, formulated his or her ethical principles through considering in some way the consequences that would result from following the principles. At least someone at the rule's genesis was framing the rule teleologically. Therefore, one might say that to a considerable extent even the deontologist in ethics is fundamentally a teleologist.

But journalists must be cautious about straying too far over into teleology, thinking too much about consequences. It is easy to become simply a majoritarian thinker, making decisions on the basis of numbers alone. For example, accepting as a guide the utilitarian principle of the greatest good for the greatest number is questionable in journalism because acting on this principle can be tantamount to ignoring the desires, feelings, or fate of the minority or minorities. In cases in which this rule is followed, it leads to a lowering of the general level of journalism out of the effort to please a larger and larger segment of the population.

So according to deontelic ethics, the journalist must consider as his or her ethical guide something besides utilitarianism, the ethical egoism espoused by Ayn Rand, and other teleological orientations. And this ethical guide must include a deontological loyalty to some principles that stand above and beyond a concern for consequences. This may not be easy for many journalists to accept, for the great majority of modern ethical systems—Kant's duty ethics is an exception—are more or less teleological.

At the same time, however, there seems to be a deep-rooted desire in journalists to have definite rules, norms, and codes to guide them in their activities. This is why so many codes of ethics are found among journalistic societies and organizations and why there is a clamor for guidelines and prescriptions in various news media.[3] Among journalists there is considerable mistrust of personally determined moral norms. Also, this desire for precise rules explains somewhat the growing trend toward institutionalization and, even more, toward professionalization.

Journalists generally are ambivalent concerning these two inclinations—leaning toward basic, definite rules and codes in a kind of absolutist way and, at the same time toward flexibility and a concern for consequences and the specific situation or context. In short, there is a widespread moral schizophrenia that naturally results in deontelic ethics—or at least it does if the journalist is willing to recognize the weaknesses of each and the strengths of both major ethical systems and to see the benefit of a synthesis.

In accepting this synthesis, the journalist must be cautious. As Kant never tired of stressing, simply thinking only of consequences before making an ethical decision is likely to lead to a solely expedient action. And as Kant also said, the motivation of expediency leads to what might be called a "nonethics." Or to put it another way, seeking particular consequences from an action may well wash away any real ethical value in the action. This means that deontology—or the desire to follow a maxim out of duty—is a deep-seated consideration in journalistic ethics. When one talks of a "principled newsman" or of a journalist as a "person of principle," one is implying a strong dedication to a Kantian deontology. This position stresses that the journalist should accept the duty to do what is right *always*—even when there is no inclination to do it.

Therefore, what appears to be the best position for the journalist is a

---

3 Maxims such as "Do not take government junkets" and "Keep your source confidential if you say you will" are typical principles in codes of ethics for American journalists. The code of ethics of the Society of Professional Journalists is typical of a normative code that tries to give the individual a few broad ethical guidelines. There is a critique of this Sigma Delta Chi code in John C. Merrill, "A Semantic Analysis of the SDX/SPJ Code of Ethics," *Mass Comm Review*, IX (Winter, 1981–82), 12–15.

deontelic ethics, the synthesis of the two systems. Deontelic ethics takes the strict legalism of Kant to a more flexible—and rational—stage and at least relates it to specific, and differing, human situations in which exceptions and modifications to the general principles can be made by the concerned journalist. The journalist is thus fundamentally a deontologist, but at the same time assumes the characteristics of a thinker—a teleologist willing to depart from basic loyalty to maxim from time to time in order to achieve what is considered to be a higher morality.

Journalistic Ramifications

What are some of the practical ramifications in journalism of such an ethical synthesis? 1) The journalist can in certain cases withhold information from a story while still being basically dedicated to an ethics of full disclosure. 2) The journalist can still be acting ethically, on occasion, by refraining from identifying a source, even while at the same time declaring an allegiance to the principle of providing the audience with the source of information. 3) The journalist can, at times, ethically justify some tampering with quotes in a story and still retain a sense of duty to the principle of accuracy in reporting. 4) The journalist can, from time to time, refrain from publishing a story, thus going against the principle of the people's right to know, on the ethical grounds that the evil consequences of publication would outweigh the good.

Most journalists pay lip service to being deontologists—to believing in and following rather specific basic principles. For instance, journalists say they believe that the people have a right to know; yet they keep the people from knowing on many occasions. They say they believe in maximum pluralism in their media, but they regularly restrict in some way the expression of views and opinions that would increase such pluralism. They say they believe that the press should be an adversary—a watchdog—of government, but they find plenty of occasions to serve as an apologist or supporter. They say they believe in objective reporting, but in their actual reporting, they bring their opinions and values to bear on stories with great frequency. They claim that they are, or want to be, a part of a profession, but they scorn minimum entrance requirements, licenses, and the like. They claim they are for maximum individual autonomy, but they calmly submit to various kinds of control from editors, publishers, and owners of media chains. Thus, in spite of their manifestly deontological orientation, most journalists in their daily overt actions prove themselves very loosely tied to deontology.

The point is that it might be better for journalists *not* to talk so much about the specific things they stand for. If they are too specific and too insistent on their dedication to deontological norms, they are likely to be considered weak and unprincipled when they depart from these standards, as they frequently do. They will certainly be considered at least inconsistent, and they might be accused of flagrantly unethical actions.

There is no doubt that the journalist does, at times, compromise principles, but this is often done in the name of, and for the sake of, a higher ethics, one that has been arrived at conscientiously, rationally, and in good faith. If the journalist is trying to be ethical, such deviation will at least be done with great seriousness and for good reason. Compromises of principle are surely to be found among journalists for less than ethical reasons, and many such arbitrary, spur-of-the-moment compromises are exactly what causes the moral dilemmas and credibility problems of the press.

The strict deontologist should not seriously object to a teleological departure from time to time if the motivation or intent is serious and ethical. Why? Because such departure shows a *good will,* and even for Kant there is nothing better than a good will. So the deontologist puts great stock in a good will, in the motive of the actor. Besides, it might even be argued that this deontelic ethicist *is* dedicated to a basic principle, one that he or she could accept absolutely. Such a basic principle could be stated in this way: "Accept a basic maxim that you can act on out of duty, deviating from it when, and only when, using reason, you feel that the probable consequences stemming from such a deviation will result in a more moral action. If you are uncertain that such deviation will better the moral situation, then stick by your deeply held ethical maxim."

So dedication to this principle is a kind of deontology that in itself permits the journalist to act teleologically—to consider consequences or make exceptions in some situations. In other words, by following the above maxim, the journalist in an ethical situation is permitted to be fundamentally a deontologist and at the same time to be rational and flexible, so that it is possible to make a teleological readjustment in the cause of a higher good. This synthesis of deontology and teleology—this deontelic ethics—seems a sound one for the journalist of today who treasures loyalty or commitment and at the same time desires to bring his or her individual thought processes to bear on the particular ethical situation.

Most journalists have adopted, perhaps without realizing it, this deontelic ethics. Often, however, they are apologetic or defensive about it, for they feel they are in some way guilty of subscribing to a watered-down or inauthentic ethics—a "situation ethics."

This attitude is unfortunate, and it should be abandoned. The synthesis arising from deontology and teleology is both rational and ethical. Just because this ethical stance does not yet have a firmly established label or name in the literature of philosophy does not mean that it is not a valid and sensible position.

There are several philosophical strains that have been important in the development of deontelic ethics. To begin with, of course, is a kind of synthesis of polar emphases that are usually referred to as the deontological and teleological theories. Deontelic ethics combines these polarizations, synthesizes them, and indicates the dialectical process that can be brought to bear in many sensitive and controversial areas of journalism.

Moral Absolutism: Kant and Rand

Moral absolutism is one philosophical strain that has significance for deontelic ethics. Moral absolutists have strict deontological proclivities. Immanuel Kant proposed an ethics of "duty for duty's sake," the following of a maxim or principle without considering consequences. Kant, a deontologist, was a subscriber to a legalistic or absolutist theory of ethics. Some absolutist theories make it sound as if one can simply intuit what is good and what is right by exercising human sensitivity; others are more religious and have moral answers depend on the nature of God. Others, such as Kantian ethics, see principles of morality coming to a person rationally in absolute imperatives that are universal laws.[4]

Kant's idea of "duty for duty's sake" seems to mean that persons should act blindly in accordance with some rigid rule, without examining what the probable consequences of their action will be in terms of happiness or misery, good or evil. According to Henry Hazlitt, in his excellent book *The Foundations of Morality*, this Kantian position is irrational,

4   Abraham Edel, *Ethical Judgment* (New York, 1955), 31.

mainly because it is inflexible and does not consider consequences. According to Kant, nothing is truly and unconditionally good except the good will. The only act that deserves to be called moral, in his opinion, is an act done from a sense of duty, an act done because it is thought right and for no other reason.[5]

According to Kant, one should not judge the rightness or wrongness of acts by their consequences to oneself or anybody else. But if actions or rules of action are not judged by their probable consequences, how does one know what actions are right and wrong? Kant's position does seem a little strange. He does not think that a person knows his or her duty in each case in an a priori way or from direct intuition, but he does believe that one can determine that duty from certain principles that are accepted ahead of time.

And this leads to Kant's famous categorical imperative, a prescription for generating our ethical maxims. The categorical imperative says simply that in a moral situation we should do only what we would, as rational beings, desire everyone to do. We may morally do what we would universalize, and we can develop principles for various occasions from such a general rule. The wording of the categorical imperative is as follows: "Act only according to that maxim by which you can at the same time will that it should become a universal law." If, for instance, a journalist is willing for *all* reporters to have the power to change words in a direct quote, then this journalist would be ethical in indulging in this practice.[6]

The contemporary philosopher R. M. Hare has shared Kant's dedication to universalizing moral principles. He has long argued that it is one of the central characteristics of moral judgment; he has applied the term *universalizability* to the basic idea embodied in both the Christian Golden Rule and Kant's categorical imperative. It means that simply a moral judgment must conform to universal principles—those applying to everyone alike—if it is to be acceptable. One other basic and very important principle of Kant's should be mentioned. It is often referred to as the "practical imperative": "Act so that you treat humanity, whether in your own person or in that of another, always as an end and never as a means only." This principle should have some meaning to journalists, who often

5 Hazlitt, *The Foundations of Morality*, chapter 16, esp. p. 139.
6 For a good discussion of the categorical imperative, see H. J. Paton, *The Categorical Imperative: A Study of Kant's Moral Philosophy* (New York, 1967). For Kant's wording, see Immanuel Kant, *Foundations of the Metaphysics of Morals* (Indianapolis, 1959), 422.

find themselves using certain persons connected with their stories as means to the pragmatic fulfillment of their objective, the pragmatic end of "getting the story."[7]

How, the journalist might ask, do we know what our duties are? Through intuition, through divine revelation, through basic instinct, or through bringing Kantian reason or rational insight to the immediate question? Or as a contemporary ethicist, W. D. Ross, has proposed, is it through certain self-evident or obvious principles of ethics that we simply know we must follow in order to be ethical? He calls these principles "prima facie duties."[8]

The philosopher Ayn Rand would probably be incensed at the idea that she belongs in the same camp with Kant, whom she generally seemed to detest as a moral philosopher. And it is true that Rand was an Aristotelian in basic stance, whereas Kant evidenced a kind of mysticism or romanticism more closely associated with Plato. Nevertheless, Rand was a stickler for standing by principles or rules, for not washing away any moral meaning of an action by submitting to various pressures.

Rand is similar to Kant also in that she had little use for utilitarian ethics, which she saw as demeaning the basic integrity of the individual actor, enthroning altruism, and deprecating personal rationality and decision making. Certainly Rand is related to Aristotle. She, like him, saw herself as a practical, hardheaded thinker. Aristotle believed, and Rand agreed, that a good man lives according to his intelligence, by reason: "He is not the irrational self-lover, who is subject to his own passions."[9]

Although Rand resembled Aristotle in some ways, she scorned his emphasis on sacrificial altruism. Aristotle pictured the good human being as willing to give up wealth and honors in the desire to play "a noble part." Such a person might even lay down his or her own life for others. Rand does not go along with that idea. According to Virginia Mollenkott, who has compared the philosophies of Rand and Aristotle in great detail, the thing that is wrong with both their ethical systems is that they ask of human beings more than human beings can deliver: a total adherence to rationality. Aristotle recognized this difficulty far more clearly than did

7 R. M. Hare, "Euthanasia: A Christian View," *Philosophic Exchange*, II (Summer, 1975), 45; Kant, *Foundations of the Metaphysics of Morals*, 47.

8 W. D. Ross, *The Right and the Good* (Oxford, 1930), 19–20; Ross, *Foundations of Ethics* (Oxford, 1939), Chapters 4–6.

9 Virginia R. Mollenkott, *In Search of Balance* (Waco, 1969), 90.

Rand, according to Mollenkott, for he wrote, "We ought, so far as in us lies, to . . . live in conformity with the highest thing within us (that is, with our reason)."[10]

Opposed to the firm, legalistic ethics of Kant and Rand is what is probably a more popular stance—teleology—the emphasis of which is on the probable or actual consequences of an action. The teleologist's major concern is good consequences, and the most important type of teleology is utilitarianism, which was first propounded by Jeremy Bentham and then popularized by John Stuart Mill.[11] The "greatest happiness principle" is a teleological concept that postulates right action as that which brings the greatest happiness to the greatest number. It has been modified in recent times into what might be called the "greatest good principle," according to which the moral action is the one that brings the greatest good to the greatest number.

Some have called this ethical theory a "commonsense stance in ethics." Sissela Bok, for instance, in a chapter on the role of consequences in her popular book *Lying*, has extolled the utilitarian philosophers for their commonsense approach. In addition, according to A. C. Ewing, the utilitarians—and their precursors in antiquity—"brought a great sense of freedom to those whom they would convince that what ought to be done was not necessarily what the soothsayer or the ruler or the priests required, but rather quite simply, what brought about the greatest balance of good over evil."[12]

Whereas Mill's brand of utilitarianism can be considered a hedonistic type, Bok is obviously referring to "ideal utilitarianism"—the kind that makes the production of good as the criterion of the rightness of an act. And it should be noted that "good" is not identified with happiness, or evil with pain. Perhaps the leading modern exponents of this "ideal utilitarianism" have been G. E. Moore and Hastings Rashdall.[13] According to A. C.

10 *Ibid.*, 91.

11 Jeremy Bentham, *An Introduction to the Principles of Morals and Legislation* (New York, 1948); John Stuart Mill, *Utilitarianism* (Indianapolis, 1957). There are many other editions of these books.

12 Sissela Bok, *Lying* (New York, 1979), 50–59; A. C. Ewing, *Ethics* (New York, 1953), 51.

13 See especially G. E. Moore, *Ethics* (New York, 1965), Chapter 1, which contains a good defense of nonhedonistic utilitarianism and shows how Moore's utilitarian views differ from traditional foundations of that theory. See also Hastings Rashdall, *The Theory of Good and Evil* (London, 1907). For an additional look at Moore's ethics, see his well-known *Principia Ethica* (New York, 1959), esp. Chapter 3 on hedonism.

Ewing, a leading contemporary moral philosopher, such a stance has the advantage over Kant's of stressing consequences and over ordinary (hedonistic) utilitarianism of recognizing other examples of the good besides pleasure. Among them might well be that of moral character, on which Kant insisted, and also the good of human love and intellectual and aesthetic experience.[14]

Certainly the teleological stance, especially the utilitarian variety, is an altruistic one. Ayn Rand is about the only writer who has seriously opposed such an emphasis and has espoused an ethics of "self first." She has argued uncompromisingly for selfishness, which she defines as rational concern for one's own interests. Rand has attacked altruism as being "responsible, more than any other single factor, for the arrested moral development of mankind."[15] To Rand, as a moral absolutist, the teleological ethics of Mill, Moore, and others would be absurd. She would see such an ethical system as a surrender of what is true and good to what is false and evil, an abdication of moral responsibility. In this, she certainly sided with Kant.

Mollenkott has said that for Rand, Christ's injunction "Judge not" should be changed to read, "Judge, and be prepared to be judged." Not judging, for Rand, would be morally irresponsible, and certainly, as Mollenkott admitted, there is "something attractive about Rand's views."[16] Journalists who write editorials or critical pieces must, in the main, agree with Rand on this point. In fact, it seems that the very ideas of a "free marketplace of ideas" and an "open society" reinforces the position that Rand took.

Another egoist, Thomas Hobbes, proposed a kind of psychological egoism that contends that "good" is those things we desire or like and "evil" is those things we dislike or have an aversion to. Nothing, according to Hobbes, is either good or evil in itself. It only becomes so when it is liked or disliked.

Hobbes would say that journalists, for instance, act in order to attain some good—something they desire—or to avoid something to which they have an aversion. Therefore, Hobbes suggested that we have egoistic reasons for acting as we do; he insisted that always, in consideration "of the

14 Ewing, *Ethics*, 61.
15 Ayn Rand, *The Virtue of Selfishness: A New Concept of Egoism* (New York, 1964), ix–x.
16 Mollenkott, *In Search of Balance*, 49.

voluntary acts of every man, the object is some good to himself." Just why a person acts egoistically is something Hobbes neglected to expound upon. But a fellow egoist, Moritz Schlick, three centuries later, formulated what he called "the law of motivation" for this egoistic human proclivity. By this he meant that a person, choosing between ends, always selects the most pleasant. So in effect, Schlick's rationale has hedonist overtones.[17]

Aristotle and the Retreat from Extremes

Aristotle's ideas about ethics have a close relationship to the spirit of the dialectical dissolving of antinomies that I propound in this book. His *Nicomachean Ethics* is the basic guide to ancient Greek moral thinking. The emphasis is, as in all Greek moral thought, on being virtuous as opposed to merely following rules. And for Aristotle, virtue is rational activity. According to Aristotle, people are essentially rational beings, though this does mean that they always act rationally. But when they do not, they are not virtuous.[18]

Aristotle's rational person is happy, and his happy person is virtuous. Aristotle saw happiness not as what we usually mean when say we "feel happy." Instead, his concept of happiness is similar to what we mean by "living well," and it includes such things as enjoying one's status in society, performing virtuous acts, and having good feelings. The virtues, for Aristotle, are socially defined, and the good life must be taught to us by society. Therefore, Aristotle places much emphasis on good education and on being brought up properly. Virtues are acquired by practice; the virtuous person desires to do good acts and to do them naturally and habitually. The virtuous person is one who acts as he or she is supposed to out of a pure desire to act right, because good action has become an intrinsic part of the person's character. The virtuous person simply enjoys being virtuous.

Aristotle's most famous doctrine is that virtues are "means between the extremes."[19] According to Aristotle, virtue is a moderation or middle state

17 Thomas Hobbes, *Leviathan,* ed. H. W. Schneider (Indianapolis, 1958), 112; Moritz Schlick, *Problems of Ethics* (New York, 1939).

18 For a good discussion of Aristotle's ethical theory, see Anthony Kent, *The Aristotelian Ethics* (New York, 1978).

19 Allen, *From Plato to Nietzsche,* 24–43, contains a good discussion of the Golden Mean of Aristotle's ethics.

between two vices—of excess on one hand and of deficiency on the other. Virtue is a kind of mean, or middle way, but from one perspective (in relation to what is best and right), it is the extreme position of perfection.

Aristotle is often considered, especially by the Korzybskian semanticists as a nondynamic, either-or philosopher. He may well belong in a scientific realm, but certainly his ethical philosophy does not evidence this static, legalistic nature. He did, indeed, see some actions and feelings as absolutely evil—feelings such as malice, envy, and shamelessness, and actions such as theft, murder, and adultery. These, said Aristotle, are "evil in themselves." But his best-known moral formulation is the Golden Mean, according to which just behavior is the mean—or point of balance—between doing injustice and suffering it. Exactly where this mean is for each of us, in a particular situation, is an open question. Aristotle is not specific about such things; he want us to be rational and to come up with our own answers.

So for Aristotle, human beings must individually accept the responsibility of reaching this Golden Mean by themselves. Morality is a constant struggle, and life is a constant becoming, a constant process. His ideas about the Golden Mean show that he was, indeed, a "process philosopher"—in the area of morals, at least—and not the hidebound, nondynamic thinker often depicted by the non-Aristotelian General Semanticist of the Korzybskian type.[20]

Aristotle's is a very practical ethics; he wanted us to think and to work out our own moral salvation. His outlook is a combination of absolutism and relativism. He believed that some things are intrinsically wrong—absolutely—but also that the majority of feelings and actions are to "be governed by individual reason in a relativistic set of shifting relations."[21] In other words, for most ethical decisions, Aristotle would have us search for the Golden Mean; this search, this moral quest that each of us must undertake is a constant struggle.

Clifford G. Christians has called Aristotle's position "a middle-level theory" and even traces it back to the grandson of Confucius in fifth-century China, who conceived it as a moral theory of equilibrium and

---

20 The basic text of General Semantics is Alfred Korzybski, *Science and Sanity*. A more popular and understandable summary of the basic principles of Korzybski is S. I. Hayakawa, *Language in Thought and Action* (New York, 1939).

21 Mollenkott, *In Search of Balance*, 88–89.

harmony. Christians used this Aristotelian concept (with supporting references to Milton, Jefferson, and Solzhenitsyn) to argue that press freedom is not an unconditional right and that such freedom does not justify unethical acts.[22]

Aristotle, according to Christians, inherited a deep concern for moderation (along with three other cardinal virtues—justice, courage, and wisdom) from Plato, and this led to his promulgation of the Golden Mean. Concerning the Golden Mean, Christians went on: "I suspect we are aware of the basic idea in journalism. We deride sensationalism and generally recognize the virtue of balance, fairness, and equal time. When faced with a decision of whether to ban all praising of tobacco and allowing unregulated promotion, the FTC took the golden mean—banning ads from TV and placing warning labels on cigarettes."[23]

Aristotle's basic moral ideas have some resemblance to the concept of the dialectic. He emphasized a kind of moderation, a retreat from extremes of excess and deficiency, the seeking of a higher synthesis. Although Aristotle is not generally looked upon as a philosopher of flux and merger (in his scientific thought) his philosophy is certainly related to the dynamic school—even the dialectical school—when it comes to ideas about morality.

Blaise Pascal, in the mid-seventeenth century, provided Aristotelianism with a more balanced orientation. Like Aristotle, he was concerned with growth and becoming and stressed that people must find truth in opinions radically different from their own. This is the "open" or dialectical stance toward truth and ethics.

According to Pascal, paradoxes are everywhere; a person must learn to encompass opposite poles of truth and establish the reality revealed by each. Because a person sees only relatively, he or she must be willing to admit what is true about a view held in opposition. Pascal was fully aware of the paradox of reason which states that the highest knowledge is that one does not know. But he also recognized that thinking is the essential dignity of a person. "By thought I comprehend the world," Pascal wrote. "To think well; this is the principle of morality."[24]

In the contemporary world, there is another advocate of compromise

22 Clifford G. Christians, "On Penultimates and Golden Means in Media Ethics," Hodges (ed.), *Social Responsibility*, 9.
23 *Ibid.*
24 Blaise Pascal, *Pensées*, trans. W. F. Trotter (New York, 1958), 97.

and synthesis—Iris Murdoch, whose ideas are similar in many way to Aristotle's. Murdoch believes that we must steer a middle course between what she calls, on one hand, the "hidebound inflexibility" of the person who never adjusts rules to situations and on the other, the "neurotic indetermination" of one who always hesitates in the fear of not fully understanding the situation. "To steer the middle course," writes Murdoch, "is itself a moral choice."[25] This strong middle-course philosophy reflects Aristotle's moral concerns and ties in with the synthesis and dynamic emphasis of dialectical journalism.

Situationism

Finally, there is an important related moral stance—situationism. The negative connotation that "situation ethics" often has is a sign of the continued appeal of Kantian legalistic ethics and the natural pull toward absolutism. Such a negative connotation is unfortunate and perhaps unwarranted. Situationism in ethics has a certain logical connection with deontelic ethics. Both situationism and deontelic ethics reflect a desire on the part of the journalist to *think* about ethical acts and not simply follow a rule in any and all circumstances.

The journalist who functions within this moral system of deontelic ethics not only has some guiding principles but also has an appreciation of situations, of the here and now. Situationists are "open" and therefore are at home with an "open journalism" practiced in an "open society," such as the United States. Situationism in ethics is quite consistent with the spirit of free journalism, individualistic journalism, existentialist journalism—the three kinds of journalism that traditionally have shaped the American press. It is also consistent with socially concerned journalism, resulting in a responsible and disciplined press system.

The situationist journalist is hard to classify. Such a person is not always or entirely this or that, not liberal or conservative, not an objectivist or a subjectivist, not an egoist or an altruist, not an activist or passivist. Such a journalist is neither doctrinaire nor ideological, but is cautiously, rationally flexible about all normative journalistic principles— about such issues as the people's right to know, the adversary relationship between journalists and government, and the public's right of access to the

25   Quoted in Mollenkott, *In Search of Balance,* 80.

press. The specific situation will likely determine how the situationist journalist makes an ethical decision, or at least it will affect the way a decision is made. In today's parlance, it is likely that this journalist will be neither a dove nor a hawk; instead, the situationist will take the middle way of wisdom and thus could probably best be characterized as an owl.

Liberalizing Ethics

The psychiatrist Carl Rogers has said that situation ethics is far sounder than an absolute ethics. However, under situation ethics a person does give up "the consolation of knowing" that he or she is absolutely right or wrong. According to Rogers, a situationist ethic "is the only conceivable kind of ethics in a world that's changing so rapidly that the absolutist's formulas in almost every sphere do tend to go by the board."[26]

What is called "situation ethics," "contextual ethics," or "the new morality" is often associated with certain theologians, especially Rudolf Bultmann, John A. T. Robinson, and Joseph Fletcher.[27] For these contemporary theologians, the context determines the rightness or wrongness of an action. Taking issue with Kant, for example, these philosophers would not necessarily condemn a journalist's action of lying in a story if the circumstances called for it. For the situationist, no ethical principle is universally right; rather, each one gains sanction from a certain context that gives it validity. Fletcher has stated that we must "tailor our ethical cloth to fit the back of each occasion."[28]

Fletcher has written much about situation ethics. He takes a position against Kant and his duty ethics. Fletcher's position is, by and large, in keeping with dialectical moral reasoning and with the thrust of this book. It is also in agreement with the comments of Nikolai Berdyaev, the Russian existentialist, on Christian morality: "The gospel morality . . . is the direct opposite of Kant's formula; . . . you must *not* act so that the principle of your action could become a universal law; you must always act indi-

26 Quoted in Richard I. Evans, *Carl Rogers: The Man and His Ideas* (New York, 1975), 102.

27 Fletcher, especially, has popularized this form of ethics, mainly in his *Situation Ethics: The New Morality* (Philadelphia, 1966). Harvey Cox (ed.), *The Situation Ethics Debate* (Philadelphia, 1973), contains a series of responses to Fletcher by authorities such as John C. Bennett, Harmon L. Smith, James A. Pike, Paul Ramsey, and Vernon Weiss.

28 For a good discussion of situation ethics, see Porter, *The Good Life*, 200ff. See also Fletcher, "Six Propositions: The New Look in Christian Ethics," *Harvard Divinity Bulletin*, XXIV (October, 1959), 17.

vidually, and everyone must act differently. The universal law is that every moral action should be unique and individual, i.e., that it should have in view a concrete living person and not the abstract good. Such is the ethics of love. Love can only be directed upon a person, a living being, and not upon the abstract good."[29]

A position opposed to Fletcher's and Berdyaev's is that of Virginia Mollenkott. She especially disagreed with Fletcher's belief that guilt should not accompany the desertion of a maxim or principle. "I think he is wrong to deny the guilt involved in breaking a moral law because of the needs of a specific situation," Mollenkott has written. "Guilt inevitably (rightly or wrongly, consciously or unconsciously) accompanies the deserting of any values a person has been taught all his life." She summed up her thoughts on the situationism of Fletcher and others in these words: "Some lies, for example, may be justified—may result in a greater good (or a lesser evil)—but it is still unethical to lie. The situation does not make the lie right—only justifiable. The liar is still a liar and will—and should—feel some guilt."[30]

Thus, Mollenkott would tell the journalist that he or she may stretch the truth from time to time, depending on the situation, in order to try to reach a higher good. But the journalist must remember that, even though such an act may be justified, the readers or listeners are still being misled. Perhaps this is ethical, Mollenkott would say, but the journalist should feel guilt for deserting a rationally held moral tenet.

In spite of Mollenkott's caveats, situationism is a needed corrective for a traditional overemphasis on laws, codes, and rules. In each moral situation the basic question that must be asked is, Are there special circumstances in this particular situation that demand that the rules of the ethical code not be followed? Or does this situation—this set of circumstances and facts—lead rationally to the setting aside of the rules? If the journalist does deviate from the ethical rules, he or she must do so very carefully, deliberately, and after much thought. It can be only a rational, responsible deviation; it must not be a haphazard, spur-of-the-moment nihilistic deviation.

In conclusion, it should be stressed that journalistic ethics can remain situational or contextual without dispensing with principles. What I have

29 Nicholas Berdyaev, *The Destiny of Man*, tr. Natalie Duddington (New York, 1960), 106.
30 Mollenkott, *In Search of Balance*, 76, 77.

called deontelic ethics might also be called "principled situationism." The journalist is guided by principles but takes the particular situation into consideration, recognizing that certain situations demand that guiding principles or rules be set aside—not for always, but for a particular time.

Neither situationism nor its companion ethical stance—deontelic ethics—is easy for most journalists. Why? Because they are not concrete enough, legalistic enough, or strict enough. Legalism is a comfortable ethics. Most journalists are happy—or at least comfortable—when they have escaped from freedom, when they are excused from making hard decisions, when they can rest in ethical safety and certitude provided by the publisher's or editor's norms. They like to be free from having to make moral decisions, from having to take personal responsibility for their acts.

Journalists also appear to like ethical codes, with fancy printing and frames—specific, impersonal guides to action that shift journalistic responsibility from self to institution or profession. But these codes depersonalize ethics; they institutionalize, formalize, and trivialize morality by collectivizing the concept of responsibility. They certainly are not in keeping with a liberal, situational, rational morality.

Rather than such a "code morality," what I recommend is an individual and rational ethics, one that will center moral judgment and responsibility on the personal level, that will help sustain journalistic authenticity and integrity, and that will combine a respect for tried and tested moral principles with a rational flexibility. Such an ethics has nothing to do with obedience to a code of press ethics or with following some set of guidelines out of a sense of duty. Rather, deontelic ethics is a theory that assumes that the individual journalist can think and make personal moral decisions exclusive of predetermined norms passed down from some elite to be followed within an institutional or professional context.

Deontelic ethics is for the journalist who is both morally concerned and rational, who respects generalized ethical principles but who is willing to depart from them, and who is aware that absolutes and universal norms are fit only for "operatniks" functioning in an authoritarian system and not for self-valuing journalists of "open" societies. Deontelic ethics is a broad moral grounding, not a set of specific rules for right action. As such, it emphasizes the journalist's own reason, not his or her ability to conform or follow orders. It is truly a socially concerned, individualistic ethics that respects the journalist's own freedom and reason but is built on a respect for others, too, and for the continued moral progress of journalism.

Ten

GLOBAL CONCERNS

In Vienna in the midsummer of 1975, a group of us were gathered in the office of Otto Schulmeister, publisher of *Die Presse,* one of the oldest and most prominent daily newspapers in Europe. Several of the editors of the paper were present, among them Thomas Chorherr, the chief editor. The talk had turned from the characteristics of great newspapers of the world to press responsibilities that might have application across the entire globe. Such a conversation led into a discussion of ethics and the degree to which (if it is possible at all) there could be an international journalistic ethics.

Schulmeister suggested that "a great newspaper in Austria might very well be a mediocre or poor one if considered by the critical standards of the Soviet Union." To his mind, expectations vary with the journalistic context. When the topic shifted to ethics, Schulmeister made a similar statement, maintaining that standards of press morality reflect the social and political realities of the particular country in question. The group in the *Die Presse* office generally agreed with this position.

This relativistic approach, manifested in the group's consensus, was intellectually satisfying and meaningful. Yet there was something vaguely disturbing about it. In a practical sense, of course, political realities do tend to impinge on ethics, to splinter moral standards throughout the world, and to militate against globalizing a sense of journalistic responsibility. But surely, beyond certain politically induced differences in media responsibility, there must be something universal about journalistic ethical concepts and practices. And though the discussion in Vienna dealt with the difficulty of talking meaningfully about international press ethics, it reflected the belief that there might well be some common denominators of journalistic morality—certain universal moral principles appropriate to the press—and that journalists should try to find them and follow them. Such discussions as this one in Vienna were taking place sporadically from place to place in the 1970s and portended the great interest in the globalization of press ethics that burst forth in the 1980s.

Globalizing Journalistic Ethics: A New Priority

From such scattered discussions as these, the point has now been reached at which it is not in the least unusual for speakers, authors, and journalistic societies to advocate international principles of press ethics. Many persons have recognized the possibility and appropriateness of some kind of universal concept of journalistic ethics. In the broad arena of the multifaceted New World Information and Communication Order, a new phase of discussion and debate now centers on the perceived need for the world's journalists to professionalize and to develop global codes of ethics. The new emphasis is being championed mainly by UNESCO and most of the Third World nations.[1]

By and large, journalists in the West, especially in the United States, do not have much interest in professionalizing journalism or trying to develop any kind of global ethical code for journalism. But the many loud, persistent voices from the Third World and UNESCO in favor of journalistic "professionalization" seem to be carrying the day. The skeptical position expressed so well by Schulmeister is increasingly declining in influence.

In spite of the difficulty of finding crosscultural and international commonalities in journalistic ethics, press critics and practitioners continue to make an effort to find them. Kaarle Nordenstreng, a Finnish journalism

---

1 Many books and articles have appeared dealing with the New World Information and Communication Order. See, for example, Glen Fisher, *American Communication in a Global Society* (Norwood, N.J., 1979); D. R. Mankekar, *Media and the Third World* (New Delhi, India, 1979); Rosemary Righter, *Whose News? Politics, the Press, and the Third World* (London, 1978); William Read, *Rethinking International Communication* (Cambridge, Mass., 1980); Jim Richstad and Michael Anderson (eds.), *Crisis in International News* (New York, 1981); Kaarle Nordenstreng, *The Mass Media Declaration of UNESCO* (Norwood, N.J., 1984); and International Commission for the Study of Communication Problems, *Many Voices, One World* (London, 1980), a report sponsored by UNESCO.

professor and president of the International Organization of Journalists, in a book published in 1984, suggested many points that might be incorporated into an international code of ethics.[2] For example, he argued that all people have a right to a truthful picture of objective reality. This right, he maintains, stems from "the universal values of humanism." Very few journalists would object to this ethical commonality. A problem arises, however, when one speaks of journalistic neutrality; many commentators, including Nordenstreng, believe that a journalist should avoid "neutrality," especially as it relates to "universal values of peace, democracy, human rights, social progress and national liberation."[3] Exactly what a journalist should do in respect to each of these abstract concepts in his or her daily journalism is something that Nordenstreng neglects to discuss.

Nordenstreng has asserted that an international journalistic ethics "implies two significant steps beyond what is typically held in the libertarian tradition with its passion to remain free from any socio-political obligations other than the pursuit of truth": 1) an invitation for the journalist to support a number of universally recognized ideals and to fight corresponding evils, and 2) an awareness that universal values are vital constituents of the profession of journalism—such values being a commitment to truth, integrity, and other characteristics of professionalism.[4]

Hamid Mowlana, of American University in Washington, D.C., is also hopeful. He has argued that we "must move to create and promote a set of principles or considerations that is not culture bound but universal, strives for the dignity and potential of human beings, and prevents the world from a catastrophic war and destruction." Mowlana admits that narrowly defined ethical codes are "irrelevant, inconsistent, and ineffective," but he believes there are broad principles that can be helpful. According to Mowlana, " confluence of historical factors has produced . . . disorder in

2   The International Organization of Journalists (IOJ) was established in 1958 with headquarters in Prague, and it is currently the largest of the world's press organizations, with more than 150,000 members in some 120 countries. Its "principal function is to support Soviet peace campaigns, human rights campaigns, and other causes through publications, conferences, and similar activities." Richard H. Shultz and Roy Godson, *Dezinformatsia: The Strategy of Soviet Disinformation* (New York, 1986), 27.

3   Nordenstreng, *The Mass Media Declaration of UNESCO*, 257. See also Thomas Cooper et al., *Communication Ethics and Global Change: International and National Perspectives* (New York, 1988), for a good discussion of many of these ethical concerns around the world.

4   Nordenstreng, *The Mass Media Declaration of UNESCO*, 258.

the moral dimension of our communication process," and until "some synthesis of the moral system is achieved, our conduct at home and abroad will continue to be indecisive."[5]

Mowlana speaks of various principles that might be emphasized by journalists throughout the world. He suggests four general ones: 1) the prevention of war and promotion of peace; 2) respect for culture, tradition, and values; 3) promotion of human rights and dignity, and 4) the preservation of the home, human association, family, and community.[6] Again, however, as was the case with Nordenstreng, Mowlana does not discuss how journalists can institute these lofty principles, including the first.

The whole idea of a universal ethics for journalism is probably naïve in our diverse world, in which bitterness and inequality are so evident, but proponents of such an ethics see it as "idealistic" or even largely possible. Common ethical principles, proponents believe, are to be found and will be useful. But a pessimistic, or perhaps realistic, note is exemplified by Herbert Read, who has said, "There are many competing ethical systems but one cannot expect the world in general, or people in the mass, to make a critical estimate of them and agree to accept the best one."[7]

Like Nordenstreng and Mowlana, the International Commission for the Study of Communication Problems, also known as the MacBride commission, in its report of 1980 sponsored by UNESCO, maintained that there are universal principles or values that should be accepted by all journalists. In their report the commissioners listed four main responsibilities for the journalists of the world, and one of the four is "responsibility towards the international community, relating to respect of universal values." But Elie Abel, a commissioner from the United States, argued that a global ethical code is neither attainable nor desirable in today's world. He was reflecting the typical Western position when, during the commission's deliberations he said: "There are indeed 'two essentially distinct conceptions of journalism' in the world today. Where the press is an arm of the state, there can be no room for the exercise of independent professional judgment by journalists. A code of ethics that would be com-

5 Hamid Mowlana, *Global Information and World Communication* (New York, 1986), 219.
6 *Ibid.*, 220–21.
7 Read, *Anarchy and Order*, 194.

patible with such a system of political control must necessarily be rejected by journalists who see their role as independent of the state and, indeed, as decently skeptical of governmental authority."[8]

UNESCO-related Principles

Since 1978, UNESCO and certain international and regional organizations of professional journalists have taken the lead in advocating global ethics in several consultative meetings under the auspices of the United Nations. Such meetings were held in Prague and Paris in 1983. The following organizations participated in the drafting of a list of principles of professional ethics in journalism: the International Organization of Journalists, the International Federation of Journalists, the International Catholic Union of the Press, the Latin American Federation of Journalists, the Latin American Federation of Press Workers, the Federation of Arab Journalists, the Union of African Journalists, and the Confederation of ASEAN Journalists. The list was presented "as a source of inspiration for national and regional codes of ethics," and it was printed and distributed by the IOJ Publishing House in Prague in February, 1984.[9]

Ten principles form the body of this ethical document. Principle I states that people and individuals have the right to acquire an objective picture of reality as well as to express themselves freely through the various media of culture and communication. Principle II describes the journalist's task as serving the people's right to an objective account of reality and advocates good, thorough, unbiased, and accurate reporting. Principle III says that information in journalism is a social good and not a commodity and that the journalist is accountable not only to those controlling the media but to the public at large, "including various social interests." Principle IV sets forth the notion that the profession of journalism should maintain high standards of integrity.

Principle V states that the nature of the journalistic profession demands that the journalist promote access by the public to information. Principle VI urges respect for privacy and human dignity and calls on journalists to

8 International Commission for the Study of Communication Problems, *Many Voices, One World,* 241, 244n.
9 Sean MacBride (ed.), *International Principles of Professional Ethics in Journalism* (Prague, Czechoslovakia, 1984).

conform with international law and national laws concerning protection of the rights and reputations of others. Journalism should have due respect for the national community, according to Principle VII, and for democratic institutions and the public morals.

Principle VIII mandates respect for universal values and cultural diversity, saying that a true journalist stands for the universal values of humanism, above all "peace, democracy, human rights, social progress and national liberation." This principle also calls on the journalist to respect the right of each people freely to choose and develop its political, social, economic, and cultural system. Principle IX states that the journalist should be ethically committed to the elimination of war and other great evils confronting humanity, "especially racialism and apartheid, oppression by tyrannic regimes, colonialism and neocolonialism, as well as . . . poverty, malnutrition and diseases." Finally, Principle X declares that the journalist should promote the New World Information and Communication Order, which proposes a new structuring of the international communication system that is favored by the socialists, the Third World, and UNESCO and opposed by the capitalist world.

In the eyes of Western journalists, most of these principles seem to go beyond the scope of journalism and reach into areas of national policy and political ideology. For example, the Western journalist generally does not feel any great commitment *as a journalist* to the elimination of apartheid, tyrannical regimes, colonialism, disease, or malnutrition. Western journalists may personally be against such things, but they usually feel that this opposition does not need to be expressed in an ethical code for their profession. In short, they do not see it as a journalistic matter. And why should a Western journalist's ethical code prescribe that he or she be in favor of "national liberation," whatever that phrase means. In addition, most Western journalists see little to recommend Principle X as an international ethical principle when there is such widespread disagreement with the ideas put forth in the New World Information and Communication Order.[10]

Unlike this UNESCO-supported list of principles reflecting a non-Western political and economic orientation, many of the concepts we discussed

---

10 For a good discussion of perspectives of Western journalists on this document, see *The Media Crisis: A Continuing Challenge* (Washington, D.C., 1982). See especially the essays by Leonard Sussman, Jerry Friedheim, Leonard Marks, and George Beebe.

in Dr. Schulmeister's Vienna office in 1975 are basically principles free of political or ideological rhetoric. They are broad, general mind-sets relating to international communications behavior that are not readily fashioned into a list or code of ethical principles for the global journalist. Instead, they are working tools for the journalist of *any* ideology or political system—tools that might help in global communication and understanding.

Of course, there will never be complete substantive agreement among journalists on particular points of ethics. That is why specific and normative global codes of ethics are unreasonable. But perhaps there are some broad ethical principles that transcend particular cultures or nations and are universal. These are not easy to isolate, but communication specialists and journalists with a moral consciousness can search for them. It seems that, to be successful, these principles would need to be fundamental concepts of ethical behavior to be employed by those journalists who accept them and feel that they can be useful in global journalism.

The Search for Nonpolitical Commonalities

How does the journalist ever know what is the right or ethical thing to do in activities related to global communication? Generally the right thing is not known, but the journalist does know enough to avoid doing many or most of the wrong things. Ethical journalists solve moral problems as they do nearly all practical problems—not by finding perfect solutions but by finding solutions that make their situation and the situations of others a little better instead of a little worse.

Journalists who act internationally probably can never really go very far beyond their own value systems. Even the most caring, careful, and diligent journalist, empathic and open-minded, cannot help injecting many of his or her own values, in politics, religion, and other areas, into global communication. All journalists are to some degree "missionaries." The very fact that the journalist is communicating—or trying to communicate—with those of another nation indicates a kind of missionary spirit. In other words, the journalist speaking to an international audience is injecting alien ideas and information into other cultural contexts and value systems, and this is a kind of mission. Seldom do we as individuals or we as nations communicate internationally without some selfish and ethnocentric motivation. Even when we do not intend it, we are pushing some idea, principle, area of concern, technique, set of data. It is hardly surprising that some nations call other nations "communications imperialists." And such labeling tends to force the indicting nation itself to become a type of communications imperialist.

Journalists are normally disposed to champion their country's moral values and their own private ethical standards. But private or personal morality is usually scorned as not being socially relevant; it is often considered a kind of nonethics or pseudomorality. However, Alasdair MacIntyre, who has written extensively on "private morality," has argued that it is a legitimate stance, even though most philosophers have virtually written it off. MacIntyre believes, in other words, that a person can be ethical without in any way claiming that his or her morality should be universalized. It seems that the same could be true of a state's ethical actions. According to MacIntyre: "The fact that a man might on moral grounds refuse to legislate for anyone other than himself (perhaps on the grounds that to do so would be moral arrogance) would by itself be enough to show that not all moral valuation is universalizable. . . . In other words, a man might conduct his moral life without the concept of 'duty' and substitute for it the concept of 'my duty.' But such a private morality would still be morality."[11]

Such private morality, on the part of either individuals or states, is certainly a viable idea when looked at from the perspective of MacIntyre. American journalists, for example, can be ethical without adapting in any way to the morality of Soviet journalists. Morality is morality, and when journalists conform to their country's ethical standards, then they can be spoken of as moral. But in a broader sense, journalists have to rise above their own personal moralities and the moralities of their group or nation in order to have any real relevance to morality on the global level. Compromising, connecting, and adapting—these concepts must be a part of any international morality that deserves wide respect. The spirit of the dialectic should lead the journalist to a global sensitivity to ethics and give him or her a sense of integration with a moral world that is larger than personal, ethnic, national, or cultural loyalties.

It is probably impossible to state a good down-to-earth ethical guide for the global journalist. The most basic one might be something like this: The journalist should think of "the other" in the communication situation.

11   Alasdair MacIntyre, "What Morality Is Not," in Gerald Wallace Arthur and D. M. Walker (eds.), *The Definition of Morality* (London, 1970), 30.

The journalist should ask himself or herself not only what should be communicated, but whether anything should be communicated at all. A basic maxim might be: "Communicate only with those who wish communication, and then only about common interests." Such a maxim—as a basic attitude—would help keep to a minimum any propagandistic emphasis. It would help develop a dialogue rather than a monologue. Monologic communication is generally considered ethically inferior to dialogic communication. The global journalist should not talk *to* another nation's citizens, but rather *with* them. This implies mutual respect and interest in the subject of the journalism on the part of both parties, which should lead to the most ethical communication situation. Certainly it would eliminate much raw and self-centered polemic. A consideration of such ideas leads to a kind of minimaxim for the international journalist: "Communicate with others only in the way that you would have them communicate with you." Or, in slightly expanded version: "Communicate only to willing others and employ only those techniques that you would be willing for others to use in communicating with you." This is little more than paraphrasing the Golden Rule and adapting it to journalism, but in morality it is difficult to improve on the Golden Rule. Kant's categorical imperative, also, might be adapted to read "Communicate only in such a way that you would be willing to make what you do a universal rule."

Absolutism or Relativism?

In a discussion of ethics the matter of absolutism and relativism always comes up. Should global journalists follow absolute ethical rules or principles, or should they tailor their ethics to the particular situation or context? Ethical communicators must be flexible. Therefore, they must consider situations and contexts, but they should also have some basic rules or principles of ethics to which they are dedicated and from which they deviate only after much deliberation and perhaps only when they can reach a higher good.

But would not a journalist be compromising basic ethical principles by rationally deviating from them? In such a case, there is no doubt that he or she would be compromising personal principles, but the principles would be compromised rationally and for the sake of a higher ethics. In other words, the motives—the will—would be good, and even Kant would approve of such a compromise, since it indicates ethical motivation. It is a sound ethical stance for the global journalist who treasures loyalty or commitment and at the same time desires flexibility of action based on reason.

Of course, the international journalist can be too flexible in ethics. As important as an open-minded attitude is, the global journalist must not be too ready to adapt. Recently a student of mine suggested that a good maxim might be: "When in Rome, follow the general Roman ethics." The journalist must be wary of such a maxim, however intriguing it appears on the surface. Of course, it might be accepted if such a principle would not seriously compromise one's ethical standards. But it is a sign of weak ethical commitment if one adapts too easily to the ethics of another culture or nation. This is true in spite of the relativist's position that the same acts can be good in one setting and bad in another.[12] It is often possible to follow one's own ethical principles and at the same time not do harm to the ethics of the other society. There is, however, that point or line over which the ethical journalist must not cross.

Just what is meant by ethics in global journalism? Certainly one concern is right and wrong action or, at least, better and worse ones. This issue leads at once into the problem of different systems of cultural values and national ideologies.[13] A nation, like an individual, is usually tied rather tightly to its own set of values and finds it very difficult, if not impossible, to deem ethical any other set of values.[14] This, of course, means that it is nearly impossible to consider ethics in any meaningful sense without acknowledging the relativity of value systems.

But if one makes such an acknowledgment, then a frustrating question immediately arises: If international journalistic ethics is relative, how can any agreement ever be reached as to what a journalist should do when in another cultural or national context? Are there not at least *some* ethical principles that are transcultural? If so, communications specialists and journalists must find them. One place to start is in the area of empathic

12 See Edward Westermarck, *Ethical Relativity* (Westport, Conn., 1970), esp. 145, where the author argues that "the same act can be both good and bad, according as it is approved of by one individual and disapproved of by another."

13 Although relativity of value systems is generally acknowledged, much more research needs to be done on similarities among these value systems. Little or nothing has been written on the subject.

14 See L. John Martin and Anju G. Chaudhary (eds.), *Comparative Mass Media Systems* (New York, 1983), for a good survey of journalistic values worldwide.

concern, stressing what might be called "cooperative attitudes," such as open-mindedness, understanding, sincerity, honesty, and mutual respect. The development of such attitudes in journalism should impel one to formulate certain ethical maxims that would be a start in the direction of universalizing at least a core of ethics.

In summary, thinking about ethics in international journalism is a healthy enterprise; attempting to formulate a global code of specific ethical principles is probably an unrealistic and fruitless endeavor. Discussing press-related ethical principles that form a part of the canopy of global morality—without forgetting the overriding importance of individual and national value systems—can certainly be useful to the empathic and cosmopolitan growth of the journalist. But normative ethical codes, with their beguiling invitation to a kind of "one-worldism," is not only destructive to basic and important political and social differences in the world community, but also may well cause the demise of an individual journalist's own values.

Why Global Ethical Concern?

Why should the global journalist even desire to be ethical? For one thing, ethics leads to some predictability of action. We can have some idea of what another person will do if that person is concerned about ethics and if we have some idea of the values or ethical precepts involved. The minimal purpose of ethical principles is to prevent needless conflict and collision between individuals, nations, and cultures. The broader purpose is to harmonize our attitudes and actions so as to make the achievement of everyone's aims as far as possible compatible. Thus, social cooperation is at the very heart of ethics, at least on a global scale.

Although actions in journalism must be judged by their probability of promoting happiness and well-being, it would be a mistake to apply this utilitarian criterion directly to an act or decision considered in isolation. For it is impossible for the journalist to predict all the consequences of a particular act. The journalist *can* judge the probable consequences of applying established general rules of action—of acting "on principle." It is a reasonable assumption that cooperation is more likely to result in well-being than is noncooperation; therefore, the ethical journalist in global communication will strive for social cooperation rather than social friction. People need to be able to anticipate and to depend upon one another's behavior in order to achieve cooperation. So we all have a very pragmatic reason for being ethical. Ethics gives everyone a basis for this anticipation of the behavior of others.[15]

When considering ethics in global journalism, one needs to look carefully at the basic elements of the situation: the journalist, his or her motives, the ends he or she wants to achieve, the means being employed to achieve those ends, and the audience. Special attention must be paid to motives, ends, and means. Do the ends justify the means, and are the journalist's motives virtuous or generally admirable? One might also ask: Should the journalist communicate at all? If so, to what degree? With what purpose? To which persons? Over what time period? With what techniques?

Surely one must give special consideration to the journalist's motives. The journalist is trying to be effective or successful—and ethical—in journalism, but why? Is being ethical a priority, or does the journalist simply want to accomplish a limited, personal, nationalistic, or ethnocentric objective? Also, one must try to ascertain the journalist's means for achieving his or her purpose. Are the means ethical in themselves? Such questions depend on sophisticated research for answers, and so far little of that has been done. Research into motivations in journalism is, of course, difficult, but so far not even much serious thought has been given to it.

One thing is certain: ethical systems clash. Such a clash among opposing ethics can make cooperation difficult and "ethical action" all but meaningless, but the global journalist should not lose hope. For there is, indeed, some common ground in ethics. The well-meaning and concerned journalist—in whatever country—will walk on that ground whenever possible. If the clash of ethical standards becomes too great, the journalist can always break off communication. And it may well be, in many instances, that breaking off communication is really the ethical thing to do.[16]

Why should journalists be ethical at the level of the international press? This question is the same as asking, Why be ethical within one's own press system? We have to live with one another, both nationally and interna-

---

15 To what degree are citizens of one country really affected by, and concerned about, the behavior of others in another country? Research to date has provided no real answers.

16 See John C. Merrill, "Ethics: A Worldview for the Journalist," in Anne Van der Meiden (ed.), *Ethics and Mass Communication* (Utrecht, the Netherlands, 1980), 108–18.

tionally. In many ways, it is more important that we live peacefully and ethically with one another on the global level than on the national level. Global frictions can lead to more than bad feelings, hostile statements, and nationally oriented intergroup polemic; they can lead to international violence, which, because of modern destructive capabilities, can endanger the very survival of life on earth.

Thus, at the root of the need to be ethical at the global level lies what in a sense is a selfish motivation—survival. The ethical journalist not only wants to survive, but wants others to survive. Others' survival affects one's own survival. So an ethical motivation on the global level for the journalist is both egoistic and altruistic. As history moves forward, the interrelatedness of people and nations is becoming ever more obvious. And it is having an impact on global ethics. Or it should be having such an impact. The survival of humankind depends on it.

Personal and Global Press Ethics

The temptation is great for journalists to project their own press ethics to the global context. There is a basic desire to see every journalist accept the same ethical standards. The historian Arthur Schlesinger, Jr., has dealt with this proclivity and has issued the following warning: "The righteousness of those who apply personal moral criteria to the relativities and complexities of international politics can degenerate all too easily into absolutism and fanaticism." But Schlesinger is in favor of searching for common ethical ties. He has written, "The quest for values common to all states and the embodiment of these values in international covenants and institutions is the way to establish a moral basis for international politics."[17]

Schlesinger is not very optimistic, acknowledging that it will be a long time before such a moral basis for international politics comes to pass. The reason is that the differences dividing the world are "too deep for quick resolution." Yet he believes that a kind of merger or synthesis of the national interest of one's own country with an "unremitting respect for the interest of others" can bring about a much greater "restraint, justice,

---

17 Arthur M. Schlesinger, Jr., "National Interests and Moral Absolutes," in Ernest W. Lefever (ed.), *Ethics and World Politics* (Baltimore, 1972), 42.

and peace among nations" than would result from an "invocation of moral absolutes."[18]

Although many people tend to identify personal morality with the morality of nations, Reinhold Niebuhr insisted that a distinction must be drawn. According to Niebuhr, governments are not individuals; instead, they are trustees for individuals. As such, the state cannot be unselfish, for as Niebuhr said, "No one has a right to be unselfish with other people's interests." If this is true, trying to project individual ethics to nation states is at least questionable. A certain selfishness is to be expected in global morality or in daily relations among nations.[19] The main question, of course, is: Are journalists tied to the morality of nations, or do they have at least an equal responsibility to citizens of the country as well as to the government? This is a primary metaethical question, one that I cannot hope to answer in this book.

Reflecting Niebuhr's perspective, Schlesinger has observed that an important aspect of an individual journalist's ethics is self-sacrifice, or altruistic adaptation to his or her institution or to the public at large. But according to Schlesinger, this ethical stance is in conflict with the government's duty of self-preservation, which "makes it impossible to measure the action of states by a purely individualistic morality."[20] In a way, Winston Churchill made the same point when he said that though the Sermon on the Mount may be the last word in Christian ethics, "it is not on those terms that Ministers [of government] assume their responsibilities of guiding states."[21]

In spite of the undercurrents of optimism that are found in Schlesinger's views on internationalizing ethics (or at least certain values), there is also a note of caution or pessimism, especially concerning the area in which ethics impinges on international law. According to Schlesinger: "Until nations come to adopt the same international morality, there can be no world law to regulate the behavior of states as there is law within nations to regulate the behavior of individuals. Nor can international institu-

18 *Ibid.*

19 Reinhold Niebuhr, *Moral Man and Immoral Society* (New York, 1932), 267; Altschull, *Agents of Power,* 320.

20 Schlesinger, "National Interests and Moral Absolutes," in Lefever (ed.), *Ethics and World Politics,* 24. See also Cooper *et al., Communication Ethics and Global Change.*

21 Winston Churchill, *The Gathering Storm* (Boston, 1948), 320.

tions . . . produce by sleight of hand a moral consensus where none exists. World law must express world community; it cannot create it."[22]

Whereas Schlesinger is concerned about a universal ethics serving as a foundation for international law, many moral philosophers would be satisfied with a moral reawakening on a global scale that would enable people (including journalists) to make limited progress on an ethical plane without affecting legal structures of the various countries. Certain ethical principles are not intended to contribute to "world law." Schlesinger's point that world organizations are unable to produce moral consensus is well taken, and UNESCO and other global groups would be wise to avoid getting deeply into normative ethics.

Ethics is vitally important, but it is best that journalistic moral responsibility be forged within states primarily, only gradually working up to the global level, rather than be injected at the international level with hopes that it would filter down into the various national contexts. Just as the individual journalist must formulate his or her own ethics within the national context and hope that it will become socially contagious, so also must individual states formulate their own ethical values and, through practicing them, hope that they will become globally contagious.

The Middle Way of Ethics

It is my view, of course, that the global journalist would be wise, in trying to find a reasonable ethical ground upon which to stand, to consider combining teleological and deontological stances. Such a journalist would start with basic principles or maxims that he or she feels a kind of duty to follow. An example of such a maxim might be: "Be dedicated to the truth." Its corollaries might be that the source for important information should always be given, direct quotes should never be tampered with, and any pertinent information in hand should never be omitted.

Such basic principles are important to the global journalist, and deontology thus seems the foundation for ethical philosophy in journalism at the global level as well as at other levels. But when reason demands another course, the journalist must deviate from such principles in order to

22 Schlesinger, "National Interests and Moral Absolutes," in Lefever (ed.), *Ethics and World Politics*, 25.

achieve a higher good. The important point is that journalists must not abandon the idea of basic principles, for such principles are what gives their ethics a sense of meaningfulness and predictability.

But it is important to stress that global journalists must not blindly and unthinkingly follow these basic maxims. They must consider particular ethical situations and be willing to modify these principles in the interest of a greater good. Henry Hazlitt has expressed it; "Always follow the established moral rule, always abide by our prima facie duty, unless there is a clear reason for not doing so. . . . The burden of proof must be upon the exception, or upon the alleged moral innovation."[23]

It is easy to swing too far over into the field of teleology when trying to be flexible and not tied too tightly to rigid maxims; journalists tempted to think too much about the consequences of their actions must be cautioned. The possibility is great for them to become simply majoritarian thinkers, making decisions on the basis of numbers alone. The rational journalist who is morally concerned will not place too much faith in trying to please the majority. Certainly there is more to ethics than that. Although "You can't please everybody" is a cliché and the journalist almost certainly will always please someone, the journalist who tries to please everybody may actually end up pleasing nobody. But what is probably more important is that the journalist, even in a situation in which it is possible to please everybody, might well do so but end up being unethical.

What this means is that the global journalist must have as an ethical guide something other than utilitarianism or some other teleological variant. And this something other would include a deontological loyalty to ethical principles that stand above and beyond a concern for consequences. As Immanuel Kant never tired of stressing, simply thinking of consequences before making an ethical decision is likely to lead only to an *expedient* action, and this, of course, is a kind of "nonethics." A synthesis of deontology and teleology—the middle way of ethics—appears to be the best position for the global journalist, for the person who treasures loyalty and at the same time desires freedom of action, to pursue the highest ethics based on reason.

Finally, it is worth noting that this synthesis of deontology and teleology is a stance that indicates a natural desire on the journalist's part to be ethical in the sense of both having convictions and having a capacity to

23   Henry Hazlitt, *The Foundations of Morality* (Los Angeles, 1972), 184.

deviate from them. This evidences a synthesis of important facets of the journalist's ethics—freedom, will, and rational consideration of the concept of duty.

Toward a Kantian Supermaxim

Political and cultural relativity should not militate against there being some basic universal ethical principles and standards. I have already suggested some, and undoubtedly, there are many more that could be agreed upon by conscientious global journalists willing to give this problem serious thought. However, ethnocentrism rears its head even among persons who are fond of claiming to be against it. Some maintain that there cannot be any universal or absolute ethical principles in international journalism, that ethics must be considered from the standpoint of a particular country and its cultural values, and that any talk of global ethics must simply be just a cataloging of cultural and political values of this or that country.

It seems, however, that nations need not be tied too tightly to their own values; if they are, their peoples will never understand ethics. They will merely believe, "Our way of doing things must be right because we do them." This is hardly a reasonable treatment of ethics. Nations must at least partially break out of this nationalistic, culture-bound, and traditional concept of ethics and reach for common ethical ties and a certitude that goes beyond borders and cultures. If we say there are none of these common ties, then we might as well become accustomed to thinking about ethics in the world context as simply a multiplicity of ways of doing things, of making value judgments—all being more or less morally equal.

Of course, it would be unreasonable to expect journalists of any particular country to abandon their basic ethical principles simply for the sake of global harmony. But it is not unreasonable for them to search out certain global principles that are compatible with their own value systems. Viewing ethical principles as based on cultural difference might force global ethics into a wide diversity of ethical systems, each with an equal claim to being "right." In such a situation there might come to be a field of study called "ethnoethics." If carried very far, of course, ethnoethics would be no ethics at all, given its extreme relativism. What today's global journalists need to search for is an international ethics of journalism, not an ethnoethics of journalism.

Finding a reasonable international ethics is far more than formulating

231

and distributing printed codes. Such codes have failed nationally, and they will fail globally. In the United States, for example, there are many journalistic codes tied to some particular organization of journalists, advertisers, public-relations experts, and the like. In every case the code is controversial, and many journalists, even those who belong to the organization that approved the code, do not accept all the tenets and proscriptions contained in it. The main reason is that journalism in a country such as the United States is pluralistic. Objectives and methods of journalism are diverse. In systems in which pluralism is a reality, codes of journalistic ethics are naturally relegated to ornamental status. And certainly the world constitutes such a pluralistic press system.

If ethical codes and other directive forces such as the National News Council (now defunct) cannot be meaningful and successful in a single nation, such as the United States, how can anyone seriously propose that there be an international code of journalistic ethics? Either such a code will be politically biased (such as the one published by the International Organization of Journalists), or it will be a collection of generalized aphorisms and abstract maxims, so devoid of substance and specificity as to be useless. When one considers the differing systems of ownership and direction of the press found throughout the world, along with the various editorial philosophies and definitions of "news," the notion of an international code of ethics begins to take on the dimensions of fantasy.[24]

But we can have global dialogue about ethics, and we may even be able to arrive at some common moral principles that will provide journalistic guidance in a broad way. For obviously there is some common ethical ground for journalists engaged in international activity. But in spite of the common concepts and principles that may be found globally, there is still much to be said for Schulmeister's opinion, expressed in 1975, that a journalist's morality stems from his or her background and value system, and is closely tied to the national political and social context. Recognition of this reality does not give much support to the idea of international codes of ethics, but it does not preclude global concern for universal moral precepts or principles in journalism.

Journalists should want to project to the world stage basic personal and

---

24 On the various concepts of journalistic ethics throughout the world, see John C. Merrill, "Governments on Press Control: Global Attitudes on Journalistic Matters," *Political Communication and Persuasion*, IV (1987), 223–62.

traditional values that they feel are universalizable. If such overriding concepts of journalism are important to journalists within their own countries, there is no reason why such concepts cannot be important to them when they deal with people and news in other countries. In short, attitudes are what is important in global morality, and it is really on moral attitudes that journalists should focus.

I believe that there are several basic attitudes that are needed by the international journalist who wants to be ethical. He or she will be empathic, having a deep desire to understand the perspectives, needs, and hopes of people of other countries. He or she will want to deal with real and substantive issues and important ideas and will strive to be honest, forthright, sincere, and clear. Such journalists will respect those with whom they are communicating, never turning the argument toward the person or the political system. Conscientious global journalists will be dedicated to their own ethical standards, which arise from their own culture, but they will be willing to be flexible when it is important to be.

These, it should be remembered, are not rules, but basic attitudes. They will help spawn ethical principles or maxims that in turn can be used to bridge cultures and nations and give some common tone to international morality. Finally, in spite of the weakness of supermaxims, which can be thought of as having universal validity, I present the following as a kind of Kantian supermaxim that in a way is a synthesis of legalistic ethics and an existentialist demeanor, providing a "duty-bound" guideline with room for both individual and international journalistic flexibility:

> Treat the people of other nations not as objects to be moved, used, changed, or managed, but as subjects with basic personal dignity: subjects and consumers of journalism with their own minds and values, capable of decision and action. Recognize them as members of humanity who can sense a universality in many of the major dimensions of morality and who recognize that while ethical principles are tied to the traditional mores of a people, they are more than simply ethnocentric whims.[25]

25 Merrill, "Ethics: A Worldview for the Journalist," in Van der Meiden (ed.), *Ethics and Mass Communication,* 118.

CONCLUSION: THE FREE AND
ETHICAL JOURNALIST

Nationalism has to be merged with internationalism for the journalist to have a proper perspective on both freedom and ethics. One must think of other nations and their people while considering the values of one's own nation. The journalist who is enslaved by ethnocentrism cannot provide adequate journalism even to his or her own fellow citizens. And at the same time, journalists throughout the world must value freedom without putting it ahead of socially responsible journalism. The dialectic must become an important concern for journalists everywhere, so that journalism will grow progressively through a spirit of dynamism that comes from the interconnections and the clashes of useful antinomies.

A central aspect of a journalistic dialectic is involved in the problem of freedom and ethics. Journalism needs ethical direction to guide its freedom. Just as life is useless to a person without a brain, so freedom is useless to journalism without ethics. Journalists need to recognize that they must be both free *and* ethical. There is little doubt among philosophers that only a will that is free—not in subjugation to another—can be morally good. So when one talks of ethics, one must assume freedom—of both the negative type and the positive type. Freedom, in the sense of having command over oneself and responsibility to oneself, is the precondition for a journalist to engage in moral action.

We can imagine journalists who obey their editor and conform to their newspaper's policy because they believe them to be just and right, and we can conceive of others who decline to obey, even at peril to themselves, when they think the editor and policy are wrong. Both sets of journalists have given up no freedom at all, for they bow only to their own wisdom and goodness. On the other hand, let us imagine other journalists who obey their editor even when it is against their own sense of what is right, acting out of fear of what will happen if the editor is not obeyed. These are journalists who have surrendered their freedom and are without moral worth, for their obedience is from fear, a fear that makes the journalists no more than automatons acting not from free will, but from fear.

So the degree to which a journalist uses free will is the important matter. Obeying, following orders, conforming—this in itself is not an abdication of freedom nor a sign of inauthentic or immoral action. The important consideration is whether the journalist is conforming autonomously and from principle or out of a fear of the negative consequences of not conforming. Of course, all journalists—by the very nature of their being journalists—are to some degree free and to some degree subject to the will of others. The extent to which the journalist is free defines the extent of his or her bondage, for what the journalist must do, or refrain from doing, against his or her will, is what marks out the bounds of the journalist's freedom and bondage.

There is considerable doubt that Americans generally, and journalists specifically, really value freedom highly. They seem to value it in their rhetoric, but in their actions they fail to manifest much of a concern. Perhaps they agree with Hobbes, who believed that people really seek neither freedom nor happiness, but security and material possessions. And it is also possible that most American journalists illustrate Aristotle's view that people are really "slaves by nature" and find freedom a burden because of the added responsibility it brings.[1]

Benjamin Constant, a leading liberal of the French Enlightenment, was insistent that we preserve as much personal freedom as possible in spite of the temptation to surrender it. Known as "the most eloquent of all defenders of freedom and privacy," he believed that we must preserve at least a minimum area of personal freedom if we are not to degrade or deny our nature. He recognized that "we cannot remain absolutely free, and must give up some of our liberty to preserve the rest; but total self-surrender is self-defeating." Constant especially prized negative freedom. Herbert Read's belief is similar to Constant's. He has said that "freedom, in its positive sense, implies an obligation"—a kind of nonfreedom.[2]

To be free from everything—other people, laws, morality, thought,

---

1   Isaiah Berlin, *Four Essays on Liberty* (New York, 1977), 20.
2   *Ibid.*, 126; Read, *Anarchy and Order*, 161.

emotion—is to be nothing. Unrestricted freedom is in fact impossible and should not be demanded by reasonable people. The truth is that any freedom that is desirable has some limitation. Realistic freedom must have some moral grounding. An example of such grounding can be found in Confucian ethics, in which a limitation to freedom is goodness. A person should choose good, not evil. If evil prevailed, freedom would disappear. Hence, from an ethical perspective, we should permit only the freedom to choose good and not the freedom to choose evil. In Confucian ethics, freedom to choose is only freedom to choose good—not evil.

In his own life Confucius confirmed this principle. He recognized a form of freedom of speech; he opposed only the speaking of bad words or empty words, that is, words without moral significance. Incipient authoritarianism? Certainly one might speak of a degree of authoritarianism in Confucius in the same way, and only in the same way, that one might speak of a degree of authoritarianism in any religious or philosophical leader. The categorical imperative of Kant and the Golden Rule of Christ carry authority, but this authority is self-realized and is in no way externally imposed.

So there are self-determined restrictions within an environment of freedom. And despite such restrictions, we can still have freedom of the press. Walter Berns is a contemporary Confucianist in this respect. In *Freedom, Virtue, and the First Amendment* he issued an articulate call to public virtue, even favoring, from a moral perspective, certain censorship. Salacious and pornographic publications, he maintained, should be censored. According to Berns, American communists should have no claim to free expression since they are disloyal, and like Confucius, he has contended that "bad" speakers and "bad" speeches deserve no protection. Government should be engaged in raising the moral quality of the society, he maintains, and therefore must limit public utterances. For Berns and others who stress positive freedom and have little respect for negative freedom, there is a set of moral principles that are obligatory for all reasonable persons.[3]

Aristotle's *Nicomachean Ethics* is a particularly valuable guide to positive ethics. Virtue, according to Aristotle, is rational activity; hap-

---

3 Walter F. Berns, *Freedom, Virtue, and the First Amendment* (Baton Rouge, 1957). For an excellent perspective from the 1980s on censorship and the press, see Herb Greer, "Who Censors What, Where, and When," *Encounter,* LII (July–August, 1986), 166–67.

piness is what all people desire for its own sake and is a natural good for them. For Aristotle, rationality will not permit the evil use of freedom. The person who is happy will live in harmony with reason. Aristotle believed that it is rational to seek the Golden Mean—the middle point between vices. And Walter Lippmann, who believed that Aristotle was really describing the attributes of a gentleman and was setting forth the rational prototype of all humanistic codes, had this to say about "means" as they were proposed by Aristotle: "Between rashness and cowardice the mean is courage; between prodigality and niggardliness it is liberality; between incontinence and total abstinence it is temperateness; between ostentation and meanness it is magnificence; between empty boasting and little-mindedness it is magnanimity; between flattery and moroseness it is friendliness; between bashfulness and impudence it is modesty; between arrogance and false modesty, it is truthfulness."[4]

Lippmann, Berns, Confucius, and Aristotle would all probably agree that if the journalist would seek the moderate position—the Golden Mean in journalism—there would be no need for censorship or other restrictions on freedom. Positive freedom, used ethically, would never deteriorate into license and would need no restraint for the sake of public morality. Self-realization would, through positive freedom, be projected onto the social scene and become social realization. Thus, with Constant we can insist on a comfortable degree of negative freedom, and with Aristotle and others we can strive to use our freedom from restraint to virtuous ends—for ourselves and for others.

In this book I have presented a series of philosophical syntheses, melding them from seemingly hostile antinomies clashing on the ideological battlefields of journalism. From the usual adversarial or antagonistic models of journalistic discourse, I have tried to move to positions more moderate and useful by connecting beneficial aspects of antithetical positions, by merging antinomies that can be used constructively and responsibly by the journalist, and by stressing the changing nature of journalistic reality. The most significant dialectic is the one in which freedom clashes with ethics and results in responsible freedom. This dialectic is, in essence, the very foundation of journalism. The rational journalist cannot choose freedom and disdain ethics, nor can he or she hope to be ethical without valuing freedom.

4 Walter Lippmann, *A Preface to Morals* (Boston, 1960), 166–67.

A certain attitude of mind is important for the responsible journalist. The journalist must be selfish in that he or she must cherish freedom for self and for the press generally, but at the same time, this selfishness must be tempered by an unselfishness that projects this respect for free expression to others. Voltaire, one of history's leading champions of freedom of the mind and of expression, gave this attitude classic expression in these words: "I disagree absolutely with what you say, but I will defend to the death your right to say it."[5]

As important as such an attitude is, it is not—or should not be—absolute. Such freedom must be merged with a deep and realistic sense of ethics. In some, perhaps many, cases this noble and charitable Voltairean attitude might work well, but in others it might be untenable and even immoral. For instance, what about the newspaper editor who decides not to use a story—true and needing to be published—because it does not have a sufficiently sensational "news value"? How would Voltaire defend this decision and even more dubious ones? Or what about the television personality who each day exercises his or her "inalienable right" to misrepresent a certain product being offered for sale? Or the writer for a news magazine who consistently slants and biases news accounts from the Middle East to suit a personal ideological position?

The point is that press freedom does not necessarily contribute to a search for truth or any other lofty or practical function so dear to the hearts of Enlightenment philosophers. As Carl Becker has pointed out, it often contributes to nothing more than "private profit" or a philosophy of "anything to win the election."[6] In other words, the rational journalist must consider the importance of ethics when trying to determine the proper use of freedom.

In my treatment of definers of journalistic ethics I considered four main such definers. I omitted one that may be of major significance: journalism education. The journalistic academic establishment should be able to exert considerable pressure concerning the issues of press ethics and the utilization of press freedom. Theoretically, a journalism school is in a knowledgeable and neutral position and should be able to influence the broad field of journalism to a considerable degree. But when such an influence is

---

5   Quoted in Carl L. Becker, *Freedom and Responsibility in the American Way of Life* (New York, 1960), 38.
6   *Ibid.*, 39.

suggested, it is usually met with silence or antagonism. Journalism education seems to be too closely tied (financially and otherwise) to the American press to provide much leadership. Press-financed scholarships, endowed professorships, grants of various kinds, and many cooperative programs militate against an independent and frank appraisal of media activities by journalism faculties. Henry T. Price of the University of South Carolina has written, "Any [journalism] program that does not have good relations with the press of its state is asking for trouble."[7]

It may be just as well that academic programs in journalism generally avoid criticizing the press. Practicing journalists have little respect for journalism professors anyway and feel that they are unqualified to judge press practices. Thus, even if more criticism were forthcoming from academe, journalists probably would not take it seriously. Michael Ryan has offered perhaps the safest course for journalism professors. Professors should be concerned mainly with their students, not the press, he has declared, and if media practices are ever criticized, the professors should be sure that the criticism has unanimous faculty approval.[8] Such a demeanor by journalism education bodes poorly for any educational impact on the press, other than a long-term impact through students.

The journalist who cares only for freedom becomes detached from reality, from society, and hovers ultimately on a narrow beach of solipsism where waves of egoism wash away any meaning that freedom might have had. Freedom is like communication—meaningless outside a social context.

We need to remind ourselves of something the Enlightenment philosophers tended to forget—that we are not completely autonomous beings, that we live in a society with other persons. We do indeed have emotions, and many of us have spiritual or mystical connections with God. In effect, we are individuals who create ourselves as we interact with others; we use our freedom to enhance ourselves and others simultaneously. We live in at least two worlds—the world of the self and the world of others—and we must constantly synthesize these worlds.

We must learn to be worthwhile egoists by being sensitized altruists. We must learn to be objective by being subjective. We must learn to be

7 Quoted in Michael Ryan, "To Judge or Not to Judge the Media," *Journalism Educator*, (August, 1986), 23.
8 *Ibid.*, 25.

liberal by conserving what is good, true, and pure. We must learn to be collectivist by merging our individualism with the tide of human progress. We must become not only loyal to the truth, but to ethical practices that might, in some cases, take precedence over the truth. We must learn to respect reason and empiricism while at the same time revering intuition and spiritual insight. We must, as journalists, recognize that we are making mere scratches on the slate of history, that these scratches are largely reflective of our own backgrounds and ideologies, and that they are only the briefest and most unreliable pictures of reality around us. In short, as journalists, we need to take ourselves and our work less seriously.

Journalists should also be able to understand the wariness, skepticism, and even cynicism with which most of the public sees them. They should try to laugh while being serious, cry while exposing skulduggery and tragedies of others, see their own failings when they point out sins in their fellows, and feel a loss of part of themselves at the death of another. What journalism needs is a dialectical emphasis. Either-or journalism is outmoded, simplistic, unfair, and juvenile; it is unproductive, and unworthy of twentieth-century journalists with intellect. In spite of the language that augments the either-or world of nondialectical journalism, today's journalists must force themselves to combine concepts and conceive of entities and ideas as many-sided and constantly changing.

The responsible journalist desires to use freedom to bring about benefits—to himself or herself, to others, and to society generally. The responsible journalist, concerned with positive freedom, does not want to hold passively and contentedly to freedom, but rather to *use* freedom in a positive, constructive, and ethical way for the creation of pockets of value, goodness, stability, and happiness that did not exist before. This is the constructive use of freedom, the ethical use of freedom. It is in so viewing freedom that the free journalist becomes the ethical journalist, profiting from a rational dialectic that seeks to develop a higher level of journalism and a more exalted persona for the journalist.

There are, assuredly, checks on journalistic freedom, even on this positive variety. I have discussed some of the obvious checks—institutional demands, forces of the marketplace, employers' desires and needs, peer pressure, legal and professional pressures, and others. But probably far more important are the checks on a more personal level. Freedom is constrained by the human dignity of the moral person who has a sense of journalistic responsibility. Self-actualization for the journalist demands a certain suspicion of society's definers of responsibility. But the journalist must also understand that the self cannot properly develop in a vacuum and that only in merging self with society will a proper sense of proportion develop that will combine social expectations of morality with personally developed ones. Dialectical journalism considers opposites and their merger and does not seek mutually exclusive answers to complex problems of press and society.

Being a dialectical journalist today is not easy. Extremists and ideologues are constantly grasping for converts and fellow true believers. Moderates, synthesizers, and the like are often disdained as weak-willed or cowardly individuals who do not have definite convictions. The journalist is called on to be either an A or a B, when a more rational position is probably to be an AB or even an ABCD.

Achieving a sense of morality is a slow process of self-liberation: liberation from unencumbered freedom, from external controls, from self-righteousness, from thoughtless complacency, from selfishness, from a belief in objectivity, from a belief in static concepts, from emotional tirades, from prosaic expositions, from pessimism, from optimism, from hedonism, from Stoicism, from scientism, from mysticism, from egoism, from altruism, from absolutism, and from extreme relativism.

Achieving a sense of morality is also a process of movement: movement toward responsible freedom, toward hopeful experimentation, toward self-realization, toward a concern for social progress, toward rational conviction, toward cautious optimism, toward socially conscious egoism, toward rational self-interest, toward emotionally sensitive rationalism, toward absolutist-based relativism, toward objective-oriented subjectivism, toward socially inspired hedonism, toward deliberate dynamism, toward rationally determined duty, toward a belief in responsible pluralism, toward enlightened personal expression, toward warranted public expression in the media, toward informed and intelligent criticism, and toward nonsentimental forgiveness.

The moral journalist needs negative freedom—freedom from restraints. But the moral journalist also needs positive freedom—freedom in the sense of acting, of doing something positive, of making a dent in harmful institutions and ways of thinking, of creating new possibilities for society. When the journalist accepts positive freedom, he or she becomes truly free and ethical. Therefore, the anarchist strain of negative freedom must be joined with the existentialist strain—the active, creative strain—

so that the journalist can do more than just rest in a state of freedom. He or she can then freely push into new and vital areas of social concern, bringing hope where there was despair, vitality where there was listlessness, sustenance where there was starvation, knowledge where there was ignorance, progress where there was inertia, and stability where there was turmoil.

The dialectic leads the rational journalist to embrace an existentialism combined with a form of Kantianism. The Kantian strain keeps the existentialist strain under control; it projects existential freedom into a social area of concern by causing the journalist to will that his or her freedom be universalized. By willing such universalization, the journalist rationally espouses only positive freedom—freedom that is compatible with rational and ethical ends. In other words, the dialectical journalist feels duty-bound to use and expand personal freedom in a responsible way and for socially beneficial purposes. Such a journalist would say, "The kind of freedom I want for myself is the kind of freedom I want for others." This Kantian perspective on freedom automatically endows it with social responsibility. Even a utilitarian strain can be part of such a stance, in spite of Kant's opposition to a consideration of consequences. The reason is that the superiority of the consequences of the rational use of freedom over those of the irrational use of freedom are obvious, and duty to a rationality one would will to be universalized is consistent with Kant's thought.

I insisted in *The Imperative of Freedom* that journalists should shun social adaptation and cooperation in order not to lose their autonomy and self-respect, but to a certain degree I was wrong. Social adaptation is not bad per se; in fact, it may be a good thing, not only for society, but also for the individual journalist. Voluntary surrender of individual freedom is not necessarily inauthentic; it depends on many factors, especially the purpose behind giving up the freedom. The very nature of journalism demands socialization—a sacrifice of considerable individual autonomy. Journalism is a social activity, not a private activity. The journalist is connected: to employer, to other journalists, and to audiences. The impact of the journalist's work falls not just on the journalist, but on many others. The person seeking complete autonomy had best never enter journalism—an activity that is, to a great extent, socially oriented.

But in spite of this fact, the journalist must not deprecate a love for freedom and should be alert to combat all forces tending toward depersonalization and alienation. Cooperation and social concern do not mean abdication of the self; the self-respecting journalist is one who gets much of that self-respect from contributions he or she makes to others. There is no need for the journalist to embrace extreme altruism to fulfill social obligations. To be altruistic does not mean totally sacrificing oneself, as Ayn Rand and others have argued. One can care for self, respect self, and nurture self, and at the same time, one can desire good for others, be cooperative in social causes, and attempt to please social constituents. It is not an either-or situation; it is a dialectical situation.

The journalist who is committed to freedom is a free journalist. The one committed to ethics is an ethical journalist. The one who is committed to freedom *and* ethics is a rational, existentialist journalist, or, in other words, a dialectical journalist. This journalist's authentic commitment to a responsible freedom defines his or her very essence. This journalist is free because there is the will to be free, and is ethical because there is the will to be ethical. Freedom does not mean that the journalist can do whatever he or she wishes. It means that the journalist is free to expand his or her horizons of thought and action if such an expansion is in line with the rights and freedoms of others. The freedom of others impinges on the freedom of the journalist. Social rights circumscribe the journalist's freedom, but if the journalist chooses to use his or her freedom in accordance with, and for the augmentation of, the rights of others, then the journalist will have no restraints on his or her personal freedom.

In conclusion, only when the journalist realizes that both freedom and responsibility are equally necessary for authentic journalism will journalism reach a maturity that will be satisfying to everyone concerned. Only when the journalist recognizes both self-directed responsibility and other-directed responsibility will journalism stand on a truly moral base. Only when existentialist, humanist, utilitarian, and Kantian moral strains combine will journalism reach its potential. In sum, press freedom is vitally important, but a viable ethics must control or limit this freedom.

SELECTED BIBLIOGRAPHY

Adkins, A. W. *Merit and Responsibility*. Chicago, 1975.
Adler, Mortimer. *Six Great Ideas*. New York, 1981.
Adorno, T. W. *Negative Dialectics*. New York, 1973.
Allen, E. L. *From Plato to Nietzsche*. New York, 1964.
Allison, Henry E. *Kant's Transcendental Idealism*. New Haven, 1983.
Altschull, J. Herbert. *Agents of Power: The Role of the News Media in Human Affairs*. New York, 1984.

Baier, Jurt. *The Moral Point of View: A Rational Basis of Ethics*. New York, 1965.
Barnes, Hazel. *An Existentialist Ethics*. New York, 1971.
Barrett, William. *Irrational Man*. New York, 1962.
Barron, Jerome. *Freedom of the Press for Whom?* Bloomington, Ind., 1971.
Baum, Robert, ed. *Ethical Arguments for Analysis*. New York, 1979.
Bennett, Jonathan. *Kant's Dialectic*. Cambridge, England, 1974.
Bennett, W. Lance. *News: The Politics of Illusion*. New York, 1983.
Berlin, Isaiah. *Four Essays on Liberty*. New York, 1977.
———. *Two Concepts of Liberty*. Oxford, England, 1958.
Berns, Walter. *Freedom, Virtue, and the First Amendment*. Baton Rouge, 1957.
Bois, J. Samuel. *The Art of Awareness: A Textbook on General Semantics and Epistemics*. Dubuque, Iowa, 1973.
Bond, Edward J. *Reason and Value*. New York, 1983.
Boventer, Hermann. *Ethik des Journalismus*. Konstanz, West Germany, 1984.
Branden, Nathaniel. *Honoring the Self: The Psychology of Confidence and Respect*. New York, 1983.
Brée, Germaine. *Camus and Sartre*. New York, 1972.

Carey, George W., ed. *Freedom and Virtue*. Lanham, Md., 1984.

Christians, Clifford G., K. B. Rotzoll, and Mark Fackler. *Media Ethics: Cases and Moral Reasoning*. 2nd ed. New York, 1987.

Commission on Freedom of the Press. *A Free and Responsible Press*. Chicago, 1947.

Cooney, Timothy J. *Telling Right from Wrong*. Buffalo, 1985.

Cooper, Thomas, *et al. Communication Ethics and Global Change: International and National Perspectives*. New York, 1988.

Daniels, Norman, ed. *Reading Rawls*. New York, 1975.

Dennis, Everette E., and John C. Merrill. *Basic Issues in Mass Communication: A Debate*. New York, 1984.

Dewey, Robert E., and James A. Gould. *Freedom: Its History, Nature, and Varieties*. Toronto, 1970.

Durant, Will. *The Story of Philosophy*. New York, 1961.

Elliott, Deni, ed. *Responsible Journalism*. Beverly Hills, Calif., 1986.

Fishkin, James S. *Beyond Subjective Morality: Ethical Reasoning and Political Philosophy*. New Haven, 1984.

Fletcher, Joseph. *Situation Ethics: The New Morality*. Philadelphia, 1966.

Frank, Philipp. *Relativity: A Richer Truth*. Boston, 1950.

Gewirth, Alan. *Reason and Morality*. Chicago, 1977.

Goldstein, Tom. *The News at Any Cost: How Journalists Compromise Their Ethics to Shape the News*. New York, 1985.

Gray, John. *Hayek on Liberty*. New York, 1984.

Habermas, Juergen. *The Theory of Communicative Action*. 2 vols. Boston, 1981.

Hachten, William A. *The World News Prism: Changing Media, Clashing Ideologies*. 2nd ed. Ames, Iowa, 1987.

Hazlitt, Henry. *The Foundations of Morality*. Los Angeles, 1972.

Hess, Stephen. *The Government/Press Connection*. Washington, D.C., 1984.

―――. *The Washington Reporters*. Washington, D.C., 1982.

Hocking, William Ernest. *Freedom of the Press*. Chicago, 1947.

Hollingdale, R. E. *Nietzsche: The Man and His Philosophy*. Baton Rouge, 1965.

Honderich, Ted., ed. *Morality and Objectivity*. London, 1985.

Hook, Sidney, *The Paradoxes of Freedom*. Berkeley, 1967.

Hulteng, John L. *The Messenger's Motives: Ethical Problems of the News Media*. 2nd ed. Englewood Cliffs, N.J., 1984.

Hussey, Edward. *The Pre-Socratics*. New York, 1972.

International Commission for the Study of Communication Problems. *Many Voices, One World*. London, 1980.

Irvine, Reed. *Media Mischief and Misdeeds*. Chicago, 1984.

Jaffa, Harry V. *American Conservatism and the American Founding*. Durham, N.C., 1984.

Jaspers, Karl. *Man in the Modern Age*. Garden City, N.Y., 1957.

Jonas, Hans. *The Imperative of Responsibility: In Search of an Ethics for the Technological Age*. Chicago, 1984.

Jones, W. T. *Kant and the Nineteenth Century*. New York, 1975.

Kelly, John C. *A Philosophy of Communication*. London, 1981.

Kenny, Anthony. *The Aristotelian Ethics*. New York, 1978.

Korzybski, Alfred. *Science and Sanity: An Introduction to Non-Aristotelian Systems and General Semantics*. Lakeville, Conn., 1933.

Kristol, Irving. *Reflections of a Neoconservative*. New York, 1983.

Lambeth, Edmund B. *Committed Journalism: An Ethic for the Profession*. Bloomington, 1986.

Levy, Leonard. *Emergence of a Free Press*. New York, 1985.

―――. ed. *Freedom of the Press from Zenger to Jefferson*. Indianapolis, 1966.

Lichter, S. Robert, Stanley Rothman, and Linda S. Lichter. *The Media Elite: America's New Powerbrokers*. Bethesda, Md., 1986.

Lippmann, Walter, *A Preface to Morals*. Boston, 1960.

Mackie, John. *Ethics: Inventing Right and Wrong*. New York, 1977.

McQuail, Denis, ed. *Sociology of Mass Communications: Selected Readings*. New York, 1979.

Magee, Bryan, ed. *Men of Ideas*. New York, 1982.

Martin, L. John, and Anju Chaudhary, eds., *Comparative Mass Media Systems*. New York, 1983.

Merrill, John C. *Existential Journalism*. New York, 1977.

―――. *The Imperative of Freedom: A Philosophy of Journalistic Autonomy*. New York, 1974.

Merrill, John C., and Ralph Barney, eds. *Ethics and the Press*. New York, 1975.

Merrill, John C., and S. Jack Odell. *Philosophy and Journalism*. New York, 1983.

Meyer, Philip. *Editors, Publishers, and Newspaper Ethics*. Washington, D.C., 1983.

Mill, John Stuart. *On Liberty* New York, 1975.

Mollenkott, Virginia R. *In Search of Balance*. Waco, Tex., 1969.

Moore, G. E. *Principia Ethica*. New York, 1959.

Mowlana, Hamid. *Global Information and World Communication.* New York, 1986.

Nielsen, Kai, and Steven C. Patten, eds., *Marx and Morality.* Guelph, Ontario, 1981.
Nisbet, Robert. *History of the Idea of Progress.* New York, 1980.
Noelle-Neumann, Elisabeth. *The Spiral of Silence.* Chicago, 1983.
Nordenstreng, Kaarle. *The Mass Media Declaration of UNESCO.* Norwood, N.J., 1984.
Novack, George. *An Introduction to the Logic of Marxism.* New York, 1971.
Nozick, Robert. *Anarchy, State, and Utopia.* New York, 1974.
_____. *Philosophical Explanations.* Cambridge, Mass., 1981.

Odajnyk, V. W. *Jung and Politics: The Political and Social Ideas of C. G. Jung.* New York, 1976.

Peikoff, Leonard. *The Ominous Parallels.* New York, 1982.
Pell, Eve. *The Big Chill: How the Reagan Administration, Corporate America, and Religious Conservatives Are Subverting Free Speech and the Public's Right to Know.* Boston, 1984.
Phelan, John M. *Disenchantment: Meaning and Morality in the Media.* New York, 1980.
Picard, Robert C. *The Press and the Decline of Democracy: The Democratic Socialist Response to Public Policy.* Westport, Conn., 1985.
Poole, Roger. *Towards Deep Subjectivity.* New York, 1972.
Popper, Karl. *The Open Society and Its Enemies.* 4th ed. 2 vols. New York, 1963.
Porter, Burton. *The Good Life: Alternatives in Ethics.* New York, 1980.

Rand, Ayn, *For the New Intellectual.* New York, 1961.
_____. *Philosophy: Who Needs It?* New York, 1982.
_____. *The Virtue of Selfishness: A New Concept of Egoism.* New York, 1964.
Rawls, John. *A Theory of Justice.* Cambridge, Mass., 1971.
Read, Herbert. *Anarchy and Order.* Boston, 1971.
Richstad, Jim, and Michael H. Anderson, eds. *Crisis in International News.* New York, 1981
Rivers, William L. *The Other Government: Power and the Washington Media.* New York, 1982.
Rivers, William L., Wilbur Schramm, and C. G. Christians. *Responsibility in Mass Communication.* New York, 1980.
Rorty, Amelie, ed. *Essays on Aristotle's Ethics.* Berkeley, 1981.
Rubin, Bernard, ed. *Questioning Media Ethics.* New York, 1978.

Rusher, William A. *The Coming Battle for the Media: Curbing the Power of the Media Elite*. New York, 1988.

Scheffler, Samuel. *The Rejection of Consequentialism*. New York, 1982.
Schmidt, Benno C., Jr. *Freedom of the Press vs. Public Access*. New York, 1976.
Schultz, Richard H., and Roy Godson. *Dezinformatsia: The Strategy of Soviet Disinformation*. New York, 1986.
Schutte, Ofelia. *Beyond Nihilism: Nietzsche Without Masks*. Chicago, 1984.
Siebert, Fred S., Theodore Peterson, and Wilbur Schramm. *Four Theories of the Press*. Urbana, 1956.
Solomon, Robert C. *In the Spirit of Hegel*. New York, 1983.
Stapelevich, L. W., ed. *The Young Hegelians*. Cambridge, England, 1983.
Stolen, Peter. *The War Against the Press*. New York, 1986.
Swain, Bruce M. *Reporters' Ethics*. Ames, Iowa, 1978.

Tataryn, Lloyd. *The Pundits: Power, Politics, and the Press*. Toronto, 1985.
Taylor, Richard. *Freedom, Anarchy, and the Law*. Englewood Cliffs, N.J., 1973.
Thayer, Lee, ed. *Ethics, Morality, and the Media*. New York, 1980.
Toulmin, Stephen. *The Place of Reason in Ethics*. New York, 1950.
Tucker, Robert C. *Philosophy and Myth in Karl Marx*. London, 1961.
Turner, R. H., ed. *Robert E. Park on Social Control and Collective Behavior*. Chicago, 1967.

Van Alstyne, William W. *Interpretations of the First Amendment*. Durham, N.C., 1984.
Van der Meiden, Anne, ed. *Ethics and Mass Communication*. Utrecht, the Netherlands, 1980.

Wheelwright, Philip. *Heraclitus*. New York, 1968.
Williams, Bernard. *Ethics and the Limits of Philosophy*. Cambridge, Mass., 1985.
Williams, Francis. *The Right to Know*. London, 1969.
Wolfson, Lewis W. *The Untapped Power of the Press: Explaining Government to the People*. New York, 1985.

INDEX

Abel, Elie, 218
Absolutism: in journalism, 56; moral, 203–208 *passim*
Active freedom, 131. *See also* Positive freedom
Acton, H. B., 198
Acton, Lord, 104
Adler, Mortimer: on freedom, 135; mentioned, 20
Age of Reason, 4, 32, 184–85, 195
Aiken, Henry, 134
Alienation in journalism, 151–52
Allen, E. L.: on Nietzsche's yea-saying, 79; mentioned, 144
Aloof orientation in journalism, 59–60, 84–86
Altruism: in existentialism, 141; in ethics, 171
Altruists as journalists, 56
Altschull, J. Herbert: on market forces in journalism, 196; mentioned, 42
American Society of Newspaper Editors (ASNE), 88
American University (Washington, D.C.), 217
Angst and the journalist, 149–51
Antinomianism in journalism, 173–74
Antinomies: in journalism, 11, 12–13, 55–57; Dionysian and Apollonian, 59–60; poetic and prosaic, 60–61; existentialist and rationalist, 61–62;

personalist and factualist, 61–62; absolutist and relativist, 69–78
Antithesis as part of dialectic, 7
Anxiety in journalism, 149–51
Apollo, 78
Apollonian journalist, 59–60
Apollonian objectivity, 84–86
Apollonian tendency in journalism, 80–82
"Apollonysian" synthesis in journalism, 82–83, 91–94
Approbative press theories, 31
Aquinas, Thomas: as a realist, 2; on morality and natural law, 163
Areopagitica, 26
Aristotelian individualism, 2
Aristotelian-Lockean tradition, 49
Aristotle: as democrat, 2–4; as realist and individualist, 2–3; as father of logic, 3; as opponent of supernaturalism, 3; and philosophy of moderation, 9, 210; and Golden Mean, 11; on ethics, 38, 209; on personal desires, 44; adapted to journalism, 50; on rationality and ethics, 209; mentioned, 50, 137, 205
Artistic journalist, 58
Audience types as described by Hitler, 112
Augustine, St.: as an idealist, 2; on love of God in ethics, 163; mentioned, 3, 4

Authenticity in journalism, 153–55
Authoritarianism: in all countries, 69; of Plato, 103; as state press freedom, 109–13
Authoritarian press, 102

"Bad faith," 24
Barnes, Hazel: on existentialist ethics, 62; on Nietzsche, 77, on ethics, 167
Barrett, William, 62, 123
Barron, Jerome, 33–34
Barzini, Luigi, 88
Becker, Carl, 239
Being and Nothingness, 133
Bentham, Jeremy: on freedom, 27; on hedonistic ethics, 45
Berdyaev, Nicolas: on freedom, 133; on Christian morality, 212–13; mentioned, 119
Berlin, Isaiah, 133
Berns, Walter: on press responsibility, 187–88; mentioned, 129, 237, 238
Bok, Sissela, 206
Bolsheviks, 110
Boston *Globe*, 88
British Broadcasting Corporation, 165
Brzezinski, Zbigniew, 104
Buber, Martin, 87, 119, 133
Buckley, William F., Jr., 49
Buddha and the ethical path of feminine virtues, 157
Bultmann, Rudolf, 212
Butler, Joseph, 163

Camus, Albert: existentialism of, 121; as a journalist, 136–37; Orphic orientation of, 138; on freedom, 147; mentioned, 24
Capitalist concept of the press, 113–18 *passim*
Casuist ethics, 159–60
Categorical imperative of Kant: description of, 204; adapted to global journalism, 223–33; mentioned, 122, 172, 237
Centre for the Study of Communication (London), 193
Centrist Hegelianism, 15
Checks on press freedom, 241–42
Chiaromonte, Nicola, 11

Chomsky, Noam: on power and authority, 67–68; on journalistic individualism, 146
Chorherr, Thomas, 215
Christian ethics, 228
Christian existentialists, 133
Christians, Clifford: on five basic ethical paths, 166–64; on Aristotle's "middle level" ethics, 209–10; mentioned, 49, 197
Churchill, Winston, 228
"Clear and present danger" concept, 27
Codes of ethics, 36
Combat, 136
Commonalities in global journalism ethics, 221–23
Confederation of ASEAN Journalists, 219
Confucianist ethics, 209–10, 237–38
Consequences in ethics, 161
Constant, Benjamin, 236
Cooper, Kent, 84
Cranston, Maurice, 174
Creative urge (Dionysian), 79
Critical Theorists on press responsibility, 191–94
Cuba, 109
Cyclic theories, 10

Democratic socialist press theory, 98–99
Dennis, Everette: on journalistic objectivity, 85; on American press freedom, 127
"Deontelic" ethics, 195–214 *passim*
Deontological ethics, 171–73; emphasis on duty in, 198; in journalism, 201–202
Descriptive ethics, 159
Determination of content as press freedom, 30–31
Dewey, John, 168
Dialectic: of Hegel, 6–8; in Nietzsche's Apollo and Dionysus, 80–83; in existentialism, 155; as journalism's foundation, 238
Dialectical thinking, 6–7; synthesis in, 11; and Herbert Spencer, 74; tendencies in journalism toward, 147–49; and journalists, 241; and journalistic ethics, 242–44

Dionysian journalist, 59–60; probable attitude of Nietzsche toward, 78–79
Dionysian objectivity, 86–91
Dionysus, 78–94 *passim*
Dissanayake, Wimal, 49
Distrust of press by the public, 39
Dizard, Wilson, 49
Dualistically oriented journalists, 55
Durant, Will, 7
Duty as an ethical path, 163

Edel, Abraham, 45
Editorial self-determination, 128
Egoism in ethics, 171
Eiffel Tower, 91
Either/Or, 119
Either-or journalism, 241
Ellul, Jacques: on journalistic deprecia-
tion of self, 124; on alienation, 151
Emerson, Ralph Waldo, 135
Enlightenment, 144. *See also* Age of
Reason
Entitlement theory in ethics, 47
Epictetus, 163
Epicurus, 163
Establishment journalism, 92
Ethical dialectic in journalism, 238
Ethical freedom, 141
Ethical Model, 57, 69–73
Ethical paths, 163–64
Ethical perspectives, 159–61
Ethical theories, 62–64, 159–60
Ethics: implication of, for freedom, 23–
24; and social adjustment in jour-
nalism, 38–39; existentialist, 61–62;
definition of, 67–68; nature of, 161–
63; respect for, 166–67; relativism in,
173–75; Machiavellian expediency,
174; dialectics in, 175–76; growing
concern with, 196; and global jour-
nalism, 223; worldwide, 225–27; and
journalism education, 239–40
Ethnocentrism in ethics, 235
Ewing, A. C., 106–107
Existential freedom, 22–26, 118–22
Existentialism and journalistic characteristics, 132–42 *passim*
Existentialist orientations in journalism,
138–39
Existentialists as journalists, 61–62

Existential journalism, 147–49
Existential Journalism, 125
L'Express (Paris), 136

Fackler, Mark, 197
Factualist journalism, 61
Factuality in journalism, 92
Federal Communication Commission
(FCC), 18
Federal Trade Commission (FTC), 210
Federation of Arab Journalists (FAJ), 219
Feminine virtues of Jesus and Buddha,
157
Fichte, Johann, 6, 12
First Amendment (U.S. Constitution),
114–15, 125–27, 182, 195
First World 48
Fletcher, Joseph: on situationism, 168; on
situation ethics, 212–13
Flux, concept of, 4–6
Formalistic ethics of Kant, 51, 69–71,
172
Foundations of Morality, The, 203
Four Theories of the Press, 43, 97, 101,
113
Francis, St., 121
Frankfurt School, 191
Free and Responsible Press, A, 42
Freedom: many meanings of, 20–27;
Kant on, 21, 243; Mao on, 21;
Spencer on, 21; negative and positive,
22–24; A. N. Whitehead on, 22; exis-
tential dimensions of, 24–26; J. S. Mill
on, 27; journalistic, 97–130 *passim*
Freedom of the Press, 140
*Freedom, Virtue, and the First Amend-
ment*, 29
French Enlightenment, 236
Friedrich, Carl, 104
Fromm, Erich: on journalistic objectivity,
89–90; on dehumanization, 152; on
the tendency to escape freedom, 167;
mentioned, 93
From Plato to Nietzsche, 79

Gallagher, Wes, 84–85
Gallup survey on public distrust of the
press (1984), 39
Gannett Center for Media Studies, 85
Gans, Herbert, 49

Gardner, John W., 124
General Semantics on flux and dialectics, 9, 13
Gerbner, George, 49
German Democratic Republic, 109
German idealism, 1
Glasser, Theodore, 49
Global concern for ethics in journalism, 225–27
Globalizing press ethics, 216–19
Global journalists, ethical standards for, 233
Golden Mean of Aristotle, 11, 56, 75, 163–64, 209–10
Golden Rule of Christ, 204, 223, 237
Goldstein, Tom: on distrust of press, 39; mentioned, 197
Goldwater, Barry, 84–85
Government as definer of press ethics, 180–82
Grandi, Roberto, 49
Grenada: U.S. invasion of, 186; mentioned, 195
Gresham's law, 28
Gulag Archipelago, 22
Gulliver's Travels, 62

Halloran, James, 49
Hamelink, Cees, 49
Hare, R. M., 204
Harris poll on public distrust of the press (1984), 39
Hayek, Friedrich: on freedom, 33; on collectivist trends in society, 189–90; mentioned, 104
Hazlitt, Henry: on Kant's ethics as inflexible, 203–204; on ethics, 230; mentioned, 74
Hedonism as an ethical path, 163
Hegel, G. W. F.: on Heraclitean flux, 5; on dialectic as historical process, 6–8; impact of, on Marxism, 8; on duty to state, 15; as a statist thinker, 50; on importance of the dialectic, 71–72; on the state, 108; on the concept of freedom, 134–35; on the insignificance of persons, 142; on "vulgar individualism," 143; mentioned, 48, 114
Heidegger, Martin: as foe of collective

social identity, 142; on anxiety, 151; mentioned, 87, 133
Heraclitus on change, 4–6, 55, 107
Hermeneutics, 73
Historia como sistema, 119
Hitler, Adolf: on audience types, 112; mentioned, 71, 109
Hobbes, Thomas: on ethics, 45; as father of modern democratic theory, 116; on psychological egoism, 207–208; mentioned, 236
Hoffer, Eric, 105
Holmes, Oliver W.: on freedom, 27; on marketplace of ideas, 185
Holy Grail, objectivity as journalism's, 84
Hospers, John, 117–18
Hudson, Heather, 49
Hume, David: on morality, 45; on ethics as feeling, 162
Hutchins Commission, 30, 41–43, 129, 177, 191–94 passim
Hvistendahl, J. K., 59

Idealist epistemology of Michael Novak et al., 86–87
Ideal observer in Rawls's ethics, 47
Ideal utilitarianism, 206
Ideology and journalists, 70
Imperative of Freedom, 1, 12, 14, 37, 194, 243
In Defense of Freedom, 118
Individual: as authoritarian, 57; importance of, 142–49; value of, to Ayn Rand, Kierkegaard, and Nietzsche, 142; as definer of the ethical, 183–84
Institutional freedom mode, 113–18
Institutionalists in journalism, 63–64
Inter American Press Association (IAPA), 97
International Catholic Union of the Press, 219
International ethics, 216–25 passim
International Federation of Journalists (IFJ), 219
International Organization of Journalists (IOJ), 217; global ethical principles of, 219–21
International Press Institute (IPI), 97

Involved orientation in journalism, 86–91

Iran, 69

James, William, 168

Jaspers, Karl: on journalistic authenticity, 25; on journalists, 123–24; on the press, 137–38; on the ideal journalist, 138; mentioned, 119, 133

Jefferson, Thomas: as libertarian, 7, 14; on freedom and rationality, 26; on restraint of freedom, 41; as a supporter of press responsibility, 41; as a representative of press libertarianism, 114; mentioned, 65

Jesus and the ethical path of feminine virtues, 157

Johnson, Paul, 122

Jones, C. David, 73

Journalism: dialectics in, 8–15; of Jeffersonian type, 14; as a profession, 31–32, 121; as cooperating servant, 100; as equal contender, 100; as forced slave, 100; education for, 239–40; as social activity, 243

Journalistic allegiances, 63–64

Journalistic antinomies, 56

Journalistic autonomy as press freedom, 30

Journalistic conduct, standards for justifying, 164–66

Journalistic flexibility, 75

Journalistic freedom, 97–130 passim; as contrary to press freedom, 34–36

Journalistic orientations: Apollonian, 60; Dionysian, 60; poetic, 60; prosaic, 60; existential, 61–62; rationalist, 63

Journalistic profession as definer of ethics, 182–83

Journalists: as dualistically oriented, 55; as situationists, 211; as missionaries, 221

Jung, Carl: on Wotan (Odin), 79–80; on authoritarianism, 112; on autonomy, 121; as an Orphic existentialist, 144; on psychic alienation, 152

Kant, Immanuel: as a statist, 2; on freedom, 21; and moral philosophy of duty, 44–45; formalistic deontology of, 51; and appeal to reason, 60; on self-respect, 140; opposition of, to consideration of consequences, 198; on duty for duty's sake, 200; ethical absolutism of, 203–205; warning of, against expedient ethics, 230; mentioned, 51, 65, 198, 243

Kantian supermaxim for global journalism, 231–33

Katz, Elihu, 49

Kierkegaard, Søren: on personal freedom, 119; criticism of society by, 123; on being an individualist, 125; opposition of, to collective identity, 145; mentioned, 24, 48

Kirkpatrick, Jeane, 49

Koestenbaum, Peter, 25

Korzybski, Alfred, 5, 7

Korzybskian semanticists, 209. See also General Semantics on flux and dialectics

Laski, Harold, 20

Latin American Federation of Journalists (FELAP), 219

Left, Hegelians of the, 15

Levels of freedom and authority, 66–69

Leviathan, 45, 116

Libertarian journalism, 113–18

Liberty as distinguished from freedom, 22

Lindsay, Robert, 49

Lippmann, Walter: on press freedom, 28; on the importance of change, 168; on Aristotle, 238; mentioned, 129

Locke, John: as realist and empiricist, 2, 4; on negative freedom, 49; mentioned, 48, 50, 114, 116, 125

Logic (Hegel), 71

Lonely Crowd, The, 123

Lowenstein, Ralph L., 98

Loyalty Model, 63–66

Luther, Martin, 143

Lying, 206

MacBride Commission (1980), 218

McDonald, Donald, 88

McHale, Tomás, 49

Machan, Tibor, 118
Machiavelli, Niccolò, 157
Machiavellian ethics, 39, 174
MacIntyre, Alasdair: on universal ethics, 222; mentioned, 104
McQuail, Denis, 49
Macquarrie, John, 147
Magic Animal, The, 90
Mailer, Norman, 86
Man for Himself, 89
Man in the Modern Age, 127
Mao Tse-Tung, 21
Marcel, Gabriel: on shunning masses, 124; on alienation, 152; mentioned, 119
Marcuse, Herbert: on freedom, 20; on freedom of expression, 104; mentioned, 129
Market as definer of ethical action, 184–86
Marty, Martin, 40
Marx, Karl: on Hegel's political philosophy, 108–109; as humanist, 145; on individualism, 145; mentioned, 48, 71, 107
Marxist-communist press theory, 101, 110–11
Masculine virtues of Machiavelli and Nietzsche, 157
Master morality of Nietzsche, 76
Maxim for "deontelic" ethics, 202
Media Ethics, 197
Media-government relationship, 99–101
Melody, William, 49
Mencken, H. L., 87
Metaethics, 161
Meyer, Frank, 118
Middle Ages, 4
Middle East, 239
"Middle way": of freedom, 130–31; of ethics, 229–31
Mill, James: on freedom, 27; on "watchdog function" of press, 42, 179
Mill, John Stuart: as libertarian, 7; on freedom, 22, 27; as utilitarian, 45; on ethical consequences, 161; and the principle of greatest happiness, 163; and the principle of utility, 163–64; on conscience and responsibility, 179; mentioned, 51, 114

Milton, John, 114
Moderation in journalism, 242
Modern Times, 122
Mollenkott, Virginia: on Ayn Rand's and Aristotle's ethical concepts, 205–206; in opposition to situation ethics, 213
Moore, G. E., 206
Moral and ethical compared, 61–62
Moralists as ethicists, 160
Movement and morality, 242
Mowlana, Hamid, 217–18
Muller, Herbert, 20
Multivalued orientation of General Semantics, 5
Murdoch, Iris, 210–11
Mussolini, Benito, 7

National News Council (U.S.), 187, 231
Negative freedom: different from positive freedom, 19; as passive, 131; mentioned, 49, 133, 242
Neoplatonism of Kant, 50
Neutralism in journalism, 64
New Journalism, 63
News at Any Cost, 197
Newsweek, 39
New World Information and Communication Order (NWICO), 216, 220
New York *Times,* 39, 170, 187
Nicomachean Ethics, 38, 237
Niebuhr, Reinhold, 228
Nietzsche, Friedrich: as an Aristotelian individualist, 45–46; attack on truth, 72; on Apollonian and Dionysian stances, 76–94 *passim;* and anti-Kantianism, 77; as ethical egoist, 77; as existentialist, 78; on objectivity, 87–88; on individualism, 141, on authority, 154; mentioned, 106
Nietzschean antinomies, 78–80
Nisbet, Robert, 177
Noelle-Neumann, Elisabeth, 49
Nomenklatura, 110
Nonpolitical ethical commonalities, 221–23
Nordenstreng, Kaarle: on international codes of ethics, 216–17; mentioned, 49
Normative ethics, 160
Normative relativism of Marx, 110

Novack, George, 6
Novak, Michael, 86–87
Nozick, Robert: and entitlement theory in ethics, 47; as follower of Locke, 48; on government as night watchman, 116–17

Odin (Wotan), 79–80
Ombudsman, 36
Open journalism, 211. *See* Situationism, moral
Open Society and Its Enemies, The, 107
Organization Man, The, 123
Orientations in journalism, 58–83
Orphic journalist, 121, 138–39
Ortega y Gasset, José: on the authentic self, 119; on journalism, 137; mentioned, 154
Overman of Nietzsche, 53, 72, 159. *See also* Superman of Nietzsche; *Übermensch* of Nietzsche

Padgaonkar, Dileep, 20
Paradox in dialectics, 6
Paradox of freedom, 134
Paraguay, 69, 109
Pascal, Blaise, 210–11
Passive freedom, 131. *See* Negative freedom
Peikoff, Leonard: as an Aristotelian, 2, 4; as a critic of John Rawls, 47–48; in opposition to Plato, 107; pro-Aristotelian view of, 108
People-centered freedom, 129
People's freedom, 32–34
People's right to know, 34
Personalists in journalism, 61, 63
Persuasive individualism of Locke, 116
Peterson, Theodore: on press freedom, 178; mentioned, 97, 99, 100
Phenomenology of Mind, 71
Picard, Robert, 98–99
Plato: as collectivistic symbol, 2–4; as idealist, 2; mystical epistemology of, 3; on interest of the state, 103; on morality, 107; and paradox of freedom, 134; on virtue, 169; mentioned, 48, 103, 114–15, 157
Pluralism, 10
Poetic journalistic orientation, 60

Political synthesis in journalism, 238
Poole, Roger, 90
Popper, Karl: on two societal types, 106–107; mentioned, 103
Populist view of press freedom, 128–29
Porter, Burton, 121
Portugal, 109
Positive freedom: contrasted to negative freedom, 19, 22; mentioned, 49, 130, 131, 242
Power in journalism, 104
Prague, 219
Present Age, The, 123
Pre-Socratic philosophy, 1
Press: public distrust of, 31; public access to, 33; authoritarianism of, and Norm Chomsky, 67–68
Press-centered freedom, 128
Press councils, 36
Presse, Die (Vienna), 215
Press freedom: Jefferson on, 26; Locke on, 26; Adam Smith on, 26; Voltaire on, 26; Jeremy Bentham on, 27; O. W. Holmes on, 27; James Mill on, 27; Walter Lippmann on, 28; Walter Berns on, 29; changing American concept of, 29–31; as people's freedom, 32–34; as distinct from journalistic freedom, 34–36; as institutional concept, 35; the A-L Model of, 97–100 *passim*; Ralph Lowenstein's model of, 98; Robert Picard's model of, 98–99; Lowenstein's PICA index for, 101; as state freedom or authoritarianism, 101–109 *passim*; as expressed by state, 109–13; and mode of personal freedom, 118–25
Press responsibility: and the Hutchins Commission, 41–43; Jefferson's support of, 41; Kant on, 44–45; Hume on, 45
Price, Henry T., 240
Prince, The, 174
Professionalism as a trend in journalism, 31–32
Professionalization as a definer of press ethics, 188–89
Promethean journalist, 120, 138–39
Protestant ethic, 185
Proudhon, P. I., 106
Psychic isolation in journalism, 155

Public Philosophy, The, 28
Public's right to know, 211–12

Radical Libertarianism, 32
Radin, Paul, 85
Rand, Ayn: as an Aristotelian, 2; on the conflict between reason and emotion, 81–82; on ethical egoism, 199, 207; on Kant's ideas, 205; mentioned, 48, 81, 135, 142, 244
Rashdall, Hastings, 206
Rationalism: in journalism, 61–62; in ethics, 73
Rawls, John: on egalitarianism, 46–49; in opposition to Nietzsche, 46; on "veil of ignorance," 47, 163–64; as follower of Rousseau, 48; mentioned, 51
Read, Herbert: on merging with the collective will, 105; on Nietzsche's individualism, 145
Reason and discipline, 79
Reformation Christianity, 143
Relativism: in journalism, 56; in ethics, 173–75; in global ethics, 224–25
Republic, 106, 169
Responsibility in journalism, 41–44, 54, 178–79, 186–91
Responsible freedom, 130
Responsible journalism, 241
Revel, Jean-François, 49
Revolution of Hope, The, 89
Riesman, David: on individualism, 143–44; mentioned, 123
Right, Hegelians of the, 15
Rilke, Rainer Maria, 121
Road to Serfdom, The, 104, 189
Robinson, John A. T., 212
Rogers, Carl, 212
Rosengren, Karl Erik, 49
Ross, W. D., 205
Rousseau, Jean Jacques: on morality, 45; on negative freedom, 49–50; antithetical ideas of, about individualism and authority (Rousseau's quandary), 64–66; on journalism, 65–66; on ethics and feeling, 162; mentioned, 48, 49
Russell, Bertrand, 198
Ryan, Michael, 240

Sartre, Jean-Paul: on freedom, 20; moral philosophy of, 78; and existentialism, 121–22, 133; as a Promethean, 138
Schelling, Friedrich von: as a relativist, 71; mentioned, 6
Schiller, Herbert, 49
Schlesinger, Arthur, Jr., 227–28, 229
Schlick, Moritz, 208
Schramm, Wilbur, 43, 97, 99, 100
Schulmeister, Otto: on relativism in press ethics, 215; mentioned, 221
Scientific journalist, 58
Second World, 48
Self-actualization for the journalist, 241–42
Self-enhancement, 108
Self-Relatedness Model, 57, 64–66
Self-respect in journalism, 140–41
Self-righting process: of Milton, 114; of O. W. Holmes, 185
Semantic "noise," 116
Sermon on the Mount, 228
Shaw, William, 110
Shield laws, 269
Siebert, Fred, 97, 99, 100
Situation ethics, 168, 174, 211–14
Situationism, moral, 197
Skinner, B. F., 62
Slave mentalities, 141
Smith, Adam: on freedom, 26; theory of laissez-faire capitalism, 185
Smythe, Dallas, 49
Snow, C. P., 93
Social adjustment in ethics, 52
Social-centralist theory of Lowenstein, 98
Social concern in journalism, 30–31
Social Darwinism of Spencer, 31
Social existentialism, 131
Socialist concept of the press, 110–11
Social-libertarian theory of Lowenstein, 98
Social responsibility: in post–World War II press theory, 41–42; growing popularity of, 196
Social scientists as ethicists, 159
Socrates, 157
Sola Pool, Ithiel de, 49
Solzhenitsyn, Alexander: on freedom, 22; Nobel Prize lecture of (1972), 104

South Africa, 91
Soviet journalists, 70
Soviet Union, 69, 215
Spencer, Herbert: on freedom and social Darwinism, 21; on relativism and absolutism, 74
Spinoza, Benedict: on the ethical journalist, 157–59; as reconciler in ethics, 157–59
Stalin, Joseph, 109
State authoritarianism, 67
State freedom: as authoritarianism, 102; mode of, 109–13
Statist utilitarianism of Plato, 103
Stephenson, William, 92–93
Stevenson, Robert, 49
Stranger, The, 152
Strict constructionist view of press freedom, 127
Subjectivists in journalism, 56
Sulzberger, Arthur Ochs, 187
Sunday Times (London), 169
Superman of Nietzsche, 76–77, 145. See Overman of Nietzsche; Übermensch of Nietzsche
Supermaxim of Kant, 233
Sussmann, Leonard, 49
Swift, Jonathan, 62
Synthesis in ethics, 74–75, 82–84, 191–94, 199–201
Synthesizing stances in journalism, 240–43

Taylor, Richard, 24
Teleological ethics, 170
Teleology as opposed to deontology, 206
Ten Commandments, 161
Theory of Justice, A, 46–47
Thesis as part of dialectic, 7
Third World, 193, 216
Thus Spake Zarathustra, 154
Tillich, Paul, 87
Tornillo case, 33
Towards Deep Subjectivity, 90
Trueblood, D. Elton, 71–72
Tuccille, Jerome, 32–33

Tuchman, Gaye, 85–86
Tucker, Robert: on freedom, 21; on Hegel's political philosophy, 108
Tunstall, Jeremy, 49
Twilight of the Idols, The, 87–88

Übermensch of Nietzsche, 53, 72, 124. See also Overman of Nietzsche; Superman of Nietzsche
Unamuno, Miguel de, 133
UNESCO; conferences and member groups of, 219; and related ethical principles, 219–21; mentioned, 20, 182, 216, 220
Union of African Journalists (UAJ), 219
United Nations, 219
University of Chicago, 82
University of Missouri, 92
University of South Carolina, 240
Utilitarianism in ethics, 164–65
Utilitarians as ethical socialists, 170–71

Van den Haag, Ernest, 38
"Veil of ignorance" of John Rawls, 47, 163–64
Vienna, 215, 216
Virtue and journalism, 168–70
Voltaire, 239

Wall Street Journal, 39
Warnock, Mary, 133
Weber, Max, 185
Whim ethics, 173–74
White, Robert: on participatory communication, 193; mentioned, 49
Whitehead, Alfred N., 22
Whyte, William, 123
Wiio, Osmo, 49
Winship, Thomas, 88–89
Work-oriented Model, 57
World War II, 19, 136
Wotan (Odin), 78–80
Wylie, Philip, 90

Zassoursky, Yassen, 49